A YEAR AT HIGHCLERE

ALSO BY THE COUNTESS OF CARNARVON

Lady Almina and the Real Downton Abbey
Lady Catherine and the Real Downton Abbey
At Home at Highclere
Christmas at Highclere
Seasons at Highclere
The Earl and the Pharaoh

A YEAR AT HIGHCLERE

Secrets and stories from
THE REAL DOWNTON ABBEY

THE COUNTESS OF CARNARVON

CENTURY

UK | USA | Canada | Ireland | Australia
India | New Zealand | South Africa

Century is part of the Penguin Random House group of companies
whose addresses can be found at global.penguinrandomhouse.com

Penguin Random House UK,
One Embassy Gardens, 8 Viaduct Gardens, London SW11 7BW

penguin.co.uk

First published 2025

002

Copyright © Lady Carnarvon, 2025

The moral right of the author has been asserted

Extract from *Four Quartets* by T. S. Eliot © Set Copyrights Limited, 2019.
Reprinted by permission of Faber and Faber Ltd
Extract from *I Went to a Marvellous Party* copyright © NC Aventales AG 1938
by permission of Alan Brodie Representation Ltd
www.alanbrodie.com
First plate section, pp. 4–5: *Downton Abbey* photography © Carnival Film & Television Limited.
All Rights Reserved

No part of this book may be used or reproduced in any manner for the
purpose of training artificial intelligence technologies or systems. In accordance
with Article 4(3) of the DSM Directive 2019/790, Penguin Random House
expressly reserves this work from the text and data mining exception.

Set in 13.4/16pt Garamond MT Pro
Typeset by Six Red Marbles UK, Thetford, Norfolk

Printed and bound in Great Britain by Clays Ltd, Elcograf S.p.A.

The authorised representative in the EEA is Penguin Random House Ireland,
Morrison Chambers, 32 Nassau Street, Dublin D02 YH68

A CIP catalogue record for this book is available from the British Library

ISBN: 978–1–529–96393–9

Penguin Random House is committed to a sustainable future
for our business, our readers and our planet. This book is
made from Forest Stewardship Council® certified paper.

To the Highclere Team

Contents

Introduction   1

1. January: New Eras   3
2. February: The Home Team   26
3. March: Living with a Film Crew   53
4. April: Telling Tails   84
5. May: The Secret Gardens   105
6. June: 'I Went to a Marvellous Party'   133
7. July: Nature and Nurture   159
8. August: Mr Darcy   183
9. September: What It Takes   211
10. October: Entertaining Royally   238
11. November: Curses and Ghosts   265
12. December: Christmas at Highclere   287

Acknowledgements   311

Introduction

This is a book about what it is like to live and work in a castle today. Built as a home in another time, and for a very different world, Highclere has become one of the most famous castles in the world courtesy of its alter ego Downton Abbey.

Whilst there is obvious visual appeal in the architectural harmony of the Castle and the beauty of its natural surroundings, the real heartbeat of any home comes from the people who live and work there as well as those who have contributed so much to it in the past.

Highclere is about storytelling – the history of the house, the timelines of the ancient trees, the farmland, wildlife, and how they all fit together. The desire to tread lightly on this time-steeped corner of England is intrinsic to this place. From stories about living with a film crew, to the four-legged friends we share our lives with, marvellous parties and ghosts we meet en route, there is never a dull moment.

Life at Highclere, and this book, proceeds in step with the calendar, and as in many communities in England the primary topic of conversation is the weather. There is usually something wrong: it is too cold and wet, too grey, too snowy, which affects horses, gardens, farm and visitors, or else too hot and dry, which affects horses, gardens, farm and visitors; it may be too windy or too still – which could presage hot or cold weather – and there is constant perusal of forecasts and reciting of traditional adages. As the Dowager Lady

INTRODUCTION

Grantham remarked when asked, 'What do you think makes the English the way we are?': 'I don't know. Opinions differ. Some say our history. But I blame the weather.'

It seems hugely appropriate therefore to draw on the structure of the year to introduce some of the stories about those who live and work here. Highclere is a way of life and, just like the famous TV series and films about *Downton Abbey*, this book celebrates the eccentric, kind, hard-working people, full of good humour, who enable it to continue.

CHAPTER ONE

January: New Eras

*'For last year's words belong to last year's language
And next year's words await another voice'*
— 'Little Gidding', *Four Quartets*, T. S. Eliot

Each January, for six fabulous years, the New Year at Highclere began with a series of recces as the film team returned to plan scenes and once more familiarise themselves with the real Downton Abbey. The TV series was filmed over the first six months of the year and the whole ensemble of cast, crew, white lorries and vans would soon be winding up the front drive. The much-lauded TV series was followed by two feature films with a third awaiting release in 2025. The first film, released in 2019, carried on the Grantham family saga from the point where the TV series ended.

The years 2020 and 2021 were indeed a different era. The second film, emerging in 2022 with fresh trials for the Grantham family, was echoed in real life by an even more challenging new era that affected the entire planet; one of tragedy, swift change and the need to adapt to survive.

Highclere Castle, its estate and landscape, has however travelled through many new eras over several thousand years, and the efforts of the families living here to adapt and change are written in the terrain, on ancient rolls of parchment, in centuries-old letters, modern diaries, and now in digital records as well. In some ways, *Downton Abbey* itself was a new era for the Castle in that it threw an international spotlight on an estate that had attracted little public notice since the 5th Earl of Carnarvon's discovery of the tomb of Tutankhamun a hundred years before.

The oldest stories, however, begin outside, under the skies, in contact with the land, nature and wildlife.

Standing on the flanks of Beacon Hill at sunset, the current Castle lies a mile away, rooted in the woodlands to the northwest of this chalk hill and just touched by the last long streaks of light as the sun sinks down to rest. Here on the hillside, the spun-gold tendrils of winter sunlight briefly illuminate a mosaic of windswept grasses which, in that moment, seem fitting embellishments to a perfect Arcadian landscape.

The summit of Beacon Hill is defined by the ruined stone walls and foundations of the half-buried, grass-covered Iron Age homes, remnants from a time when people were more connected to and dependent on the natural world. This ancient fortified community marks just one of the many new eras witnessed by the ancient landscape surrounding Highclere.

Iron Age man farmed and lived around Beacon Hill, or Weald Setl as it was called then, for perhaps 800 years, shaping a landscape of pasture and arable land together with managed woodland. They worked their fields and reared their animals: pigs, cattle and sheep, essential for food and survival. Settlements were enclosed for safety and land ownership was important. Weald Setl – which translates as 'settlement of the chieftain' – was a communal gathering place, perhaps even a stronghold. Iron Age architecture is characterised by hillforts, designed to make an impact; they were impressive undertakings, built and achieved through teamwork.

Not much is known of the structure of Iron Age communities. They marked the seasons of the year under the auspices of their religious leaders, druids, beginning with Imbolc, a celebration of light and renewal which took place in February after the darkest days had ended. Beltane on 1 May heralded moving the cattle to summer grazing; Lughnasadh in August was a time to pray for and celebrate the ripening crops, whilst the three days of Samhain marked the return of the dark time of year when the barriers between this world and the spiritual world temporarily opened.

The passing of the days of the year was marked in a different fashion from today. For convenience, mankind now divides up the year into months and weeks, aligning time across the world and across the past on a uniform scale. In reality, of course, the precise beginning and end of any timespan are difficult to distinguish, but the systems of nomenclature and mathematics that we now observe enable these distinctions to be made in ways that would have been surprising to our ancestors.

To Iron Age man, the natural world was fundamental. Then as now, Highclere had good trees – oaks in particular. The word 'druid' means 'oak knower', and such epithets connected the ancient sages to the earth and nature. Their wisdom was seen as sacred and god-given.

From the vantage point of the tall steep hill on which they lived, the Iron Age farmers would themselves have looked down onto the ancient tumuli of their ancestors, who had settled here several thousand years before. The Neolithic or later Bronze Age burials in the tumuli would still have been respected as sacred places and ancestors would have been left undisturbed long after the tumuli were built, used or even understood. Still visible on the estate today, they suggest that then, as now, our ancestors found solace in congregation and ritual.

In turn, these Bronze and Iron Age communities would have followed in the steps of even earlier eras, which saw the arrival of the Mesolithic settlers who discovered these newer, warmer lands as the last Ice Age retreated around 10,000 BC, but no traces of these peoples have been found here.

The land around Highclere was first settled and farmed around 4,000 BC. The round Bronze Age barrows date from circa 3,000–2,000 BC and are thought to have been built near groves of oak. It is therefore possible that druids lived here too, and a later Anglo-Saxon document which references the 'bounds' of Highclere details a track leading '*wiðig grafas*', towards graves or groves, which suggests a joint inherited linguistic reference.

Prehistoric cultures existed in various parts of the world for over two and a half million years, meaning that 99 per cent of our human experience was gained in the Palaeolithic era (or Stone Age) alone. The Bronze Age tumuli and Weald Setl (Beacon Hill) of the Highclere Estate represent a history and architecture that is just 5,000 years old. Nevertheless, in terms of being able to touch the past, this hill marks a unique inheritance for us and offers a valuable yardstick to earlier lives in this place.

The golden age of these Iron Age forts, with their ramparts, timber palisades and elaborate fortified entrances, was about 600 BC, and the dismantlement of these communities was the result of the Roman invasion of Britain that began in AD 43–7 under Emperor Claudius. The Roman General Aulus Plautius arrived in England on the south coast with four Roman legions, numbering towards 20,000 soldiers, as well as cavalry and auxiliary troops. Well trained and well armed, the Romans steadily advanced northwards, easily overcoming small and fragmentary settlements such as Weald Setl.

Part of our understanding of life in such settlements is due to a Greek traveller and explorer, Pytheas. He sailed around the British Isles in 325 BC and excerpts from his diaries remain, quoted and paraphrased by later Roman authors. He called Iron Age Britons the '*Pretanoi*', Greek for painted ones, a linguistic link to '*Britanni*'. He described Britons as renowned wheat farmers, but a simple people who live in thatched huts, stored their grain in subterranean caches and baked bread. The TV series *The Great British Bake Off* clearly has ancient antecedents.

Apart from bread wheat and spelt, they also grew '*eincorn*', '*emmer*', uncultivated oats and naked and hulled barley, with the latter being the predominant grain. Today, the landscape around Beacon Hill still clearly shows the British 'square field' system from this time. Whilst our ancestors found patterns in the sky and the seasons of the year, so we find sustaining patterns in our historic landscapes.

Weald Setl and the modern-day Highclere lie on the border between the Belgae tribes to the south and the Atrebates to the north, and an Atrebates coin found at the foot of Beacon Hill suggests at least some inter-tribe trade or influence.

The Atrebates tribe threw in their lot with the Romans, who gradually developed the town of Calleva Atrebatum, or Silchester, just to the east of Highclere in the centre of their territory. There are also traces of a Roman villa settlement at the foot of Beacon Hill, sheltered from the prevailing south-westerly winds and weather, which may have recycled and reused existing building materials in the area.

For the next 450 years, the land around Highclere was a division of the Roman administration of this new province of Britannia, forming part of its Western Empire until its collapse in AD 500. The Romans built towns and forts linked together by a network of roads, many of which are still in use today, if tarmacked and full of cars rather than soldiers and chariots. The rather prosaically named A34, which passes right by the Highclere Estate, is part of the original Roman route from modern-day Winchester to today's Manchester.

The same fields were also continuously cultivated. There may have been vines as evidenced in the Roman period at Silchester, but by using the new Roman ploughs, the larger cultivated strips to the east of Highclere could produce better yields and a granary was certainly built there. The Romans introduced domestic fowl, including pheasants, and changed the traditional farm layout of buildings. Previously, animals and humans would have either shared a space or, at best, there would have been one room for animals and one for people. Romanised farms, on the other hand, show a devolution of agricultural functions into outbuildings, which were placed around one, two, or even three yards.

Prosperous estates owned by an urban aristocracy were based on wealth from agriculture, and literary evidence indicates that Britain regularly exported grain to the Continent. This is borne out by the grain-drying furnaces widely found in villa excavations, but perhaps they were also connected to the increased need to dry wet-cut crops as the climate began to cool after around AD 400. Roman agriculture also understood the agricultural principles of reseeding meadows as part of a crop rotation, the three-crop rule, and the value of oats, legumes and roots.

For 200 years, in this country at least, the Roman Empire

enjoyed a stable government with an established judiciary, military security and a vast improvement in communications which opened it to new markets. Yet already by the second half of the third century, the towns were finding an insufficient basis for their economic activities in the rural life of the provinces, and by the fourth century many villas were in decline.

By the sixth century, the chalk and limestone uplands of much of southern England had been drained of their Romano-British peasantry. There is no single reason why this happened, but in part it must have been due to the changing climate and agricultural practices. Higher rainfall and lower temperatures in the latter part of the Roman occupation would have made these upland soils unworkable in autumn, leading to crop failures. There is evidence of a transition to stock-farming and an increased production of wheat in the lower lands, which is better fitted to moist conditions than barley. Combined with state pressure to produce wheat and wool, increasing maladministration, inflation, over-taxation, political insecurity and social disturbance in consequence, economic disintegration was inevitable.

Today, rough stones from the ramparts of the Iron Age fort tumble down the steep northern slope of Beacon Hill, to be hidden in the undergrowth and woodland. Only faint traces of the buildings within the fort, whether domestic or administrative, remain. Grain-storage pits have reverted to earth and the contours of the walls following the line of the terrain are just a muted reminder of the enormous team effort of construction. The signs of Roman occupation are even fainter.

The Anglo-Saxon historian Bede gave a precise date, AD 449, for the beginning of the next new era at Highclere, which was the arrival of the Anglo-Saxons. They came from three tribes, the Angles, the Saxons and the Jutes, who originated in different parts of Germany and Denmark, so the name Anglo-Saxons was really the simplification of a complex series of migrations into a single term.

Over the first half of the fifth century, the political collapse of the Roman Empire led to the gradual withdrawal of Roman military and civil authority from Britain. In AD 449, there is a record of an appeal from the Britons to Rome for help following the arrival of ever-more armed migrants from the north. However, from as early as the fourth century there are records of Anglo-Saxons being employed and paid by Romans to guard towns and roads in England, so not all were unwelcome.

According to Bede, the West Saxons were originally known as the Gewisse and were based in the Upper Thames Valley, which in turn was part of Wessex. Highclere lies within this region.

Cerdic was the head of a partly British noble family, with blood ties to existing Saxon settlers, who had been entrusted with the defence of Wessex in the last days of British sub-Roman military power, relying on a mixed population of assimilated settlers and British natives.

Various records confirm the presence of British landowners in Wessex over a hundred years after the beginning of the Saxon conquest, suggesting a steady pattern of assimilation in the area.

This period of history is often referred to as the Dark Ages because of the lack of records to chronicle it. It was also a dark period because of the so-called Justinian plague which, by AD 543, had spread to every corner of the Roman Empire. This was the same bacterium that some 800 years later would be responsible for the Black Death, and research has shown that it too originated in Tian Shan, Central Asia.

JANUARY: NEW ERAS

As the old way of life collapsed, archaeological records reveal a drastic reduction both in the population and in the standard of living of the British in south-eastern and central England, including obviously Highclere.

Needing a fresh start away from plague-ridden burials and tired land, the centre of life at Highclere moved north, a mile away from the old Roman villas and homes around Beacon Hill. The new site was slightly higher, with good views, and old maps suggest it formed a convenient crossroads.

Wells were made to draw up fresh chalk water, new ovens and farmyards built, and the settlement came to be called High-Clere. By AD 749, the buildings and lands were sufficiently established to be described in an Anglo-Saxon charter. King Cuthred of Wessex, seeking favour from Bishop Hunfrith of Winchester, granted Highclere, the buildings, land and woodland, including what is now called Old Burghclere, to the bishopric, keeping only Kingsclere for himself. The agricultural land at Burghclere was now the focus of farming endeavour and the settlement still had a Roman granary, with a church and village built next to it.

The charter defines the estate at Highclere in just eight lines. The southern boundary was formed from the *'hunig weg'* (honey way), which then turned down to find the watery 'wash' and the (River) Enbourne, before it described the eastern extent as passing the *'coferan'* (tree), and then *'withig grafa'* (towards graves), these words implying both the ancient graves and the oak tree groves of their all-knowing forebears. Amazingly, it is still possible to physically 'walk the bounds' of this original estate and find much the same heritage bar the northern part, and to observe the archaeological remains from this period.

Over the next 200 years, the population was gradually

re-established and a church was built at Highclere next to the farm buildings, with a cemetery to the north. Before long, a walled garden and orchard were built by the bishopric and streams dammed to create five fishponds two miles to the north of the bailiwick or district. By 1208, and the first real administrative records, the bishop had already established a residence at Highclere and a centre for collecting and measuring agricultural harvests.

The first Bishop of Winchester to construct fishponds was Henry de Blois, who was well known for being in the vanguard in terms of estate management and producing high-status food:

> In 1315–16 a new fishpond was made ... and a wooden channel and sluice were constructed ... in 1350–1 two channels were dug between the ponds ... In 1352–3 a weir was built beside the great fishpond ... A new fishpond was constructed at great expense in 1372–4 ... a new fishpond was made and enclosed in 1381–2 ... These ponds were within their own enclosures. [Sourced from the Bishops' Rolls of Winchester]

Carp was the mainstay of fish farming and records testify that four acres of ponds would return 1,000 carp per year if bred to fourteen or fifteen inches long (about two to two-and-a-half pounds in weight). Other fish that would have been farmed were tench, bream, perch, rudd, roach and pike.

Presumably one pond would have been a stew pond, not manured or cycled as the other ponds were. This would be used to store live fish and feed them oatmeal in order to improve the taste so that they were ready for eating.

The monks, lay brothers and agricultural workers populating Highclere would have been experts at maintaining the fish-farm cycle, ensuring there was sufficient water-flow and filtration. In turn, each pond would have been drained and the next one filled, with the surviving fish transferred there. In the meantime, cattle would have puddled and muddled the second pond, which helped to foster the growth of weed on which pond life could flourish. The carp would then eat the pond life.

In the thirteenth and fourteenth centuries, the catch from the Highclere fishponds was reserved exclusively for the use of the bishops and their royal and aristocratic associates, and it was almost always eaten fresh. However, fish could be preserved and Bishop William of Wykeham's household account roll, which survives from April to September 1393, shows that during this period the episcopal household mainly had to make do with smoked and salted fish.

The Winchester Pipe Rolls dating from 1209–1711 detail income and expenditure across the bishop's estates and thus provide insight into daily life at Highclere during this period. What is clear is that Highclere was gradually transformed from one of many manors within the bishopric into a significant medieval palace under first Bishop Edington and then Bishop William of Wykeham (1324–1404).

William Edington, Bishop of Winchester (1346–66), Treasurer of the Realm (1346–56) and Chancellor of England (1356–63), began the substantial rebuilding works of the administrative buildings at Highclere, as well as improving the agricultural buildings. It was a significant commitment to invest in an area that had previously been devastated by the plague.

However, Highclere really stepped into the hall of fame when it was transformed into a palace by William of Wykeham in about 1360.

Highclere Palace and the surrounding buildings reflected the traditional status and hierarchy of a princely home, and different chambers or rooms in the palace were allocated to the different ranks in the household. For example, the esquires would be allowed to gather together in the Lords' Chamber in the evening to talk of the chronicles of kings, to play the harp or sing in order to occupy strangers until their departure.

Wykeham's works at Highclere began with fairly modest repairs and refurbishments using a few thousand tiles in 1367–8 and 1368–9, rising to a crescendo of further expenditure over the following four years.

The hierarchy of the medieval world was based first upon birth and secondly upon service. William of Wykeham was unusual because he achieved the highest rank of royal adviser, architect and Chancellor of England, through service to King Edward III rather than being born of any rank at all. In fact, he was the son of a poor yeoman farmer in Hampshire, near Winchester.

King Edward III was a handsome man possessed with both natural ability and good fortune. Thomas Walsingham described him as 'a shapely man, of stature neither tall nor short, his countenance was kindly'. The king enjoyed outstanding victories on the battlefield at Crécy and Poitiers in the war with France, was blessed with many children and was also interested in technological advances. For example, he installed a clock on the bell tower at Westminster and initiated the shift from liturgical to mechanical time. William of Wykeham was closely associated with him, granted the rare privilege of private access to the king's chambers and inner rooms or cabinet.

Most of the entries in the rolls for Highclere are for repairs – of roofs, locks, sills and beams. There are references

JANUARY: NEW ERAS

to various rooms including a hall and a chapel. Although the estate supplied oak to other building projects, given it was used by the bishop and had a deer park, Highclere itself would probably have been built of stone. The hall would have been on the ground floor but the chapel may have been at first-floor level and have had an apsidal end. By 1240, further buildings were added so that the bishop's retinue could also be housed at Highclere. There was the chamber for the knights and the squires, for example, along with a wine cellar, dovecote, gatehouse and larder. Over the next decade, a long chamber, a stewards' chamber, a kitchen and a series of stables were built, along with the inevitable slew of necessary repairs. Some things never change. One courtyard became two courtyards, the outer one for the working areas and an inner one for more refined activities.

These centuries form an important part of Highclere's history in that they mark over 800 years of uninterrupted ownership. The stability afforded by the bishopric allowed for a period of relative prosperity and the continual development of the estate. In the wider world, it was an era which encompassed great change marked by increasing literacy, beautifully illustrated books, international cooperation in trade and ambitious building projects, both ecclesiastical and secular. With its heroes and saints together with painters such as Leonardo da Vinci, philosophers such as Galileo, explorers such as Columbus, and literature celebrating chivalry and courtesy, this era marked the beginning of the end of the Dark Ages. It is perhaps ironic that the current Highclere Castle celebrates the Middle Ages in its Gothic inspiration and homage to Wessex, from the wyverns carved into stonework of the Castle to the names of the bedrooms.

During the fifteenth and sixteenth century the bishopric's

interest in Highclere faded and the estate was sequestered by King Edward VI in 1551. It was briefly owned by the Lucy and Kingsmill families before it was acquired in 1677–8 by the current Lord Carnarvon's direct ancestor, Sir Robert Sawyer.

How much of the medieval buildings survived beyond the end of the bishops' tenure in 1550 is uncertain. The manor house, or Highclere Place House as it was then called, was completely rebuilt in an Elizabethan style in 1616, with a double front constructed of brick and freestone quoins. In 1676, records testify it had a large gatehouse opening into a courtyard, a great stable and a smaller stable, a woodyard and another yard, a long turf-house, barns and a dovecote. At this time, it also had a well-stocked garden of at least an acre in extent and two kitchen gardens, a four-acre orchard and a smaller orchard. The parish church was close by to the west of the house, set in a wholly agricultural landscape of arable fields and meadows, with the village of High Clere nearby.

Over the next three centuries the house was much altered. The parish church was rebuilt, mile-long avenues of trees planted, temple and grottos erected and extensive new gardens created for the pleasure of family and guests. Robert Herbert inherited the house from his grandfather in 1706 and improved and extended it in the early eighteenth century, giving new fronts to the south and the east. The next major phase of change took place between 1774 and 1777, when his nephew Henry Herbert, later the 1st Earl of Carnarvon, moved the main entrance of the house from the west to the north. He then built a new nine-bay front with a central pillared entrance. This period was dominated by the influence of ancient Greek and Roman classical design, and so, in the 1820s, Henry's son employed Thomas Hopper to make further alterations, which saw the house re-faced in stone.

JANUARY: NEW ERAS

Perhaps the greatest change, however, was in terms of the landscape. Led by a very innovative man of great vision, Lancelot 'Capability' Brown, it was an extraordinarily exciting new era in 'place making', which blurred the boundaries between art and nature in a completely contrary fashion to the formal and structured gardens of the previous centuries. It was no surprise therefore that, ever keen to keep up with prevailing trends, in 1770 Henry Herbert duly commissioned Capability Brown to draw up a plan for Highclere Park. His proposals are shown on a document now hanging in the Castle. Whilst many of Brown's suggestions were implemented, the work was actually carried out by Henry Herbert's own labourers in order to save some money. He himself wore out his horses riding to and fro whilst the work was being done, so invested was he in the scheme.

Field boundaries were swept away, arable land put down to grass, lakes created and trees and woodlands planted. It is worth noting that Capability Brown had spent some time researching Highclere, seeking to understand the land and its history. He was looking beyond the formal gardens and deliberately working within the bounds of the old medieval deer park.

Later on, the diarist William Cobbett praised the landscape in preference to many other comparable houses: 'I like this place better than Fonthill, Blenheim, Stowe, or any other gentleman's grounds that I have seen ... The oaks are still covered, the beeches in their best dress, the elms yet pretty green, and the beautiful ashes only beginning to turn off. This is, according to my Fancy, the prettiest park that I have ever seen. A great variety of hill and dell. A good deal of water ...'

The television opening credits for *Downton Abbey* begin with the parkland and, at the premiere of the first *Downton*

Abbey film in New York, the spires of the golden sunlit Castle rising above an autumnal glowing parkland was a breathtaking sight, which had the audience cheering and clapping. It gave us all the chance to glimpse the rural idyll that once shaped our relationship with the countryside, the remnants of which still exist if we look carefully.

The version of Highclere that is so known and loved today is the work of the pre-eminent Victorian architect Sir Charles Barry and his client the 3rd Earl of Carnarvon. Both were much travelled in the classical world, particularly Italy, and both brought back a vision inspired by the harmonious principles of Italianate architecture, from the interior's arches within the central saloon to the external pinnacles and spires reaching for the skies, as well as the Great Tower. The central saloon involved cutting-edge engineering work and its overhead leaded lights ensure natural illumination filters through to those living below. Despite the dramatic changes to the look of the house, it was however essentially a remodelling rather than a rebuilding, removing the Georgian stone facings and extending the footprint and the height.

Sadly, both Barry and the 3rd Earl died before the works were finalised and it was the 4th Earl who completed the interiors of the Castle, including perhaps one of the most glorious rooms, the library. The proportions of the room, its detailing and the collection of 6,500 books, is an enduring legacy, especially when so many great libraries have been dispersed.

At Highclere, the classical is mixed with a grand, essentially British medieval style. In addition, many of the bedrooms were named for the old Anglo-Saxon kingdoms – Wessex, Mercia, Northumberland and Kent. Apart from its influence on Victorian architecture, the ideals of medieval chivalry also inspired the literature of Alfred, Lord Tennyson and Sir

JANUARY: NEW ERAS

Walter Scott, spinning stories around a golden age of civilisation which projected a romantic morality and fascination with the tales of King Arthur. The 4th Earl of Carnarvon was himself very much a historian and antiquarian, giving lectures on Anglo-Saxon times, and could well be described as a Christian medievalist.

For all the historical associations, its place within a wider community and its longevity within the landscape, fundamentally modern-day Highclere Castle was built as a home – not only for a family but also for the many staff and agricultural workers who lived both within its walls and in the nearby cottages and surrounding villages. It may have been built with all modern aids available to ease life in 1842 yet in today's terms it is anachronistic – a family home with 250 to 300 rooms and extensive areas for a staff who no longer exist.

Thanks to increasing industrialisation, life in Highclere changed dramatically between 1842 and 1914 as it did everywhere in England. No one date marks the beginning of this new era, but steam ships speeded up global trade, railways began to stretch across countries and continents (as well as counties) and travel became possible for wider swathes of the population. By the beginning of the twentieth century, motor cars were in their infancy, telephones allowed speech through space, photographs miraculously captured images, machines heavier than air could fly and electricity was replacing gas lamps and candles.

If there is one reason why Highclere made it through the swift upheavals of the last century, it was the good fortune of the 5th Earl in choosing a wife with a fortune and the vision to match it. Almina Carnarvon was the beloved daughter of Alfred de Rothschild and he stepped in to provide a dowry of £500,000, some £60 million in today's terms. He supported his son-in-law and daughter in various endeavours as well as leaving them another legacy on his death.

Thanks to his generosity, both of them were able to embrace and enjoy the new technologies. Lord Carnarvon was one of the earliest enthusiasts of the motor car as well as a keen photographer. Almina replumbed the Castle and, in 1895, introduced electricity. Entrepreneurs and inventors such as Charles Rolls and the earliest aviators, from Charles Voisin to John Moore-Brabazon, stayed at the Castle, whilst Geoffrey de Havilland made his first flight from a flat field on the southern boundary of the estate in September 1910. Meanwhile, Lord Carnarvon had found his true passion: Egyptology. From 1906 until his death in 1923, both the Pharaohs of an antique land and the modern world of Egypt were to become an integral part of his life as he travelled to Egypt by rail and steamship for several months every year.

Highclere Castle was designed to accommodate family, guests and staff on a grand scale, which it did with tremendous flair and style during this period. Sixty indoors staff looked after the family and its guests, with gatherings ranging from weekend house parties for the grandest in the land to celebrations for 500 local children or staff parties. Always busy, all the rooms were in use, with most of the requisite food supplied by the estate. The vegetable gardens, orchards and greenhouses provided supplies for the Castle kitchens, whilst the tenants on the farm grew grains and kept cows for milking, cattle, sheep, chickens and pigs. Some 250 families lived around the Castle and were part of its various enterprises. This rural community supported and surrounded Highclere, from the foresters to keepers and farmers. Equally, they were supported by Lord and Lady Carnarvon. Even during the years of the First World War, Lord Carnarvon continued to pay salaries to the longstanding estate families whose sons and husbands had gone to fight. He also bought tea and cheese in huge quantities to help sustain the dependants.

As the casualties mounted and the British Army grew in size, the numbers working at Highclere correspondingly declined. At the same time, more women left to work in a number of different industries to replace the menfolk. With financial support from her father, Almina transformed Highclere into a hospital during the war years. Patients were welcomed into the best bedrooms with good food, beer and kind nurses whose byword was cleanliness, but who were also there to talk with them, help them write letters or venture outside to sit under a tree. Ever practical, Almina had installed an operating theatre in Arundel bedroom and the surgeons arrived by train each Monday, whilst Saturday was visiting day.

Several hundred letters record the grateful thanks sent by the patients after they were transferred elsewhere to convalesce following their hospital treatment, usually to houses by the sea where the clean air was believed to be beneficial to healing. The handwriting gave clues about each man's state of mind, wibbly-wobbly if their hand was injured, sometimes in pencil, sometimes written on headed paper from their next port of call, full of courage and of hope but also sometimes of fear. Fear for the repercussions of their injuries but also the realisation that once they had passed their medical boards they would have to return to the trenches and the theatre of war once again.

The word 'war' had been scribbled shakily across the Highclere visitors book in August 1914 when the country still hoped it would be over by Christmas. Instead, for five long years, Lady Carnarvon never ceased welcoming casualties to her home. If the scale of the wartime suffering was beyond understanding, on an individual level nevertheless Highclere offered compassion and healing.

Eventually, it was over and the Armistice was signed at 11 a.m. on the eleventh day of the eleventh month in 1918. Quite literally, the guns fell silent. Everyone hoped it was a new era of peace.

The year 1918 radically reshaped the map of Central and Eastern Europe. New nationalistic forces took the place of the previous three powerful empires – Germany, Russia and Austria-Hungary – and the early interwar years began with economic uncertainty, taxation and inflation. Lord Carnarvon sold off the Bretby Estate in the Midlands and struggled to practise economy to balance the books. Into this world came the discovery of the tomb of Tutankhamun in 1922, a golden glimpse into a distant realm. The ancient Egyptian civilisation far outpaced its European equivalents in terms of sophistication and knowledge. Whilst Highclere's Bronze Age inhabitants scraped a living in mud huts, the Egyptians built the pyramids and created incredible works of art.

The 5th Earl died too young aged just fifty-six and once more Almina came to the rescue. Her father's collections went on sale at Christie's in 1925, considered one of the great sales of the century. A number of paintings from Highclere were also included and the finest Egyptian antiquities were sold to the Metropolitan Museum of New York in order to defray death duties.

If Highclere Castle entered the 1920s and 1930s with optimism, the lack of a crystal ball to predict the next few decades can only have been a positive. The 6th Earl (my husband Geordie's grandfather) did survive two World Wars and continued to live in the Castle throughout his life. However, he often said to Geordie, 'I am the last of the

Mohicans, darling boy.' It was an amusing remark, but at heart reflected the prevailing mood in the quietly decaying great houses of England. They cost too much to staff and maintain, and perhaps as many as 1,200 of them vanished in the period after the Second World War to the mid-1970s.

The 6th Earl (1898–1987) may have believed economy was the rule of the day at Highclere but this was not financial constraint as we might understand it. His staff in the early years after he inherited consisted of a butler, a valet, a first footman, a second footman, a hall-room boy, an usher, a head chauffeur, a second chauffeur, a chef, a first kitchen maid, a second kitchen maid, a scullery maid, a still-room maid, a housekeeper, five housemaids, an electrician, a night watchman, a head groom and two under grooms.

Writing in 1972, the 6th Earl's butler Robert Taylor commented:

> I've served Lord Carnarvon for over 35 years and during that time I have seen so many changes but since World War II we are struggling to continue. I am one of the last of the old guard and none of us are getting any younger. Highclere remains as it has done for hundreds of years but now it's an island and the waters are lapping at the doorway. At 60 I feel young and strong and at 75 his Lordship is robust but our individual faults must become more obvious as each day passes though no doubt, we both make our concessions the one to the other.

As with the Great War of 1914–18, the Second World War fundamentally changed English society. In the 1940s, Churchill himself noted that it was only in hindsight that he recognised the underlying currents of socialism sweeping through the country's populace. They had all fought the war and they had all won the war, and they were entitled to dictate the conditions of peace.

The 6th Earl wrote in his memoirs:

> I have witnessed the passing of an era that spans man's first powered flight to the moment he stepped on the moon. Who could ask for anything more? I have met some of the greatest men of the century. I've been privileged to call them my friends. I have been served more faithfully than perhaps I deserved through successes and failure, through peace and in war. It is a different world but yet when I walk out onto the lawn and behold the cedars of Lebanon, I realise that all changes are relative and nature alone spans the changes that man brings about.

At the end of his life, he again wrote:

> I have loved every moment of my life and have taken great joy from my friends. Perhaps I have not loved wisely but certainly quite well . . . I sigh for the future of Highclere. Sometimes I sigh for the future of England but when I see the young people of today, I marvel and pray for their well-being. Farewell my friends.

On his father's death, the 7th Earl continued to live in his home on the estate and for the first time in a millennium the Castle was uninhabited. It was my parents-in-law who, together with my husband, first opened it to the public as the estate fought to find a new role and purpose in this modern world. Initially, it was only open for around forty days in the summer and it wasn't until Geordie and I took over that we decided it would be better to expand the opening to include spring, Christmas and other seasons.

Highclere is a 'Stately Home'. Geordie and I have taken both words to heart. It is a home once more and a gracious one, which we share each year, all year, with thousands of visitors.

As the saying goes: 'Life is a journey to be experienced, not a problem to be solved,' but life on a great estate like Highclere actually involves both. Its history is one of constant adaptation to new politics and changing social mores and, with luck and careful management, it will continue to adapt successfully into the future, as it faces each new era.

CHAPTER TWO

February: The Home Team

'You're entirely bonkers. But I'll tell you a secret. All the best people are'
— *Alice's Adventures in Wonderland*, Lewis Carroll

For many stately homes, including Highclere, February is a month devoted to much-needed repairs and restoration work, as well as finding new team members for the coming year as we look forward in hope.

One morning, twenty years ago, I opened the double doors from the red-carpeted saloon corridor leading towards my study and greeted the well-dressed man who leaped up from an armchair by the fireplace. I noticed his shock of dark hair and warm polite voice. He was wearing a pinstripe suit and clutching a folder of papers. Geordie followed me in and we all shook hands and sat down. John Gundill had sent in his CV following an advertisement we had placed in the personal columns of *The Times* and *Telegraph* newspapers in an attempt to find a Castle manager.

In most ways this is a rather arcane job, but amongst the replies to our adverts, Geordie had immediately spotted John G's CV as he had run racecourses. On a racecourse you are dealing with people from all walks of life, as well as the weather and animals, and it was therefore unlikely that any day would ever run smoothly. I was concerned that he seemed to live in Yorkshire as, despite what *Downton Abbey* later depicted, Highclere Castle is in Hampshire, some 220 miles to the south.

It emerged that his wife and her family had grown up not far from here and they wanted to relocate. John's folder of papers turned out to contain many questions for us and demonstrated his focus on detail. He accepted our offer and his very first weekend (in early May) was somewhat of an ordeal by water as he helped us get through a large outside concert in torrential rain, followed two weeks later by a country fair, also in torrential rain.

The fields in which theoretically cars could park for the fair were so muddy that Geordie and the organisers had reluctantly decided to close the grounds. This is one of our largest events with, at that time, up to 12,000 people expected to visit over two days. Dressed from head to foot in waterproofs, with a wide-brimmed hat keeping rain off his face, in the mode of Brave Horatio at the gate, John was asked by my husband to walk up the long line of impatiently queuing cars on the public road to tell them that, unfortunately, we'd had to shut the event. He was called all manner of names but kept going. Twenty minutes later, walking back the other way, John saw that the endless snake of cars was moving forward. My husband and the organisers had identified another parking field. As the same cars passed John, he was subjected to a second barrage of abuse and returned to find my husband had driven off, leaving him with a further mile-and-a-half walk back towards the Castle.

Rather amazingly, John appeared for work the next week. At that time, Geordie and I were picking up every baton in terms of roles in the Castle and one of my very glamorous first jobs had been to write a traffic-management plan. It was wonderful to have another pair of hands available and someone with whom to discuss such assessments.

It is always rather difficult to describe exactly what John does. He certainly walks an awful lot and his high step count allows him to indulge with much enjoyment in his wife Henrietta's excellent cooking and the medicinal glass of red wine at the end of the day. Every evening before leaving Highclere, he is to be found walking around the walls of the Castle looking for problems as it is often easier to hear or see something out of place from the outside. For example, on a Friday at 4 p.m., whilst walking past the Castle boiler rooms, he will find the inevitable leak that could have manifested itself earlier in the day or week but did not. Unfortunately, copper pipes today are not what they used to be; they tend to be much thinner in this century than they were in the past and it is always the hard-to-reach pipes in an awkward corner that fail first.

John's folder of notes has grown, and since every email and conversation is duly recorded, the filing cabinets, piles of paper and now leaning towers of paper in his office have expanded over the two decades. In fact, it is no longer possible to find a chair or see the table around which to have a meeting. Fortunately, we have since renovated the estate office and acquired a conference room. However, if John and I are trying to recall a point of discussion or a line on a contract, I know he will soon be saying, 'Hold the line, caller,' and after various shuffles and grunts, the correct paper will be unearthed and the scribbles triumphantly recalled.

John studied law briefly before racehorses beckoned, whilst I studied law as part of my accountancy training, and so often, in order to minimise lawyer's fees, he and I will slowly read through contracts, drafting initial replies and arguing over words and commas. Whilst we are sitting together at his desk, sometimes I ask if I can have the keyboard, which gives him palpitations. Sometimes he grabs it back so we have a bit of a childish tugging match.

However, John, Geordie and I have gained a wealth of experience since those rainy days spent slogging through mud when we began working together. Geordie had spotted a very good man.

Every week John convenes a Castle meeting and asks all the departments to attend. This Highclere term is rather grand and traditional, deriving from the old ledgers of a century and more ago, in which the household was divided into discrete departments or areas of responsibility. In perfect cursive script written upon faintly ruled lines meticulous records were kept within the copious ledgers now occupying shelves in the muniments room, an area fitted out for the 4th Earl by his guardian Sir William Heathcote, as recorded on a Latin plaque on the wall above the door. The names and salaries of every servant within all the different departments are noted. Of course, much larger numbers were employed in those days: twenty-five people in the maintenance department as opposed to four today, a similar number in the forestry department, fourteen footmen, three butlers of varying rank, chefs, housemaids, still room maids, chauffeurs, grooms, and over a hundred men and boys in gardening, all paid in pounds, shilling and pence.

The accounts were managed by the house steward, a superior sort of butler. Almina, the 5th Countess, even employed a groom of the chambers called Roberts. From reading between the lines, it appears that he helped with organising events, attended the main door, ensured writing materials were kept in good supply, and in summary was a wizard at anticipation and planning.

Travel was arranged by Fernside the valet or by Roberts, but the removal of the household between London and Highclere was organised by the house steward. Travelling with the family was a role that was much coveted by servants, yet one requiring hard work and endless organisational skills. Suitcases then were perhaps less cumbersome than the travelling chests of the distant past, but nevertheless not quite the modern rolling cases.

It all makes me feel slightly rueful as it would be marvellous to have such teams on hand to help run the Castle and grounds today. After all, Highclere is still the same size now as it was 150 years ago, the time to which many of these staff records relate, but these days, for example, there are just two of us clearing leaves out of a gutter on a winter weekend – and there are an awful lot of gutters.

I do have a little black book (or rather phone) containing the mobile numbers of David and Andy the electricians, Steve the roofer, Ben the brickie, Ashley the tree man, Mark and Geoff the plumbers, Richard with Team Withers, the painters. They of course are all independent contractors but nevertheless maintaining Highclere is like supervising refurbishment of the Forth Road Bridge and, on their part, we are probably considered a valuable contribution to their pension plan.

Fortunately, we have a human resources company to help with all the employment laws and regulations that seem to take up ever-more of John's and my time. He tries to keep up with all the courses we need to provide for employees: health and safety, use of chainsaws, diggers, risk assessments, first aid, manual-handling courses, working-at-height courses, as well as managing the fire and alarm systems, before we even approach the business side of things.

The storyline in the first series of *Downton Abbey* began in

1912, during an era when any well-ordered household knew exactly which tasks needed to be accomplished and who should be responsible for each of them. The butler and the housekeeper, the valet and the lady's maid, the cook and the chauffeur, all headed up a clear hierarchy, which was even more jealously guarded than the titles and rights of seat or lineage upstairs.

Downton gathered a cast who have become household names, but the number of central characters had to be realistic and not too large so that we could follow their stories without getting muddled. In reality, there would have been many more characters below stairs, but these days many of the positions no longer exist despite the fact that the job or activity may still need to be done.

Each room in the Castle tends historically to have a specific function, but there is also an overarching harmony that contributes to the prevailing sense of order. The library is for reading or discussion and contemplation; the dining room is where the family gathers to eat; the robing room is the best place to store clothes; the study was where traditionally you would write diaries and letters; the drawing room was used to withdraw into before or after dinner; the smoking room was somewhere gentlemen could gather together; the morning room was for the lady of the household, and so on. That sense of order and place is something that we all recognise and see as a virtue when it is depicted in households of the past, whether in books or films. In real life too it can be a blessing. After all, Highclere Castle was built as a home, albeit one with 250 to 300 rooms.

Some of the household roles are still recognisably the same. The one played by the house steward Streatfield in Edwardian times remains relatively unaltered some 120 years later and is fulfilled by Luis (Coelho). Its focus is on managing the butlering or banqueting team, looking after the wine cellar, and organising lunches and dinners. Where it is unrecognisable in terms of the past is in its interaction with our public visitors when Luis's role switches to include managing all the tearooms and the staff employed there.

Simon (Andrews) the farm manager remains in charge of growing crops and the husbandry of animals but is helped by significantly more machinery than was available in the past, though there are far fewer farm workers. Emmeline the head gardener is stepping in the footsteps of predecessors such as Mr Blake in 1912, though again with smaller numbers to help her, whilst today's kitchen team would recognise the roles of all their forerunners.

An element of John's role as Castle manager relates to the part formerly played by Mr Rutherford, who was the family agent here for decades. Both men are or were conversant with the shooting estate, the leaky castle roofs, and the larger projects concerning plumbing and wiring. Judging from letters in the archives, Rutherford was as much a trusted member of the family and staff during the time of the 5th Earl as John is today; a listening post yet someone not afraid to speak his mind.

Sitting in on the weekly catch-up sessions are all the Castle's familiar faces. John's meetings are not known for their brevity but are very detailed. Luis sits to one side wondering when he can escape, but his role is utterly key to every single event so he has to stay. His team has four full-time staff, but increases by another thirty to forty during the summer and by slightly fewer for receptions and dinners. Luis is often to be found accompanied by his spaniel Super Ted who is a true Highclere dog. Clemmie, my chocolate-brown spaniel, gave birth to three puppies and two never left Highclere. I kept one little bitch, who was soon christened Evie, whilst a male puppy found a home with Luis. Ted is good-looking, enthusiastic and happy to learn new tricks – he is just glorious.

Luis and I also meet sometimes in the middle of the night – along with a number of firefighters. There are 542 fire detectors in the Castle and each time the system is updated there are teething problems with dust, flies or spiders. Once the fire alarm had gone off as usual about 4 a.m. and I emerged to tackle the problem dressed in a most attractive ensemble of beanie hat, thick sweater, yoga pants and gym shoes, to find Luis similarly attired and accompanied by two rather smarter-looking firemen. The warning panel said the alarm was in the north-east corner tower. The fire engine was waiting in the courtyard, but we were sure it was just flies as only a single detector was flashing a warning. We ran round the top-floor corridors with the firemen, looking for the correct tower in the dark. I had thought it must be above the maids' rooms but was corrected by Luis saying, 'Lady C – this is the south side. It can't be here.' 'Bloody hell,' I replied, 'where is north, Luis?' Swiftly pursued by the firemen, we wheeled around and further on we found the offending, dusty fire detector.

Luis arrived at Highclere some sixteen years ago. He was hugely enthusiastic and leaped around everywhere. Apart from the pleasure he takes in his role as butler, in the summer months he welcomes some 1,200 visitors a day and liaises closely with the kitchens and tearooms. Either he or I will try and offer an interview to any student looking for their first holiday job. By the end of the summer, we generally have a great band of youngsters who are collectively much more self-assured and pleased to be earning their own money.

Until we launched Highclere Castle Gin, I had not quite

focused on Luis's cocktail-making skills. He is an excellent mixologist and a gifted teacher, and has developed his skills even further in helping us with our Highclere Gin. We now have 'Luis's Bar', which appears during summer opening and serves Lord Carnarvon's favourite cocktail, one dedicated to me, an Upstairs, a Downstairs, and a daily special. Luis loves football and is full of bonhomie, constantly finding new friends amongst the visitors, whilst simultaneously selling drinks made from gin – or indeed whole bottles – and doing selfies. His team rapidly pick up on his vivacity and become more confident themselves, adopting his mantra that this is another fun day and we are all lucky to be here.

None of the Highclere Castle staff of Edwardian times would recognise the social media aspect of work here today, even if the filming might be less surprising to them given the family interest in photography. I idly asked Caitlin, who helps me with social media, if she remembered her job interview here. She nodded, smiling, so I asked her if there were any questions that she had found unexpected. Her reply was that she had wondered why I'd asked if she had any welly boots.

Personally, I think it is quite a useful question as life and work at Highclere depend very much on what is happening outside. It is perhaps a contrast to the fictional family of *Downton Abbey* who are always immaculately dressed on all occasions with polished shoes, coiffured hair, and usually sitting perfectly upright on a sofa asking for a cup of tea or something stronger.

In reality, the weather is often the main topic of conversation at Highclere because we actually have to deal with it day-to-day. For example, if it is, as usual, raining, we need to know if we have enough shelter for visitors and that the tearooms are fully staffed. The gardeners survey the skies to determine whether they can mow the lawns and the farm needs to know if it is too wet for them to drill the fields with seed. Are the gutters and hoppers on the Castle unblocked, is the passageway outside the gift shop flooding, do the horses need rugs and should they be in the stable or out in pasture, and how are the car parks holding up and perhaps the car parkers may need a round of hot chocolate or similar? A pair of wellies is very helpful, if not obligatory, for much of everyday life here and, it seems, throughout the year. Computers and emails are just one part of any job or role.

Caitlin did indeed have a pair of wellies and she did join Team Highclere. Given she has her own horse, she kindly helps bring the Castle's in or out and takes the dogs for a walk with me, which is a good way of having a meeting.

———

Eighteen years ago, Geordie, John G and I were sitting in the music room looking forward to lunch. As part of the interview process for a new head chef, we had asked our prospective interviewees to come and cook. Paul Brooke-Taylor had prepared a menu of beetroot-cured salmon, followed by a partridge dish and then a chocolate fondant. Absolutely delicious. We then sat down for a chat and offered him the role. Not long afterwards, he and his girlfriend Serena moved into a white-painted cottage on the edge of Highclere's gardens.

Paul told me that he hoped to be at the Castle for three to five years – he was ambitious, always asking 110 per cent of himself and setting exacting standards. In due course, he asked Serena to marry him and, naturally, the wedding took place here; it was the happiest day, with Richard Walton, the chef who had given Paul his first job, as his best man.

Four or five years later, I was thinking about his career path and wondering when he might say something. However, in contrast to his original statement, from time to time he would say, 'Lady C, you're not thinking of asking me to move on, are you?' 'Never for my part,' I would reply. He then said, 'Good,' I said, 'Good,' and it remained a reassuring routine between us. He was happy here.

Paul said he did not think he wanted children but Serena knew otherwise, and he could not have loved his son and daughter more. Paul was a huge football fan and his son Jack has become a very able young footballer. Daughter Amelia is a gymnast and thus much of Paul's time was spent being coach, starting teams, driving to games and organising charity matches. Memorably, even Geordie played for him one freezing February. His family time was always a precious priority.

Walking out of his cottage in the morning, he would see the horizon stretching away in front of the Castle towards the hills of Oxford, a view so beautiful that it is almost breathtaking. Paul would then turn and walk down the drive to the Castle kitchens. He always said he had the best commute in the world.

I have written various books in which cooking and recipes play a major part and he and I had to learn how to get along during the writing process. He was a chef and I was, and am, just a cook. I had an AGA which he refused to cook on and I couldn't figure out his ovens. I learned about a chef's need for precision and he slightly despaired of my sometimes experimental approach. We tossed pancakes together, swapped stories and had a lot of fun. Food is at the heart of life and it is the heart of Highclere. Paul and Luis would compete to see who had the most photos in any of the Highclere books,

FEBRUARY: THE HOME TEAM

which was hilarious, but overall, I would say I probably won anyway. We often worked late and I spent a lot of time with Paul.

Lesley Nicol, who played Mrs Patmore in *Downton*, has stayed in the Castle as our guest and she cooked with Paul for a documentary about Highclere. He was also filmed cooking for other TV shows and, of course, was really thrilled to cook with Mary Berry. I think we all loved Mary Berry.

In the Castle kitchens, he ensured that there was an excellent process for producing food for general admission tours, with up to 1,200 visitors, as well as all the afternoon teas. He has created fine-dining menus for guests from all walks of life, from royalty to Egyptologists, statesmen, musicians, writers, ambassadors, racehorse trainers and actors. We have done Christmases, New Year's Eves, Burns Nights and picnics together, filling every minute with sixty seconds of life well run.

He built a team here, in particular with Will, Andy, Rob and Raj, whilst Mandy joined in more recent times. Very much part of our wider team, Paul always added to John G's Wednesday meetings with his direct turn of phrase. Sometimes he was Scary Chef. Two of us might be found at the bottom of the flight of stairs leading to his office, arguing about who was going to confess that we had inadvertently booked double the number of afternoon teas we were supposed to. If it were me, I would go up and try to soft-soap him by asking about his children and Serena before admitting to whatever the disaster was. I just needed to promise him I would manage it better in the future. Obviously, something else would then go wrong.

The Highclere kitchen has been situated in the same place for a thousand years but today it is a fully equipped modern catering kitchen. In this area we have embraced change. I would joke with Paul about how very expensive he was: wanting the best ovens, freezers and fridges, but whatever he suggested was always sensible and future-proof. The central kitchen space has a huge high-domed ceiling, which was once painted shiny cream. But then an artist and scaffold arrived and it was transformed, painted with blue sky and clouds, and a star in the east. It is lovely to see, but the star is now a rather poignant reminder that Paul has gone to live among the stars as we have lost him.

Cancer is unbearably cruel and unfair. There seems to be no rhyme or reason as to who gets it or why, or who survives and who doesn't. The treatments are brutal and awful for both the patient and their family. Paul was the bravest man we knew and he never gave up over the twenty-month span of his illness, always fighting fiercely for more time with his loved ones.

His funeral was one of the hardest of any I have ever been to and almost agonising in its intensity. Richard read a poem to say goodbye and, with extraordinary courage, Serena, Jack and Amelia all spoke as well, along with Paul's mother. He himself spoke directly to us as he had written his own eulogy, which was read by his sister and niece. He was:

> . . . *their North, their South, their East and West,*
> *Their working week and their Sunday rest,*
> *Their noon, their midnight, their talk, their song;*
> *They hoped that he would last forever, but we are all wrong.*

Once the raw shock of death is over, grief settles in, sitting with us in place of the person we loved. I'm not sure time heals so much as it teaches us how to bear the loss: it becomes a familiar shadow as we go on breathing and walking. All our thoughts remain with Paul's family – his wife and children – and, somehow, we have continued.

FEBRUARY: THE HOME TEAM

We have not found a new head chef. Instead, we have made our way forward by drawing on the strength of Andy and Will, with a part-time consultant in Rob. To begin with, we have all continued to tread the same path, meeting often to smooth out any gaps in terms of areas of responsibility within the kitchen. A year after Paul's death, I have not yet gathered myself to go up the stairs to his office – I might have to change the paint colour there first.

We have had a few muddles but that is life. We will change some of our menus and all write a new book together, and we will do our best. Paul used to humour me on Burns Night and take part in the parade of the haggis, and in some ways Robbie Burns's 'Epitaph' about the honest man who now lies at rest sums Paul up exactly:

> *The friend of man, the friend of truth;*
> *The friend of age, and guide of youth:*
> *Few hearts like his, with virtue warm'd,*
> *Few heads with knowledge so inform'd:*
> *If there's another world, he lives in bliss;*
> *If there is none, he made the best of this.*

Paul usually thought he was right and he did say it how it was. He is still part of Highclere – it takes a village past and present to nurture each other through the vicissitudes.

Another beloved member of the Highclere team whom we all miss is Les Taylor, who was 'part of the furniture' when in charge of security at the Castle for forty years, which exceeded the length of his original career with the Hampshire police force. He had joined them in 1952, spending time in Southampton and on the Isle of Wight, before being posted to Whitchurch, a town just six miles south of Highclere, as section sergeant. When he retired from the police in 1982, my father-in-law offered him a job organising security. One of his initial roles was to drive his new employer to race meetings and stable visits, often together with the Queen and, consequently, various personal protection officers.

Les also became our shoot captain and would always load for my husband. Otherwise, he loved golf and sailing, and used to keep a family fishing boat. Les sadly 'crossed the bar' when he was ninety-six years old. He never wanted to retire and stayed at Highclere until the end, ostensibly working part-time, although in reality he came in most days. He was such a familiar figure in all our lives, driving round the grounds in his little navy-blue car. He bellied that car on a tree stump in a field one winter's day, but luckily we found him, got him off and towed him back. None of us were sure why he was in the middle of the field, nor how he had found the tree stump. Later on, in 2021, he stumbled and fell whilst filling up his car at a petrol station. When he got to Highclere, we took one look at him and asked the kind nurse with the *Downton* film crew to check him over and dress his grazes. Les tried to convince her he was fine, but we got one of our team to drive him safely home and, in the meantime, hid his car.

Undeterred, the following day Les arrived in his wife's car and drove round trying to find his own vehicle, which had been put behind some greenhouses, half hidden in the laurel bushes. He was a most remarkable man and I often sat in his office to ask him for his view on something; there would always be a moment of contemplative silence before he imparted some of his wisdom accumulated over the years. There was little he had not seen.

Les said of Highclere: it is a 'family-run place and in consequence you become part of the family. It's a family job and you're your own boss to some extent, which suits someone like me.'

Compared to some of the other 'family' members, Les was a relative newcomer. One cold morning in 1960, the 6th Earl's agent arrived at Ivory Farm, Beacon Hill, and asked Pat and her father (Mr Hayes but always called Pop) if they'd like to paint the windows on the outside of the Castle. Until then neither of them had actually seen the Castle and they were somewhat stunned when they arrived in front of it. However, they accepted the job and Pat is still here, but now supported by her husband Mike (Withers) and their friend 'Young Richard', who is a slip of a thing at nearly sixty years old.

Pat has so many memories of her time at Highclere. One of the best, however, might be when she was presented to the late Queen Elizabeth II by the 7th Earl. The Castle was first opened to the public in 1988 and my parents-in-law had organised a grand ceremony. Pat had really not wanted to go as she heard there would be 800 people there and that was not her thing. However, she was persuaded to attend and was standing in the drawing room next to Stan Anstey the brickie when she realised the Queen was coming their way. Stan just had time to grab Pat's rather large handbag and thrust it out of sight, hoping that it wouldn't catch the priceless porcelain behind them and send that crashing to the floor. The Queen said she had heard that Pat had painted the Castle three times and might be painting it a fourth. Trying to curtsey and reply simultaneously, Pat responded that she would probably need a Zimmer frame by then. Lord Carnarvon promptly offered to get her one and help her push it!

Pat met her husband Mike at a dance soon after she had lost her father and been stood up by her then fiancé, so it was a most fortuitous encounter. Mike stood out like a sore thumb as he was dressed in a suit whilst everyone else was wearing jeans. They were married in Highclere Church in 1973. Mike loves bees and beekeeping and now collects the estate honey, which is used in the kitchen and sold in the gift shop. Occasionally his bees get him into trouble. On the morning they were to be married, Mike got sidetracked when he went to collect a skep of bees from an apple tree near his mother's home and then had to scramble to get to his own wedding. Pat and Mike also keep ferrets and currently have about eight of them.

Pat has worked for three generations of Carnarvons and in the early days turned her hand to many other odd jobs as well as painting. Helping out during the shooting season, she would often tiptoe up the stone staff stairs to peer over the balustrade of the gallery at the dancing below in the saloon. Her verdict?

'You can't get nicer people to work for than them Carnarvons. The three Earls were totally different and absolutely brilliant. The 6th Earl called every woman "my love" and every man "my friend". The 7th Earl would round the corner calling out "hello", and over the years he became ever-more relaxed.' I think Pat loves the current Earl most because she's known him since he was born and he is such a good man.

Pat and I remind each other that there's always something beautiful and something different to see every day. Luckily, she still loves working here otherwise she would have been long gone. She reckons she's the longest-serving member of the staff working at the Castle as Eddie Hughes the head keeper, with whom she went to school, retired after just sixty years. Pat is still painting the Castle but hasn't yet needed a Zimmer frame.

After my father-in-law died and our stewardship of

Highclere began, Geordie and I inherited two gardeners: Don and Philip. They managed the Monks' Garden, the greenhouses that were more or less still standing, and the borders in the Secret Garden. In due course, the advent of another garden area, incorporating a wilderness and arboretum, meant that their area of responsibility increased by perhaps twenty acres and they were understandably not thrilled.

Don was one of a kind, a truly skilled gardener who knew plants and the earth, but he was not a man who was easy to guide. Geordie and I would try to make a planting plan, which Don invariably said would not work, nothing would grow and it was a waste of time. In any case, he tended to plant only things he liked (usually orange), in the middle of everything and out of place, in our view. It was a constant game, but I learned so much from him.

However, the expanded garden meant it was time for Geordie and me to recruit a head gardener, and Paul Barker arrived. In the meanwhile, Philip came to help us in an area behind the Castle whilst Don stayed where he was, and so we recruited new help for Paul as well. Today our new lady head gardener Emmeline leads a larger team of five.

Don remained a legend in his own lifetime, full of stories and knowledge. He worked at Highclere for over forty years and, like Pat, over the lives of three Earls. I often sat with him and asked him for stories about Geordie's grandfather: there were so many. In one of them, the 6th Earl had decided to drive his car down the gravel footpath from the Castle leading into the Monks' Garden because it was raining and he wanted to cut some roses – presumably for a prospective girlfriend. Driving was not his forte; he had a chauffeur/batman called Bill Misson who was in charge of cars and on whom he utterly relied. His Lordship aimed his car at the gateway, which was too narrow and meant he took off one wing, both bumpers and mirrors, and dented the sides. Ignoring the damage, he leaped out and proceeded to cut all the roses, which annoyed Don. He then tried to turn the car around but got it stuck. He asked Don to sort it. Wisely, Don refused point blank. His Lordship then had to trudge back up to the Castle and admit what he had done to Misson, who apparently shouted at him and called him all sorts of names, although His Lordship gave as good as he got.

The 6th Earl was always cutting the best flowers, so Don used to try and hide all Lord Carnarvon's secateurs in an effort to limit his floristry sprees. I can only imagine that somewhere there must be a huge pile of them waiting to be found.

Towards the end, I did ask Don about retiring, but he said he preferred to come to work part-time as he did not want to spend every day with his wife Gwyn – he spoke as he thought, but then again so does Gwyn. Paul, our then head gardener, was very kind about collecting Don so that he could come and sit in the greenhouse and remain part of the team for as long as he wished. He died at home here at Highclere where he wanted to be. When Gwyn called to say he had gone, I went and sat quietly with her for few hours, with Don in his same old chair but covered by a sheet, until eventually an ambulance came. Gwyn has stayed where they always lived, walking her little dog, chatting to her neighbours or the *Downton* crew when they are around, playing bingo and, through the kind efforts of a fairy godmother, has even travelled for the first time to London to buy a lipstick from Harrods and has flown on a plane.

Not everyone at Highclere has been to London. An earlier gardener called Bill Sticker and his wife decided to catch a train to Paddington from Newbury to see what it was like.

Feeling nervous, but well dressed for the occasion, they set off. When they arrived under the huge metal gridwork of Paddington station they got out of the train and looked around. To their horror, they saw large signs saying 'Bill Stickers Will Be Prosecuted', and so they got straight back on the next train to Newbury, swiftly returning to the sanctuary of the gardens.

There is something about working with plants and the earth that is good for both body and soul, and I enjoy both planning a planting scheme and spending an afternoon weeding or planting out. Computer work and writing can wait until it's dark. Two or three times a year, I go onto Instagram or our website and ask for volunteers to help me weed the vineyard in the morning and, in return, come up to the Castle with me for the afternoon. It is an amazing day spent working with other keen gardeners until we can all look back proudly along lines of cleared vines.

Many of the people who work outside here have initially come to a meeting. We often end up, however, in the gardens, picking up a trowel or a fork whilst we talk. Without meaning to, they inadvertently start helping me and in a short time we find that we've cleared quite a lot of a bed, cut back some brambles or planted some hellebores to bring light and life to the February borders.

—

Hannah Gutteridge was already a keen gardener before she joined us to handle press and marketing. I first met her through a friend when I was looking for a yoga teacher – I love stretching out with a little yoga in the gardens and a teacher pushes me to go just a bit harder than I would on my own. It turned out that she specialised in food and drink PR and, as I was writing a cookbook and we were creating Highclere Castle Gin, this was serendipity. Hannah is very tall and stylish and of course loves dogs, so sometimes Cariad, her beloved Pekinese who is not the tallest, will appear on her desk to aid her typing. Hannah writes beautiful prose, adores her ink pen and leather diary, and is nothing if not direct. It is very clear if she does not like some suggested copy or the wrong choice of photo for a piece on Highclere.

Curiously, I also have another Hannah who came to work for me as an intern when she was studying Social and Political Science at Cambridge University. I remember her perched on a scruffy chair with a little desk before her in a doorway, helping with a huge summer charity event. She was always worried about her university results though only ever got scholarships and firsts before being accepted for law school then pupillage in an esteemed London Chambers before practising as a barrister. I always dreamed of having someone with her sort of analytic mind to work with, and I feel immensely grateful she returns to our world for a few days a month. Whilst not so tall as the other Hannah, she has the tallest dog in our world, a Great Dane called Wilma, so the 'Hannahs Squared' are a great combination.

I think many of our team are unique and one who definitely fits the bill is Paul Mactaggart – Paul Mac. He used to help me find Second World War planes that had come down on the estate – we have tried over the years to record and memorialise those who were sadly lost here, and now have a more detailed record of the airmen involved so we can pay tribute to their service during the war.

When Paul lost his job, I asked him to come and work here. I thought he was such a nice man that I found him a job welcoming visitors. He doesn't always listen, though, and once confidently announced that 'Leslie Camels' was here to see me. Everyone looked nonplussed as there are some camels that do arrive at the Castle for various Egypt-themed events. However I realised he meant Lady Camoys was here – who duly arrived, without any camels, as we were plotting related events with Stonor Park, her ancient home.

—

Laura arrived for an interview for a role as part of the estate team which she kindly accepted. Later I met her husband at our church fête and he asked me if I remembered the details of her interview. Slightly nervously I said, 'No, should I?' He replied saying Laura had returned home and, on being asked how it had gone, had told him that apparently I had said, 'It is all a bit random,' and I was not sure exactly what the job would entail but I liked her very much. Luckily for me, Laura accepted the rather vague job offer and I do like her very much. She has become a mainstay of the office although, in typical Highclere fashion, a lot of her day-to-day job requirement is indeed rather random.

I very clearly remember my father always encouraging my friends to 'have a bit of spark', not be afraid of having a go at things. Hiring at Highclere is tackled very much in that spirit and the opposite of the process by which CVs are analysed by a computer, leading to employees who are all similar and safe and tick the right boxes. I am not sure that is a healthy situation.

Jo is another, newer recruit to the estate office and initially I was worried that she might prefer a quieter workspace. The office is always noisy with the grooms constantly arriving with hot chocolate, tenants explaining that they have lost their keys again, John G trying to tell a funny story and Jo from accounts attempting to sort out a missing invoice. New Jo, however, is very much on top of the madness and during meetings is not averse to telling everyone to pay attention – mainly John and my husband as she has not yet finished sharing her PowerPoint. Simon our farm manager does listen. She is very impressive.

It is February and there are a few projects which it would be good to ask the farm to help with as it is their quieter period. Simon's team swells and shrinks depending on the seasons. In spring, part-time help arrives to aid Matt the shepherd with the lambing before they drift away again, and during harvest later on in the year we also need more hands on-deck. Simon's office is above that of the gift shop, which is useful as their flare for design helps to support the farm's endeavours to retail what we grow, from rapeseed oil to grain for chickens, horse feeds or the estate-reared lamb we sell. Simon is innovative and hugely caring, and our ethos is to tread lightly on this earth – we will always need to grow food to eat and yet we should be the best stewards we can.

In the early years, I tried to help run the gift shop as well as doing everything else. Geordie and I would both go up to the NEC by Birmingham each February to the Gift Fair Show. To start with, Jeanie, my mother-in-law, came as well, with Anne from the gift shop acting as our ears to the ground, researching what visitors might want.

After the first season of *Downton Abbey*, we found that my stock buying was woefully insufficient. I had to ask the Castle kitchens to up jam production and had a line of helpers busy doing the pricing (my son Edward and my niece Marina), whilst Nanny (part of my family since I was five years old) cut out little circles of cloth to go on the top of the jam jars.

The gift-shop girls were transitioning to new tills but sometimes resorted to a cash box in case anyone wanted to pay the analogue way, in order to reduce the shop queues. Duncan, our computer and IT colleague, was trying to take us forward into this century and would say wryly that the combined age of the gift-shop girls was older than the Castle. Anne was so polite that she would always try to insist she should be going up a ladder, not me (she was around seventy years old), but I would argue, win the point, clamber onto a chair and bring whatever was needed down from the top shelf.

We had to change gear and, looking for advice, I asked a girlfriend who I knew had a very good eye for giftware if she would mind awfully coming up with Geordie and me to the NEC fair that year. Unable to resist, she said she'd be delighted to but that, as she was a friend, there was absolutely no way she would carry on working for us as she did not want to lose a friendship. It was originally going to be for those few days, a little bit of advice and that would be all. That was in February. I then remember walking over to her desk and computer in an office in the Castle a month later. It was seven o'clock in the evening and I was waving some glasses and a bottle of wine, which was much appreciated – and fourteen years later, Sally (Popplewell) is still here and still a friend. She has transformed the gift shop and, whilst I much enjoy looking at the latest artwork ideas and products, Sally is the mastermind responsible for its stock and success. She has continued working with a mixture of gift-shop girls of all ages whilst Harry has also joined as a full-time assistant. Everyone helps unload lorries with her, John offering a non-stop commentary about the joys of working at Highclere and Sally promising biscuits.

The guides, meanwhile, tend to make their own biscuits.

The old steward's room just inside the Castle is now the refurbished guides room, where they have a radiator (a luxury in the Castle!) and a small kitchen. Alison the head guide runs a well-organised pool of perhaps forty to fifty very knowledgeable part-time guides who contribute immensely to the tours. From deputy guides to others who have been here for ages, there is a camaraderie and support system within the 'gaggle' that helps ensure Highclere feels like both family and a village. Most of them live nearby – anybody who commutes any distance to Highclere is rare.

Much of the computer infrastructure – from the online schedules in the diaries, to online tickets, guidebooks, the Egyptian exhibition interpretation, endless scanning, labels for the food produced in the cafes, shop prices and tills – has been put together by a Scotsman called Duncan who lives in Ireland. I met Duncan through my mother who told me she had just encountered 'a lovely computer man walking across the courtyard outside an office in Fulham. I think you should meet him, darling.' So I did and he ended up helping me in an early business venture, and then at the Castle when Geordie and I ventured forth, beginning with our diaries.

In 2002, if I rang the Castle office to enquire about a date, there would be a scurry around several desks to check the large office diaries and, if I had happened to get the date wrong on my first enquiry (easily done), it was simply too painful to ask again. We desperately needed to get everyone onto a shared computers system, i.e. Microsoft Exchange. This led to an invoicing and purchasing system on the one hand, whilst on the other Duncan could help me write guidebooks, which we then designed and produced. In addition, we started the lengthy process of scanning the masses of archive photos, often late at night when I was waiting to help clear up after a wedding. I was concerned that there was no back-up to anything in the archives in case of accident, whether by fire or water. The downside to this arrangement was that we were sometimes asked to be quiet as our voices carried when we chatted.

Our archive work dovetails into the continual cataloguing and research by our part-time archivist David Rymill, with whom I have explored many historical projects for my books. He has a brilliant knack for asking just the right search question.

Duncan's next project was a ticketing website so we could sell tour tickets online and scan visitors in. To start with, visitor reception was just a table and chair in a pop-up gazebo at the entrance, but when we had the funds, we bought a smart new kiosk, which makes life considerably easier as all the wiring is built in. I've often sat with Duncan for long hours whilst he's edited code to achieve a smoother booking process. He used to come and stay for a time before he returned home to Ireland, after which Skype became part of my life. Every year the systems become more sophisticated and resilient.

During Covid, if there is one person who helped Highclere, Geordie and me to survive, it was Duncan. He and his computer colleagues wrote the code that enabled us to offer transfers and vouchers, in great haste but with care. Whilst waiting for this new system to be up and running, my role was to communicate, retain goodwill where I could, and answer emails. Geordie was managing the government administration but, in the end, we have created a business that is far more resilient to future shocks, and I'm sure there will be some.

I sometimes think of Highclere as a ship sailing from London to New York: you need to keep an eye on the compass without losing the speed necessary to stick to the scheduled arrival. So, if Highclere is sailing at eighteen knots, there is no way I want it to revert to five or six. Duncan helped us achieve this process and is unfailing in his support. He travelled back from Ireland to see Paul the chef when he gathered the cancer was unresponsive, and back again six months later to say goodbye. We are still working together part-time, although there are now three further colleagues in the computer department, which would not be a department found listed in the old ledgers.

What is it like to work at Highclere? The answer is that if you get it, you love it. It is a community and, for all the lightness and individuality, it is a place where we are all the stronger for working together and sharing the load of whatever life throws at any of us.

As a leader, I try to say thank you more often, to encourage and listen to the insights, enthusiasm and inspiration of everyone who works here because, despite all the titles and supposed hierarchy, we are all just family.

CHAPTER THREE

March: Living with a Film Crew

'All the world's a stage,
And all the men and women merely players;
They have their exits and their entrances;
And one man in his time plays many parts'
— As You Like It, William Shakespeare

It was oddly quiet as Geordie and I walked through the half-lit library, now set for the very first day's filming of a new television series to be called *Downton Abbey*. Our photographs had disappeared into cupboards and drawers, whilst those of strangers took their places – the as yet unknown Lord Grantham and family now appeared in ornate frames on various tables and desks.

A green-lacquered objet de vertu (an antique box) was sitting in its usual place on top of the table opposite the fireplace. Geordie stopped, asking, 'Should we leave this here, do you think? Is it safe?' After I'd replied that I was sure it would be fine, we went upstairs to our bedroom overlooking the front of the Castle. Slightly unsettled by the thought of the months ahead of us, we drifted off to sleep before being woken at around 6 a.m. as white vans crunched to a stop on the gravel beneath our windows. Retrieving the tea tray, we listened to the sudden cacophony of sound, thoughts spinning, as we got ready for the day ahead.

Now familiar to hundreds of millions of viewers, the first episode of *Downton* began in Edwardian times with the storyline developing from the tragic loss of the *Titanic* and most of those on-board. The obvious Grantham heir had perished and a very distant, unknown cousin was now to inherit the title, to the perturbation of all. It was a rather unfashionable (then) costume drama beginning with a slightly archaic plotline, commissioned by ITV and produced by Carnival Film and Television Ltd, led by Gareth Neame, as a co-production in the USA with Masterpiece and PBS. The script was written by the immensely talented Julian Fellowes, of *Gosford Park* fame.

Undoubtedly, the commissioning was justified by marketing analysis and carefully formulated budgets but often such ideas are also due to gut feeling. Nevertheless, *Downton Abbey* was a leap in the dark. Peter Fincham, then CEO of ITV, took the gamble. The prescience of his decision, given every platform and producer has to anticipate the next big thing, only seems obvious in retrospect.

Highclere Castle was chosen as the setting – eventually – although Julian Fellowes said in several interviews that he had written *Downton Abbey* with Highclere in mind. It was therefore the first house the *Downton* team came to recce in the summer of 2009. Emma (Julian's wife) had phoned me to say something was afoot, but obviously they could not simply choose the first place they saw so they spent the autumn travelling round Britain visiting many more houses, double-checking their suitability and testing for camera-ready appeal. Emma sometimes called me to keep me updated. She was always on a train!

There were probably some practical points in our favour. We are relatively near London, which made the extended months needed to film the series more possible as eminent actors committed to London theatre could stay part of the logistical jigsaw puzzle. Highclere is not open to the public all the time so the production crew could have longer uninterrupted periods in which to make the programme. Furthermore, the coach park provided the ideal space for a unit base, this being an essential requirement of any filming project. There is no public footpath near the Castle so there is privacy. Lastly, the geography of the house works well for television and does not confuse the viewing public: the saloon is central, with the main state rooms and staircase in plain view from it, and it has a very visible green baize door connecting it to the 'below stairs'. Highclere was built as a family home and still serves that purpose; it is not a palace in which to parade through marble-lined state rooms, but instead has large family rooms with cosy fireplaces.

Throughout 2009, normal life continued at Highclere as it had in previous years and I started to wonder whether we should still delay taking wedding bookings or whether Carnival's thoughts were drifting in another direction. Before Christmas, I emailed Gareth saying I imagined he might well have found a lovely house on one of his train journeys, but could he give us the heads-up before we accepted wedding bookings for 2010? These would otherwise interfere with any proposed filming and Geordie, John G and I had gambled we were in with a chance and thus delayed. Gareth kindly replied swiftly that they would like to choose Highclere. We were, of course, absolutely delighted, but I don't think either we or our new partners had any idea what this collaboration would come to mean.

Christmas 2009 was followed by some heavy January snow, which was just magical. Given my son Edward's school term had not yet started, he and I could spend some heavenly time sledging down the front drive together. Nigel Marchant from Carnival was due to arrive for a first meeting and had driven down carefully from London in a very nice but nevertheless rather impractical sporty Audi, completely defeated by the snowy Highclere Park roads. He skidded to a stop at the crossroads just as Eddie and I were once more sliding down on a better mode of transport. Phone in hand, I called John G to ask him if he could come down in a Land Rover and pull Nigel up the drive, and perhaps Eddie and me, plus sledge and dogs, could also catch a lift back up. It was a memorable introduction.

Eventually, we were all seated in John G's office so we could sketch out dates and terms, which was, of course, the first of many meetings with various groups of the *Downton* production team. We needed to understand the parameters of what *Downton Abbey* would require of Highclere and everyone needed to be happy about which rooms would be part of the contract, where the downstairs entrance and courtyard would be, for the scenes involving 'downstairs' cast, the extent of the gardens to be used, length of days spent filming, and so on.

The world of TV and film was not completely new to us as Highclere had stood in for P. G. Wodehouse's Totleigh Towers in Stephen Fry and Hugh Laurie's TV programme *Jeeves and Wooster*, which had been a successful series from 1990–93. In addition, *Robin Hood: Prince of Thieves* with Kevin Costner had been filmed in part of the park; we had also welcomed filming for *Inspector Morse* and a few Agatha Christie adaptations, whilst Stanley Kubrick had reflected at length in the Castle as well as filming scenes in the library for his final film *Eyes Wide Shut*. More importantly perhaps, Maggie Smith had first come to Highclere to film part of *The Secret Garden* in 1993. What was very different about *Downton Abbey* was the number of filming days required for the eight episodes of the

MARCH: LIVING WITH A FILM CREW

first season and the possible continuation into the future. We all hoped that this would be a marriage of longevity.

Negotiations continued, contracts were signed and the first day of filming took place on Monday 8 March 2010.

Apart from the now familiar cast, there was to be an extraordinarily large crew, always the first people to arrive on-set each day. In total there would be about 120 crew members on-site, all arriving in cars and vans for the 7 a.m. start. A film crew is made up of many departments from Art to Props, Set Dec, Camera, DIT, Video, Grips, Electrical, SFX, VFX, Sound, Costume, Make-up and Hair, Locations, Security, Publicity, Medical, Continuity, Catering and Facilities. Each of these departments employs teams of people all with very specific roles, though often job titles only make sense to those in the know: Gaffer, Best Boy, Genny OP, Grip, Focus Puller, First AD, Runner, Data Wrangler, DOP ... but two of these people we have worked with the closest over the years are 'Sparky' from Locations, and Donal Woods, Production Designer. Both have been a part of the *Downton* team from the very beginning and both are hugely important in making the fictional world fit with the real world of Highclere.

Much of the furniture used is ours, but it is augmented to heighten the period interest. Donal's team made the cleverest card and plywood disguises to cover fire detectors, storage heaters, and even anachronistic outside drainpipes. There is not a huge amount of heating in any case in the Castle and the one very inadequate small storage heater in the dining room was taken out temporarily. The round globe lights at the front were changed to much nicer lanterns, but they did not work in reality or I would very much have preferred to keep them in place of our own.

The props team moved in to share a room with Sally's

gift-shop store in what used to be a base for the outside estate team. The upside was that there were always biscuits on offer by Sally's desk. She also usually had a large sign outside the gift shop saying 'Cast and Crew Welcome' – in case anything were needed for birthdays or other presents.

Geordie, John and I had decided that, given Highclere was chosen to be Downton, for the most part the chattels, i.e. the sofas, tables, works of art and paintings, should all remain in situ rather than being swapped in and out, which may well have been more damaging, and certainly more exhausting for all of us. Donal brought in an older carpet for the drawing room and more old-fashioned fringed lampshades, but much remained as it was. Various pieces of porcelain, china and glass were rented, which meant we could remove all our more delicate Meissen, the Chinese vases and Napoleon's desk, to rooms not included in the filming agreement. Over time, this process became part of a reasonably well-ordered way of life.

One particular period item appeared throughout the first season of filming. It was a conversation piece, also called a *divan de milieu*, which is a circular sofa that allows its occupants both to view their surroundings and to converse discreetly, thus modestly encouraging flirtation. It had a palm tree at its hollow centre. I had shown Donal and team old photos of the saloon from Edwardian times depicting such a piece, though it no longer existed at Highclere. Such sofas gradually became less fashionable and were probably sold by Geordie's grandfather, whose approaches to potential girlfriends were generally more direct.

As an early riser, Geordie tended to be the first person down into the state rooms to begin opening shutters. However, his familiarity with the Castle did not include dealing with the rather exotic palm trees now dotted around by the

MARCH: LIVING WITH A FILM CREW

set dressers. With their razor-sharp long leaves, they attacked him when he tried to find the hinged shutter arms. Luckily for him, the trees left Highclere after the first series.

John G and housekeeper Diana would also get there early to allow the crew to start preparing for their filming day, but, on the plus side, the locations team would arrive bright and early too and there were very welcome bacon butties from their catering unit for breakfast. Having allowed the morning light into the Castle and surveyed the scene, it was time to carefully read the call sheet listing, which indicated what scene plus which actors would be filmed in each room. John G and I would then have a quick word to see if plans had changed from the night before – a not unknown occurrence.

Shortly afterwards, the first shift of Highclere guides would arrive to be on hand, both to help monitor filming activities and to assist in repositioning our furniture as required. Polished black cars would start to bring the 'talent' in from the car park down the main drive. At the front of the house, actors emerged swathed in huge black puffer coats with hair in curlers or nets and Ugg boots or something similar on their feet, phones to hand, make-up experts trailing just behind. In fact, I soon learned that all the actors spent much of their time in hairnets and pin curlers, endlessly waiting, and that the 'downstairs' *Downton* characters tended to have to wait the longest. Jim Carter as Mr Carson sometimes had to wait all day on-set just to open the dining-room door or stalk into a room and say, 'Dinner is served, Milady.'

Corex mats, or boards in some rooms, were already strewn over every wooden floor and carpet. On top were trolleys with computers, monitors and other heavy gadgets. Black bags in all shapes and sizes proliferated, thick black cable runs snaked five or six thick outside the Castle before looping in via windows and doors to curl up in corners and then be unwound to sneak into various state rooms.

Lights were stabilised on tripods of varying heights. Every tripod foot would wear the obligatory tennis-ball slippers in order to protect the floors from sharp edges. As time went on, in addition to these standing lights which could become quite hot, balloon lights with the much cooler LEDs became the order of the day, especially in the dining room over the long table.

One of the best things about the saloon (or the Great Hall as *Downton* called it) is the fact that it is illuminated by natural daylight, via its windows of course but also via the leaded lights built into the ceiling fifty foot above floor level. One hundred and fifty years ago, when Highclere was rebuilt, these windows were state-of-the-art technology. Today, they still ensure that every day throughout the year, uplifting and positive natural light filters down to us at ground level. Lovely for those of us lucky enough to live here, but of course *Downton Abbey*'s DOP (director of photography) wanted to control the light at all times and natural light does change throughout the day. Therefore, riggers disappeared onto the roof to fix blackout blinds along the top of the high saloon leaded lights, which they could roll down for the weeks or days they were filming. Then, instead of natural light, a large balloon light was inflated and floated in between the sides of the gallery with various sandbag tethers at angles around it.

Each time they left, they had to roll the blackout blinds back up until the end of filming when the temporary blinds and riggers left altogether. Perhaps the crew and cast took the dimness for granted but I always looked forward to when they could be removed.

Meanwhile, the natural daylight from very tall Gothic arched windows above the main oak stairs was another problem for the crew. Depending on the time of year, they tried various different means of putting up blinds or blocking the windows from the outside so they could control the light. A scene might begin filming in the morning with other versions of it being shot several hours later, yet it all needed to look as if it was shot at exactly the same time and in the same light.

As custodians, our main priority was to establish with the production team that Highclere was 'real' rather than just an artificial set and that, as such, much of what was on the floor or walls or in the rooms was genuine and needed to be treated carefully as befitted works of art. With the crew beginning to set up for a breakfast scene in the dining room on the very first day, one of them was heading at speed through the front hall whilst carrying a long galvanised pole balanced across his shoulder. Concerned about the risk this posed, I followed as he swung in through the saloon and round into the dining room, missing the paintings and silk wall covering by a fraction.

'Excuse me – could you go a little slower and more carefully, please? You nearly hit the painting!' 'All right, love – a van Gogh, is it?' 'No, it's a van Dyck actually.' I was not convinced he was impressed so I scurried off to find the locations manager and John G. New plan: long scaffolding poles should only be moved with a person at each end. Unfortunately, by the end of the very first day, a lighting boom had been dropped on precisely the green objet de vertu that I had said to Geordie would be quite fine. The *Downton* crew were mortified, and it was just an accident, but it took some six months before I found someone to mend it. I felt dreadfully guilty because I had left it there, but Geordie very kindly did not say, 'I told you so.'

Most of the filming days seemed to me to be either about

eating or waiting, which absolutely suited our Labradors best. Alfie and Scooby, in particular, very quickly got to know the pattern of the day and soon, every teatime, were to be found lurking underneath the trestle tables set out at the front of the Castle to offer afternoon tea to cast and crew whilst they were 'on the go'. During a tea scene that was being filmed, Alfie even managed to sneak on-set and sample a little cake, which was on the table opposite the fireplace in the saloon. However, as the cast never really ate on-set but just pretended, I smoothed it down with a knife and turned it round, so I don't think they noticed.

Otherwise, the weeks and months followed the same pattern with, as always, one eye on the weather. Occasionally, clear skies suggested an indoor conversation could be re-sited outside along a garden path. Parts of the garages or sawmills were explored for other key moments. Vintage cars were driven round on the back of trailers, cameras attached, whilst various animated conversations took place inside with no worry about de-clutching. Then the cars went round again with someone else driving and more cameras mounted on other cars to follow them. Given it was the magic of the movies, it was then all edited together very successfully but even so, geographically, Team Highclere found it very confusing.

Each *Downton* season usually had one dramatic centrepiece. In the first one it was a hunting scene full of colour and tradition. My great friend, Camilla Clutterbuck, was Master of the local Vine and Craven Hunt, so she rallied her members and the hounds to come along to help provide authenticity when it was filmed. Proper clipped hunters arrived with friends who could ride side-saddle, all thrilled to be extras on-set. Michelle Dockery not only looked elegant riding side-saddle but had taken lessons beforehand. However, each part of the scene seemed to take a long time to film and after two or three hours, some of the horses knew their moves a little too well and were beginning to bounce down the slopes with riders still on-board but starting to look a little less coordinated. John G and I were standing by the bridge and tried to mark the DOP's card with our concerns but the filming had to go on. Theo James as Mr Pamuk looked admirable. Despite his very brief time on *Downton*, he made a lasting impression. Highclere's Stanhope bedroom was Mr Pamuk's room and people still ask, as they walk round the gallery outside, if this was where he was carried after the night in question.

Every week, Sparky and John G would sit down to work out diaries, with arrivals and exits, as well as what scenes were planned, where they would be filmed, the respective timings for each day's filming, how many cast were on-set and whether there were any specific requests from the various crew departments – euphemistically referred to as going through 'the Bible'. John is an exceptional member of Highclere, though not renowned for the speediness of the meetings he conducts, so it was always fun for me to try and trap Sparky in his office for a head-to-head from which he would not emerge for at least an hour or two.

The marrying and merging of Highclere Castle's 'normal events' with the newly undertaken obligations to filming days required careful and meticulous planning in order to make the revolving doors operate as seamlessly as possible. Quite often the *Downton* 'circus' – lorries and vans – would be waiting at the local service station, and as the last visitor left Highclere from a non-filming-related event, they would be coming up the driveway. My pack of Labradors, with almost psychic premonition, were always ready and waiting for the arrival of the breakfast bar and became perfectly deaf to our calls.

Looking back on the first season, it seems in retrospect to have a lightness of atmosphere and, from memory anyway, to be lit by rays of English sunshine. Curiously enough, at the beginning of the first episode, a maid is opening shutters in the main library and sunlight is illuminating particles of dust, the filming of which was the result of protracted discussions. The HD cameras of today capture images that are too clean and clear to get such a shot naturally, so there was a request to be allowed to fire oil droplets into the air. John G rang around various other houses where apparently this might have been done, to find out that they had for the most part refused and their advice was not to agree to it – especially in the library. Despite repeated requests to use oil, he and I stood firm and suggested they use old cameras to get that hazy look. We were not popular. In the end, a number of crew banged lots of cushions together to produce the dust motes required to dance in the afternoon sun, and they managed to capture the necessary atmosphere.

Following the success of the first season, the powers that be commissioned a Christmas special as well as the second series, so filming had to extend a little further into the diary at Highclere. During the first year, *Downton* returned in October to film the engagement scene of Matthew and Mary in the snow. The snow in this case was provided by various artificial means, both underfoot and in the air. The snowflakes, which were created by burning what looked like tissue paper in canisters, were collected in buckets and then floated off into the air. It did look very good, but after a while they began to eddy into the library. Luckily, it was a cold October evening, which focused everyone on completing the scene before any more ash was spread around. Nevertheless, these tiny light flakes of paper kept reappearing around the room, much to the distress of Diana the housekeeper.

MARCH: LIVING WITH A FILM CREW

Thereafter, the scenes required for the Christmas special were filmed every July. Naturally, that meant the filming took place on the hottest day of the year and any night scene on the longest day. John debated with Sparky whether this was a split day, a late day or a day overrunning? Might a late extension fee be due? Sparky would return with a long face and an air of sadness about the state of their budget, and John would ask why the only night scene in the entire series was being filmed on 21 June?

Although today the cast of *Downton* have become household names, many of the actors were less well known in 2010, apart from Dame Maggie Smith, of course. Whichever room was not being used for the day's filming or for the video village tended to serve as a green room for the actors. However, because she liked her privacy, to begin with we offered Dame Maggie a warmish sitting room to use in between takes during the February and March filming. There, Diana could bring her a cup of tea. An electric fan radiator whirred away just in front of her, offering some heat, and the watery sunshine obligingly filtered through the windows into 'her' sitting room. I rarely saw her clutching a script, although given she had already spent several hours in costume and make-up she probably knew it by heart. Her skill as an actress could be seen in the way she threw away some lines or else would turn to look at another actor, holding a moment of silence. A legend in her lifetime and a much-missed stage and screen presence today, she respected above all a professional, organised and expeditious approach to work, from everyone. From time to time, if I walked into the Castle during filming, I could feel there had been a little friction. Perhaps an AD had not got all his ducks in a row and in consequence an early lunch for crew and cast had been called.

Sometimes, however, Highclere itself incurred her displeasure. One morning the fire alarm went off and we duly evacuated the entire Castle in the middle of filming. Having identified the fault, which was not actually a fire (a carpet was being fitted), John G was placed under considerable pressure to let the crew and cast back in to resume filming – every moment was precious to them. Despite our phone calls to allay worry, the fire brigade arrived, blue lights flashing, drawing up in the mêlée of white vans on the gravel outside. John promptly met them, smiling, saying he had identified the cause and there was no fire. The building had been evacuated but, as the cause was now known, filming had resumed. The Senior Fire Officer was not amused. John was strongly reprimanded and asked to evacuate the building again, so once more the entire cast and crew had to leave. As Maggie Smith came out, she made her evident disapproval known and John endured some quelling looks and expressions. Thereafter, no pressure from any film crew whatsoever took precedence over the fire brigade's arrival and we remain super careful.

In fact, this tale is regularly quoted when undertaking practice evacuations and on internal fire-marshal training courses, and for John the enduring pain of that very public reprimand lives on!

For the Highclere team, however, it was in some ways a magical experience. They had been filming a formal dinner scene and all the 'upstairs' cast were together in beautiful evening costume in one part of the courtyard, whilst almost the full 'downstairs' cast was in another huddle. Our horses had also been evacuated from the stables and there was, coincidentally, an entire stall of prop flowers and a vintage car in the courtyard as well. It gave the team a brief glimpse of what the Castle might actually have looked like in its heyday as a private house in the previous century.

Ironically, the most recent *Downton* filming project, the third film, was subjected to another fire-alarm activation, which the fire brigade again insisted on attending, despite the cause being found to be incidental. John did not permit anyone to re-enter the building prior to the brigade's arrival on-site and, on this occasion, it was the director who was decidedly unamused that filming could not resume. It appears that if the fire alarm activates during filming, John is in for it either way!

Time was of the essence every day and in the background the clock was always ticking. The first *Downton* season consisted of eight episodes and in each nominated day, the crew hoped to achieve four to six minutes of television screen time out of an eleven-hour filming day, with an hour to set up and de-rig at either end. Inevitably, there were time slips and towards early July, when *Downton* were due to leave and Highclere's summer visitors about to arrive, there would suddenly be requests for two extra camera days, suggestions for what cottage they could shoot, or requests about whether there was a local church hall or somewhere else suitable for an operations centre so that they could double bank (film with two film crews at the same time) as they shot out all the scenes they needed. *Downton* had an ambitious and challenging timetable both to film and to edit, and it was a huge achievement to get so many beautifully filmed scenes in the can.

In 2010, none of us knew if the series would catch on and be welcomed by the viewing public, and perhaps because of this there was less inherent stress and pressure. Looking back, it seemed a relaxed spring and summer as crew and cast came and went over the weeks and months, in between other Castle events. From being here for two weeks, they might then retire to Ealing Studios so that Mrs Patmore could bustle around, bringing puddings in and out of the ovens, whilst Mr Carson was in charge of protocol in the staff dining room.

We had all mutually decided that it was not possible to film the kitchen scenes at Highclere. Although our kitchens have been in the same place for a millennium and once contained old Victorian ranges, they are now too full of stainless steel and the latest ovens. Plus, we really needed to cook in them.

As the *Downton* crew withdrew for some time off at Easter, we would be turning ourselves around to welcome visitors, finding the signs for loos, cafes and gardens, all of which had been squirrelled out of shot for the filming. Two weeks later, as the last of the Easter visitors left, long white artic lorries would be waiting until the signal was given by John to Sparky for the circus to return once more.

Given the length of the filming period, *Downton* benefited from the changing colours of the seasons at Highclere. It helped give an authentic sense of developing storylines as costumes changed with the lengthening warmer light of summer, before the first series ended with a moving scene on the lawns outside the Castle when Lord Grantham announced the outbreak of the First World War.

In September 2010, Geordie and I caught a train to London and walked across Hyde Park to Sloane Street to attend a small screening for the press organised by Peter Fincham. Sitting towards the back of the room, it was the strangest sensation watching our beloved home rise up on the screen in front of us, with a yellow Labrador waggling its tail and the Castle in a reflected image on the title card, announcing the beginning of the first episode of *Downton Abbey*. I half-watched the episode and half-watched the press. What were they thinking? Did

MARCH: LIVING WITH A FILM CREW

they like it? Peter asked us if we liked the music – which we did. We were not quite sure what everyone else actually felt and left to find a cup of tea.

Downton began with good audience viewing figures. I spoke with Emma Fellowes and asked her where the numbers should be, in case they might wish to return and make a subsequent series. We were trying to anticipate in order to offer a good clear run of weeks, rather than having the crew dipping in and out, which was more tiring for all of us. Emma replied the numbers simply needed to go up in the second week. Amazingly, they did, and then another week or two later overtook *The X Factor* – phenomenal!

The first season of *Downton Abbey* was the result of long planning and thought with a beautiful story arc. As a result of its somewhat unexpected success, the second series had to be put together at speed. The Castle had in fact been a hospital for wounded soldiers during the First World War and so Julian Fellowes created Downton as a convalescent home during the same period. Demonstrating the fundamental changes in society that occurred at this point in history, as well as following some tragic losses from the cast, the second series of *Downton* opened with various members of the family either for or against its new role. Military-grade hospital beds arrived in the drawing room, but Geordie used to find the bandaged dummies in them creepy in the mornings whilst I used to find them rather unappreciative if I played the piano in the evening. Props used to find them very heavy to move in and out, and so I think we were all quite glad to see the back of them.

The third season began with the arrival of Shirley MacLaine, whose character, Mrs Levinson, sweeps in to confront the old British ways. She had barely landed before she was on-set. Liz Trubridge, one of the executive producers, came to find me saying she had a huge favour to ask. I wondered what was coming. 'Do you have a bottle of red wine and do you by any chance have an Anubis?' Relieved, I said I did indeed have both – how could I help? Unsurprisingly, 'Mrs Levinson' felt perfectly exhausted. Luis kindly retrieved a delicious bottle of wine, which we all enjoyed, and later that day we went down to what had once been our cellars so she could discover our Anubis in part of the Highclere Castle Egyptian exhibition.

Undeniably Hollywood royalty, Shirley MacLaine explained she was the reincarnation of an Egyptian princess. An optimistic and formidable lady, it was far better to nod in agreement as she was in no doubt about this. She was also convinced that her beloved little dog, a terrier called Terry who went everywhere with her, was a reincarnation of the jackal-headed Egyptian god Anubis. She later said of Highclere: 'They had the tomb of King Tut in the basement', and that the Castle was haunted and pictures came off the wall, which I had not noticed, although, given we also had Professor Minerva McGonagall (Dame Maggie Smith) from *Harry Potter* upstairs, it might just possibly have been true.

The third season also involved one wedding, two funerals and a cricket match. Memorably for Highclere, the gift-shop store room was transformed into a very nice pub, allegedly at Lincoln station, which in fact is 160 miles north of us. It was part of the storyline of John Bates, who at the time was in jail. Everyone at Highclere wished the pub could stay. The most notable event, though, was the tragic death of Lady Sibyl in childbirth – a scene as memorable for those watching it being filmed as it was for many viewers because by now the series characters had become household names. Happily, Lady

MARCH: LIVING WITH A FILM CREW

Mary had married at the beginning of the series, but the final Christmas episode climaxed in further disaster.

The now-famous car crash in which Matthew dies occurred at the far end of Lime Avenue just as the road bends around and dips down. John had agreed that an upside-down replica car constructed of wood could be left just down the bank in advance of the upcoming filming day. It was all top secret and John still finds it amazing that no members of the Castle, farm or wider estate staff spotted the crash site over the long weekend, in spite of its amazingly realistic detail. When the scene was screened on Christmas Day it caused much outrage, but in fact the actor Dan Stevens, who played Matthew Crawley, wanted to leave the series after three years and that had been the break clause. At the Castle, Geordie and I received black-bordered letters of condolence for our loss.

The appetite for Sunday evenings with *Downton Abbey* continued unabated and soon the crew recces returned once more. On one occasion, twenty people dressed as usual in black and sporting backpacks duly arrived to explore the settings and filming options for the next instalment of life in the Grantham family. The backpacks were left in the saloon whilst they reacquainted themselves with Highclere, but on their return, they found that the older Labradors, wise now to the ways of film folk, had raided the poorly secured backpacks and there were now rather fewer sandwiches than expected. I had to hare off downstairs to see if the chefs could come to the rescue.

They came for several hours and often repeated visits, sometimes towards the end of a visitor general admission day. If the *Downton* team were trying to be discreet, I think they would not be my first choice of undercover agents, as twenty to thirty people all dressed the same, with cameras, phones and dark glasses, walking up the drive whilst huddling together, made quite a statement. There was always much excitement when the public spotted them but I could neither confirm nor deny.

Recces were numerous over the years, mainly of the Castle and surrounding lawns but sometimes of further-away places on the estate if production was looking for a specific scene or an angle of the Castle not yet shown. It became a standing joke between Sparky and John that when a new director came on-board, John or I would suggest that the exceptional temple on the hill would be a perfect and new setting. They would therefore inevitably request to visit Heaven's Gate. This is a folly high up on Siddown Hill to the south of the Castle and is neither quick nor easy to get to but, nevertheless, it was recced many more times than any other part of the estate. Inevitably, after each visit it would be ruled out as being too far away and too hard to service. Series four had a new director and the anticipated request to visit Heaven's Gate duly came through once more. Sparky and John dutifully headed off to a location where they felt the outcome was predictable – but to their enormous surprise, this time the crew did overcome the logistical challenges and a scene was filmed at Heaven's Gate to everyone's delight, particularly Sparky's and John's.

On another full technical recce (all departments are represented – the director is presenting his wishes to the crew who will then make it happen), John was asked by Sparky if it might be possible to move a particular bench? John quickly replied to say sadly not as it was fixed to the ground. Sparky reported this back to the director but film crews are not known for accepting the first answer, particularly if it is not the answer they were hoping for. So, Sparky returned again to ask if we could possibly undo the fixings? John once more replied no and Sparky walked back to the recce group to share the news. Turning to me, John then said, 'Quick, Lady C! You take that end, I'll take this, and let's walk off with the bench.' It is, in fact, a remarkably heavy bit of furniture but it was worth the effort to see Sparky's face. We moved it a few yards before John called over to the director to ask where he would like it moved to? Sparky promised to have his revenge against John.

The phrase 'Downton Abbey' has now passed into everyday language; things or events are described as 'very Downton'. I'm still not sure what caused it to become such a global success. Perhaps it was the fact that there are not many programmes to watch on TV that do not involve or focus on violence or death. Instead, *Downton* highlighted conversation and family stories, it was entertaining and, in the main, the action was simply opening or closing a door, perhaps the arrival of a puppy, the occasional fight on a sofa or fear of new technology. Nevertheless, it was very entertaining.

At different times during the series, both 'upstairs' and 'downstairs' were depicted having to get to grips with change. The Dowager Lady Grantham had to cope with electric lights, Mrs Patmore with an electric whisk, and Mr Carson was very disapproving of a new-fangled apparatus called a 'telephone'. It was fun to see how they reacted to such novelties given that for the viewers these were all everyday items in our lives. Mrs Patmore was rather suspicious of the new modern cooking equipment but the scullery maid Daisy embraced it. There was no choice about it when Lady Grantham decided to have a refrigerator installed in the kitchen. Miss Baxter took to a sewing machine, and, of course, upstairs Sibyl led the changing fashions, even if they did rather memorably make her look like a lampshade according to her family. As usual, Julian Fellowes skilfully brought it all to life.

Each of the characters developed and changed over the course of the six series, Thomas the footman undergoing perhaps the most obvious transformation. He started out almost as a caricature villain and gradually became more three-dimensional and sympathetic as his back story developed. Daisy grew up, children were born, the cast became bigger.

Julian and Emma Fellowes had often stayed with us over the years and knew how the service of any meal at Highclere worked in real life. I often quip that we won *Downton* with good food, good wines and good conversation, which is the best way to achieve most things in this world. Many of the scenes were set in the dining room and Julian masterminded the often-barbed comments and sharp expressions of meal-time clashes. However, whilst the 'pretend' food may have looked authentic, it was never actually eaten as it had usually been sitting there for hours on end and, if a piece of asparagus suddenly went missing from a plate, it would spoil continuity.

A dining-room scene always took all of an eleven-hour day to film. Every window was both blacked out and left slightly open so that lighting cables could come in, which meant it was all rather cold and most of the actors wore furry boots under the table. Although *Downton* used our table and chairs, the table was always clothed as it was simply safer that way. One of the most exciting scenes filmed there was when Lord Grantham's ulcer burst so dramatically, but with layers of blankets on the floor and table, the scene was a brilliant 'one-take' success.

Not everything went so perfectly. Every season John and I would have a few contretemps after various bright ideas had been tried by the crew. One day, walking past the studio at the back of the Castle, I glanced to the left and saw there were some wooden blocks underneath the feet of a table.

John G and I had been feeling kind and, given it was raining, had offered this large room to the costume department so nothing would get damaged or wet en route from unit base. I reversed, went along the passage and up the stairs, and looked more closely. There were indeed blocks underneath the table legs – with our cream tablecloth on the table surface. I pulled it back and realised to my horror that the crew had been using the table as an ironing board and had needed it higher, hence the wooden blocks I had noticed. It was an early-nineteenth-century dining table with a beautiful patina after decades of careful polishing. A hot iron had bleached and flattened this in some places. It was not a good moment for me, and when I went and explained what had happened to Sparky, it was not a good moment for him either. These things do happen, but what was slightly annoying was that everyone, apart from Sparky who immediately accepted responsibility, said they hadn't done it: 'It wasn't me, guv.' I only wish Highclere had an ironing ghost – that would be quite useful.

The next phone call was to Sarah Morris, my interior decorator friend, to find out where we could send the table plus all its leaves, both those that were ironed upon and those that had escaped, for restoration so that it all matched up once more. The table disappeared off to an expert restorer based in Battersea and, of course, didn't come back for some months. When it did return, I did not make the mistake of putting it back in the studio, instead finding it a new home in the music room where it is used for small suppers with friends.

Downton used the main state rooms and bedrooms as they were. The only exception was that they asked if they could repaint Arundel (Lady Edith's) bedroom. Irritatingly, I had just lined, cross-lined and repainted it the prettiest pale pink but they said it was too pale. Reluctantly, I agreed, and it became a dirty brown-pink, which may have worked on TV but definitely did not in real life. So, at the end of filming they repainted it my colour. The decorator, Nick, was charming and very tall so he was immediately christened Nick 'No Ladders' by John G, despite the fact that he seemed to spend more time painting skirting boards, which had been thoroughly bumped by *Downton* equipment, than ceilings.

The following season they returned and again asked to repaint Arundel bedroom. I told them it was fine but that this time, instead of just repainting it the original colour at the end of filming, it would have so many layers of paint that they would have to do a proper job and strip, reline and then paint. Funnily enough, they suddenly found my pale pink perfectly acceptable.

For many at Highclere, one of the highlights of the 2013 filming was welcoming Dame Kiri Te Kanawa who was appearing as Dame Nellie Melba. Whilst on-screen for barely a minute or two, she did in fact sing for much of the day with all of us sitting on the stairs listening. Her concert was a cover for a very disturbing part of the story that continued to unfold over the following series. As the horrendous rape of Anna took place downstairs – i.e. in Ealing – we at Highclere were wholly unaware of it, too intent on listening to the soaring soprano voice eddying around the saloon.

In contrast, we did all know about the much happier church fête scene, which took place as the season ended. Many of our guides had auditioned to be extras a few weeks before, but after they had all spent long hours hanging around or walking the same twenty yards for several days on end, most decided that being an extra just the once was quite enough.

The final scene of season four remains one of my favourite images: Mr Carson and Mrs Hughes paddling in the sea

MARCH: LIVING WITH A FILM CREW

on the edge of a sandy beach. Perhaps John's and my biggest regret is that we did not nip down to West Wittering where they were filming, borrow a boat and row towards the film crew, shouting, 'Coooeee – we're here!' I still think about it wistfully today . . .

By now, *Downton* had a large global audience and everyone was hoping for a few more weddings and a lot of happy endings. Thus, by the end of the last series, Mr Carson was married to Mrs Hughes, Anna was not only married to Bates but all their various tribulations were resolved, Lady Mary got married for the second time to Mr Henry Talbot, Lady Rose married Atticus and left for other shores and, finally to absolutely everyone's relief, Lady Edith got married, both happily and eligibly, as the series ended. I think *Downton* finally outdid *Four Weddings and a Funeral* in every respect.

Filming for the series finished in the summer of 2015. It felt very odd as *Downton* had come to dominate our lives. Unexpectedly, we had all been drawn together annually for six years, first for filming and then marketing. Highclere Castle had become *Downton Abbey* but *Downton* was really Highclere. Due to the fact we had been open to the public, not just the one fictional time in season six but in real life since 1988, fans of the series could touch and feel the setting and actually *be* in Downton at Highclere. I have always hoped that this helps give *Downton* added authenticity as much as *Downton* helped us market Highclere. It had undoubtedly become the most successful TV series ever.

Downton Abbey reignited ITV's reputation and its advertising revenues. In the summer of 2014, ITV filmed a 'Text Santa' skit which involved George Clooney arriving at Highclere or Downton. I sincerely believe that most women who worked at ITV came to Highclere that day. So did the press, but only as far as our gates, as they thought Mr Clooney might be considering Highclere as a venue for his wedding to then fiancée Amal Alamuddin. John was quite happy with that as he thought we might get some more wedding enquiries. In fact, at the height of *Downton* there were paparazzi looking for behind-the-scenes photos all over the place, and much excitement when one photographer was found in the azalea bushes wearing a balaclava.

From its speculative beginning, *Downton Abbey* became a phenomenon and over the years of filming the real cast and crew became a familiar team, who in their own real lives suffered sadness and joy. Some married each other and had children. Some married others and found happiness. There was illness, divorce and death, mirroring the tragedies of the fictional lives they had all sought to capture on film.

Downton had many stars but undoubtedly Dame Maggie Smith shone the brightest. Feeling that in *Downton* terms she must have attained at least 120 years of age, she had opted to leave in the second film, but by then we had had the good fortune to watch her in so many of the scenes filmed here, as well as once again on cosy Sunday evenings when the programme was shown. They were all inevitably sharpened by her natural wit and excellent comedic timing. In some ways, she said, she found the recognition she acquired through *Downton* annoying – sitting in a theatre watching a play, an excited whisper would eddy round the audience that Maggie Smith was there. Speaking on *The Graham Norton Show*, she quipped: 'I led a perfectly normal life until *Downton Abbey*. I'm not kidding.' The razzmatazz and red-carpet parts of show business were not for her.

Although there was debate amongst fans of *Downton Abbey* as well as in the press about whether the series had ended too early, we always knew there was a chance of a film or two or three.

The first was made in the autumn of 2018. It was the first time the *Downton* crew was there at that time of year and they captured the glorious changing colours and autumnal golden light – it lit up the opening scenes and titles. The weather was really quite warm and Jim Carter, dressed in overcoat and hat, marching purposefully up and down the front drive, had to be offered fans and flannels to mop his brow in between takes. Everyone else was in T-shirts and shorts. The same thing happened when, as part of another scene, Lady Mary, dressed in hat and gloves, was helping load chairs for the King's parade into a motor van at the back of the Castle whilst it was tipping down with rain (in this case, from a hose), and the camera crew were once more in shorts as it was so warm.

Perhaps unexpectedly for NBC Universal, this first *Downton Abbey* film was a great success, storming the box-office rankings. They kindly invited John G and his wife Henrietta, Geordie and I to the premiere. The credits at the end of the film thanked John and the Highclere team, but much to his annoyance and everyone else's amusement – and after years of emails with many of the *Downton* production staff – they still managed to spell his surname incorrectly. I understand the DVD credits reverted to the proper spelling.

Some of the Highclere team were able to go to the London premiere and after-party through the kindness of Viking Cruises who helped sponsor it. Luis and friends caught a taxi back afterwards, apparently, but no one really remembers . . . Through Airbnb, Geordie and I were also able to go to the New York premiere, which was entirely surreal. When the film began and the Castle's golden turrets swam into view, highlighted by rays of autumnal sun, the American audience applauded and I immediately wanted to cry. The home that we loved never put a foot wrong in a single scene. I thought Geordie's parents would have loved it. We were in the city where they married, still fighting to carry on looking after Highclere.

Given the success of the first film, a second seemed likely, but then the world came to a shuddering stop in March 2020 with the arrival of Covid. Through those strange traumatic months, *Downton Abbey* remained a reassuring safe place to visit and revisit on TV platforms all round the world, and so the second film, *Downton Abbey: A New Era*, was made during the pandemic, from April to June 2021. It was extraordinarily aptly named and a tremendous achievement given the health and safety restrictions and the onerous Covid testing that was required. Every other day, first thing in the morning, we all lined up to be tested. We had to wear masks and keep our distance from each other. Whilst filming may have been a financial lifeline for some of the actors, it was definitely so for many of the crew. Much of the self-employed artistic world did not benefit from the government's furlough scheme and it really mattered that we all held it together – which we did.

In this strangely isolated world, one of the highlights of filming was the coffee man in a van who went to work behind the Castle. We all – Highclere staff, crew and cast alike – stood awkwardly distanced, but we were together and his coffee was good. The stress, however, was immense and we could all feel it. The very last part of the film was, if possible, to be shot on location in France and they did achieve it, despite all the isolation requirements.

It was a beautiful film but its premiere and release were constantly delayed by the crisis. Cinema audiences were drastically reduced from pre-Covid figures and so the film took time to get going but, in the end, it had very respectable results and hopefully the fans enjoyed it.

Some of the *Downton* crew have remained for the full journey. Perhaps the key man for both John and me was Sparky. Over fifteen years, he has become a friend and, like other friends, he happily accepted an invitation to stay as my guest for a weekend, as a way both for us to say thank you and for him to feel what it is like to live in the actual Castle rather than just the make-believe version. Sparky and John did occasionally spar with each other, but there were also a lot of good-humoured pranks. Sparky got his own back for the bench – he persuaded the caterers to put nearly all the chillies for a chilli con carne into just one portion, which he then kindly offered to John – and sat down to watch him eat it . . .

John still has the two-page 'treatment' from 2009, which was the first information and outline we saw, secreted among the piles of paper in his office, and is immensely proud of still being able to lay his hands on it. It is just a bare outline of a few characters and gives no indication of what it would grow into.

All of us at Highclere learned a different language thanks to *Downton*. During the months of filming, new words and phrases filled every waking moment. Many of the expressions are self-explanatory, such as 'Quiet in the house', or 'Rolling', or 'Cut'. Others are less so. 'Directors stepping on . . .' meant the director was entering the room where the scene was being filmed, as otherwise he would be sitting in video village in another room. 'Travelling' meant an actor was being driven the 100 yards down the drive, whilst 'GV', 'POV' described the general or point of view. 'Reverse' was changing the camera angles, which was a particularly lengthy process in all the dining-room scenes, whilst 'Wild card' meant they were taking an audio recording only of the scene. The call 'Running over' meant extending the day, and 'Going again' meant just what it said – we did hear this rather a lot.

There was one scene in which the chauffeur was being filmed walking past some offices and storage sheds disguised as garages. The location trapped IT Duncan and gift-shop Sally in their office, and they were not allowed to open their door and leave until the scene was complete. Over three hours later, they rather apologetically had to interrupt what seemed like the fiftieth take to explain they really did need a bathroom break. Thus, 'Scene complete' was followed by 'Moving on' (to the next scene on the call sheet) and, finally, the much-longed-for 'That's a wrap' at the end of each day.

It has been an extraordinary journey but we have been fortunate to be part of it. *Downton* returns soon with a third film although it will be missing the light and wit of the one and only Dowager. But it has all the other established characters, as well as some new stars lined up.

After the first film I wrote this little ditty for John G and Sparky:

And Action!

> *There are masses of mats from Corex to boards,*
> *trolleys and dollies which arrive in their hordes,*
> *large lights on silver stilts with tennis-ball feet*
> *and black wire snaking (though really quite neat)*
> *to screens and decks with knobs everywhere,*
> *monitors with cases hold equipment with care.*

MARCH: LIVING WITH A FILM CREW

Crew in black trousers, black boots, padded coats
and stuff everywhere despite our organising notes.
Small white vans, large white vans and various trailers
filled to the brim with costumes to tailor.

Cars and buses from breakfast to tea.
Tables and bins where my Labradors can see
friendly faces and little somethings to nibble
which they far preferred to that designated kibble.

Sparky from Locations asked John G for a word.
The details and boundaries can get a bit blurred.
Can they start early? Stay late? Change the date? Have a tea?
John's heard it before, grins, and suggests a fee.

Shooting has started calls for silence and turning
whilst actors and actresses practise their pose.
It's fun and exciting, frenetic, nail biting.
Chaos that's miraculously eventually self-righting.

From Highclere scenes to the silver screen,
our honey-coloured home and the lawns have been
life-enhancing at all times from darkness to dawn
for so many fans when and wherever born.
Let's hope the film catches your hearts for the past
And for the present with this wonderful cast.

Despite all the long days and the challenges, the final 'It's in the can' was a moment of both elation and of sadness. When we part company none of us ever knows whether we will get the call again.

'It's a wrap.'

CHAPTER FOUR

April: Telling Tails

'Oh, to be in England
Now that April's there'
— 'Home-Thoughts, from Abroad', Robert Browning

As April begins, we all wait excitedly to hear that the first lambs have been born in the barn under Beacon Hill. There is nothing better than watching the tiny creatures first sit up and then stand, wobbling and bleating, wiggling their tails madly as they seek out their mother's milk. Matt the shepherd is happy to have help topping up hay or water, and his sheepdogs, Bonnie and Clyde, sit obediently in a crate on his quad bike before helping him sort out and bring in more sheep. These Border Collies are extraordinary dogs, highly intelligent and with a natural herding instinct, who just love their job. They never stop looking for something to do.

Collies are definitely country rather than town dogs. When we were young, my sisters and I dreamed of having a dog in London where we lived most of the year, but it would have to have been a breed that would cope in such a big city. Despite all our pleas, our parents did not give in until quite a few of us were older. Eventually, to everyone's delight, a little golden Cocker Spaniel called Lottie joined us. She was really my sister

Lucy's dog but was much loved by us all. An abiding memory is of our mother walking Lottie round Kensington Gardens, endlessly having to call out 'Lottie, Lottie!' in increasingly exasperated tones as the excited dog headed off to taste a family's picnic or give chase to a pigeon. She would then be put back on a long extendable lead until she was let off again, at which point the game began once more.

The first time Geordie asked me out on a date, I rushed back from the office, calling out to my mother as I sprinted along the corridor to my room to try and improve my appearance. I explained that I was running late, predictably, but a chap called Geordie was coming to take me out and I suspected he would be on time. Could she please look after him for a few minutes?' She said yes but asked me not to be too long as *EastEnders* was about to start and she didn't want to miss it. Priorities!

As foretold, the doorbell rang perfectly on time. I was as quick as I could be and reappeared to find Geordie sitting on a sofa in the drawing room, clutching a large gin and tonic and being penned in and monitored by Lottie, who was not letting him move. Having apologised and removed the dog, I left with him to go for supper.

My mother immediately decided she liked Geordie very much, which was fortuitous, and their friendship included a shared love of ridiculous songs, ditties and rhymes. This evening led to many other suppers and their friendship, whether it involved going to the theatre or for brisk Cornish seaside walks with the irrepressible Lottie, would give Ma such pleasure after our father's early death. Sadly, she too died far too young, a month before our son was born. Nevertheless she had time to name him Edward for us and there is so much joy for me in seeing some of the things in him that remind me of her, although perhaps not a love of *EastEnders*.

Lottie was such an important part of all our lives but above all Lucy's, who loved that dog to bits. Dogs slot into our lives and we take them for granted. However, their lives are so much shorter than ours and when they are no longer with us there is such a painful sense of loss from the sudden emptiness. Their love is unconditional and what is wonderful is that they do not judge us. Though I do sometimes feel Alfie the Labrador's eyes on me as I present him with a breakfast that he does not consider sufficiently interesting. One day, of course, Lottie's celebratory joy in each day was gone. Her impact on Lucy's life had been profound and the grief was long-lasting. A little later, another dog, of a very different sort, became part of Lucy's life but there was only ever one Dotty Lottie.

It is said a Labrador is born half-trained and a spaniel dies half-trained, and Lottie definitely bore that out. Geordie's father also owned Cocker Spaniels from time to time, of varying degrees of excitability, but he had one remarkably well-behaved working Cocker called Mango Sandringham. This particular dog, which had been given to him by Her Majesty, the late Queen, was incredibly well trained and one of the best working dogs ever. He also sired many litters of successful puppies and was really quite a legend for all the right reasons.

However, rather than with a spaniel, I began our family life at Highclere with a cuddly yellow Labrador puppy, who my sister Lucy helped me choose from a friend's litter. She chose the biggest, fattest puppy and Percy duly arrived a few weeks later. Edward was about three years old at that point and puppy and toddler grew up together; Eddie sat in the puppy's bed and Percy climbed into Edward's. He grew into a large dog with an old-fashioned broad head. When he was somewhat older, Percy used to pull Eddie round on a little plastic tractor with Geordie hanging on to both of them as they rounded corners on two wheels at high speed, laughing all the way. Cooking in the kitchen on winter afternoons meant Eddie standing on a chair with Percy in close attendance, lightly dusted with flour and guaranteed to enjoy a few snacks.

Percy's ears and tummy were finely tuned to the engine sounds of the various delivery vans. He would always find a timely excuse to be let out in the morning and, if we were not perfectly awake to his ploys, would nip off to inspect whatever the butcher had delivered. In his time, he snaffled several pounds of sausages destined for a cricket match, some very nice beef, the mince for a cottage pie, and so forth. In the end, we built a little wooden hatch in which all the meat deliveries could go in the short time before the chefs arrived, which was reasonably Percy-proof. He loved visitors – perhaps something to do with the remains of scones – and discovered that if he was busy looking hopeful at a table by the tearooms, one of the Highclere team would then tempt him back to his own room with a scone. So, it was a win–win strategy. He was incredibly loyal and loving to us all and adored by Eddie and Geordie.

Given Percy was rather large, Eddie then said to me he would like a little dog who could sit on his lap. I immediately thought of a Cocker Spaniel and thus began my own family of working Cockers.

Early one Christmas morning, armed with a basket and some tea towels, I drove down to the house belonging to Highclere's head keeper Eddie and his wife Val, who had been part of life at Highclere forever. Returning as swiftly as I could, I quickly tied a red ribbon onto the little willow basket and went back into the Christmas-stocking chaos.

I put the basket on our bed with my six-year-old son and my husband and left them to it. Inside was my gift to them both – a tiny chocolate-coloured working Cocker puppy with white markings on her nose and chest. They called her Rosie but, as she was only six weeks old, she had to return to her mummy for two or three more weeks before she came to us as her forever home.

Rosie was the kindest, most enthusiastic bundle of brown fur and such a welcome and loving part of our little family. Percy and Rosie became quite the duo. If dogs make us humans feel loved and a little less lonely, I also felt that Percy would like to have a friend to curl up with. Rosie was just perfect. Neither of them could ever be replaced but, as we bred from both of them (separately), it has been very special to be able to continue the link to these two dogs.

Sometime later, my sister-in-law Carolyn rang me one evening asking if our Labrador was safely at home. I had a quick look round and realised he had not come back from his last evening venture. Dipper, her dog, was missing as well. It transpired Percy had managed to cover a mile across the park and then swim a lake to find a Labrador paramour who was on heat. It was not long before a litter of puppies arrived, and not long after that Bella, a truly well-named dog, came to live with us. Like her father Percy, she was quite large but very pale in colour. She was immensely attuned to humans and kind, and spoke with her eyes as well as her body language, reflecting the way dogs can share our lives, moods and living spaces like no other animal. She was also partial to strawberries and pears, competing for her favourite fruits rather too successfully for her two-legged friends.

In 2010, Bella had an assignation with a very nice fox-red Labrador and ten heavenly puppies arrived in September

Proposed design for the Castle saloon
(Thomas Allom sketch)

(*Top*) The Georgian Highclere House *c.* 1800

Highclere Castle
library in 1895

Team Highclere

John Gundill, Castle Manager

The estate office team (*from left to right*): Jo Johnstone, Chris Bushnell, Caitlin Rennie, Laura Edinborough, Paul Minall, Paul McTaggart

The late Les Taylor, our former Head of Security

The late Paul Brooke-Taylor

The banqueting team (*from left to right*): Jorge Barbosa, Luis Coello, Tom Williams, Sam Herring

The painting team (*from left to right*): Pat and Mike Withers, Richard Crocker

The kitchen team (*from left to right*): Mandy, Will, Raj, Rob, Andy

The real Vine and Craven Hunt, behind the scenes with the *Downton Abbey* actors. Series 1, episode 3

The concert during the First World War in *Downton Abbey*. Series 2, episode 4

An icon, the late Dame Maggie Smith

Behind the scenes in the dining room

Jim Carter and Julian Fellowes discussing the script

The final episode of Series 1

The puppy journey begins…

'Dogs may not be our whole life but they make our lives whole'

The garden team (*from left to right*): Emeline Fisher, Nick Williamson, Holly Randall

The White Garden

The Secret Garden

The Monks' Garden

Lady Carnarvon in the Peach House

The 6th Earl and Countess of Carnarvon

Final adjustments to the placement

Burns Night – the Eightsome Reel

that year. Bella was an amazing mother but it was exhausting. I chose the littlest, reddest puppy, Alfie, and then we also kept Scooby Doo because Eddie and his brother, my stepson George, thought he looked most like Percy. My husband was so happy that eight puppies had found other homes that, somehow, he accepted two were staying.

Most of the puppies did not go far, finding homes with happy friends so they could come back for tea once in a while. Parting with each puppy was emotional, yet they would come to mean so much to the families they went to live with. Some came back for walks in the next few weeks as the new families found their way together.

In consequence, September is puppy-party month: any puppy born here, as well as their four- and two-legged friends, returns here and we celebrate together. Everyone runs around the lawns trying to demonstrate their perfectly trained dogs, who in turn spot the cakes, tennis balls and toys and win the prize for enthusiasm and happiness, if not for perfect behaviour. Trying to take a group dog photograph is excellent entertainment – all the humans focused on saying 'sit' and 'stay', with individual but never joint success. It becomes a little competitive.

Each puppy from each generation born here has made a difference to people's lives. They teach us to love and be loved unconditionally. We can be ourselves with no fashionable front or style. Labradors are particularly focused on their humans and all we have to do is listen. With their genuine frankness, their mild eyes and affable body language, they teach us kindness and to be on 'receive' rather than just 'transmit'.

In a world in which we spend far too much time looking at back-lit screens, dogs are often there to bring us back to today.

They are good for our health and make us exercise, although paradoxically they are often the stars of Instagram as well as being key screen-savers.

Labradors do seem to like living in England even if they originated across the ocean in Newfoundland, Canada. They are well suited to our rather damp cold climate having webbed paws and smooth, waterproof double coats. The downside is that they do shed their coat and need brushing as anyone with a dark floor and a yellow Labrador will testify, but they sort out their own coats in bad weather as the water just runs off. They sit happily in puddles and love to leap into any available pond, easily shaking off the water after a short time. They are also hard-working and love tasks, with a far longer concentration span than Cocker Spaniels.

It is a moot point how many different words they can understand. I do know that if I suggest 'Shall we all go out?' without moving so much as a fraction from where I am sitting, they leap up expectantly. Cuddled around me of an evening, the latest puppies in particular do seem to watch TV from time to time and they can certainly recognise my voice down a telephone.

Labradors do not just live here at Highclere Castle, they also live at Downton Abbey. At 9 p.m. on many a Sunday, just like 10 million other families in the UK, we used to settle down to watch the next instalment of *Downton Abbey*. Walking away from us all, across the lawns towards 'Downton', was the wiggly bottom and waggly tail of a yellow Labrador. Over the years, the Grantham family also welcomed different Labradors including new puppies, which became an intrinsic part of the fictional family's life in many episodes. They only ever had one dog as part of their family, but in real life, the number of my dogs was somehow increasing.

APRIL: TELLING TAILS

Our wonderful old friend Percy came to the end of his life, which was devastating for us all. Having lain down with him to say goodbye, Geordie was so distraught that it fell to me to carry him, wrapped in a blanket, into the car to go to the vet's. Whilst I did not doubt it was the right time, it was nevertheless no easier. For the next few days, neither of us slept properly and there was a huge empty place in our life and home. Dogs may well live with us for a decade of our lives, Percy lived a little longer, but in that decade they share all our confidences with very few expectations of us and always take us as we are. They share the best and saddest moments and are simply there. Percy's courage and size meant he had been nicknamed the 'Yellow Lion' by Geordie and so, later on, one of the racehorses born here was given the racing name 'Yellow Lion'.

Percy's daughter Bella took his place as matriarch of the Labrador family. As she too aged, she became even paler. She was kind and empathetic, and she reminded us of how to grow old gracefully. As she became ever creakier, each step became an achievement, but every now and again she made it clear that she would like to be included in a walk. Sometimes I lifted her into a wheelbarrow and sometimes she ventured out with us on foot, but I usually returned with a car to retrieve her from the various points of the garden to which she had laboriously hauled herself. When she was less and less able to bend and stretch, brushing her and scratching behind her ears or along her back meant a lot to her.

One of Bella's puppies was born with a faint mark on her forehead. She was the last to leave me but found a home where she completely changed the life of her new owner who became her devoted best friend forever. For all the complications we pile into our own human lives, Bella and her puppies were and are about the simplicity of unconditional love. It is rare to replicate this with another human being because we bring with us so many unconscious prejudices to relationships, both with our families and our friends, often expecting too much from them as well as the ability to read minds. Of course, a dog can, to some extent, read our minds. Rather than muddling up words and thoughts, however, they encourage us to enjoy the sense of touch and remind us of the power of scent and sight and hearing.

The puppy with a faint mark on her forehead stayed close by and, in time, became the mummy to eight more puppies. Needless to say, they were just adorable and my husband, wanting to anticipate my love for puppies, enthusiastically chose and named one Freya, after the Norse goddess of love.

Another puppy from this litter happened to come and stay as well – and whilst Geordie continued to ask when it was going, after a little time it did begin to dawn on him that this one was also perhaps permanent: Stella – a star, and she looked so very like her mother.

Rosie the spaniel, who grew up to have a very modern Mohican fringe, also had two puppies, Winnie and Clemmie (grandly given the surname Churchill-Carnarvon), and then Clemmie had further puppies. Evie was born on the sofa in my study, watched by Luis and his daughter Isabella, and more puppies arrived later that night in my bedroom in the Castle. Evie stayed with me whilst Super Ted, Rosie's grandson, stayed with Luis.

There was, by now, quite a gaggle of dogs, to my husband's amazement. Over time, walks with Rosie became far less frequent and quite short. Her sight and hearing gradually deteriorated, but she still enjoyed her food which I would soak to soften it as her teeth were not very good either.

Nevertheless, this funny little figure, bouncing along a bit like a teddy bear with her slightly wonky back legs and her determination to spend each day just as she wanted, was a beacon and a daily reminder to live life to the full.

Over the final few weeks, Rosie's back legs grew progressively worse but she still seemed fine in herself. Despite the fact that we know that death comes along for all of us, it is still achingly awful when a dog reaches the end. Something else went wrong somewhere in her spine and so once again it was time to ring the vet's. Matthew, one of the Highclere team, very kindly drove me so that I could hold her on her last journey. Many of you with dogs will know this moment – the phone call, the advice, the terrible decision. Neither my husband nor my son was there so, rather as I'd made that first journey with her on my own when she came to us, it was just the two of us for our last goodbye as she went gently into that good night.

Sadly, Bella too had left us and whilst another generation do not replace those you love, they do occupy you and remind you to love those who are here today.

The spaniels have always been harder to train than the Labradors. They have superb noses for scents and to see them leaping around following a trail, whatever their age, is good for the soul. On some afternoons I used to ask a lovely Nepalese member of our Highclere team, Indra, to walk the dogs for half an hour around the Castle gardens. Soon afterwards, I noticed that whenever I took the spaniels out, they never came back and rather ignored me. I asked Indra for his view and he happily replied that, 'Winston go on walk, they very good and run well.' I realised I had failed to explain that he and the dogs were supposed to walk together. Winnie was thereafter constantly 'lost in jungle' as Indra called it, which meant sending a search party into his favourite wood; he was otherwise on a lead outside any fenced area. Winnie and Clemmie still bop along on walks, curl up together afterwards to snooze and, given half a chance, will still try to nip out for their own adventure without me.

I have done better with Evie who zooms back at full speed when called, checks me out and zooms off again. Despite being a very small spaniel, she is extremely fast and bosses all the Labradors around. In fact, of course, she is really a princess – she sleeps with me every night and tells me very clearly when it is time to go upstairs as she has had a tiring day. Conversely, the next morning, she circles me, strongly suggesting that I should get dressed a little faster to take her out for her early-morning walk.

Geordie and I are by no means the first to share our home with dogs. You cannot help but notice the little terrier dog named Pinsher leaping out of the portrait of the children of the 1st Earl of Carnarvon, which hangs in pride of place above the fireplace in the drawing room. Even if the children adored their favourite dog, it is clear the terrier was none too keen on the artist Sir William Beechey.

In the smoking room there are more paintings featuring dogs, though, in these cases, more in the guise of hunting dogs than children's pets. The aristocratic breeds of those times were 'running hounds' – greyhounds or wolfhounds – which is the type of dog that Geordie's seventeenth-century ancestor Sir Robert Sawyer chose as his companion in the portrait in the dining room. They may have been fast, but it was their ability to follow a scent that was most admired. They had a job to do in that hunting was both a sport and for some a way of providing food.

By the time guests are climbing the red stairs to the gallery, it is clear that dogs have been part of family life throughout the Castle's history. On the wall leading to the top floor is an enormous portrait of a rather grand, commanding-looking ancestor of Geordie's, William Herbert, from the time of Henry VIII. Despite his fine clothes and formidable pose, he too is painted with a tiny, cute white dog, which was probably a fluffy white Bichon Frisé, making it clear that this little animal was definitely part of his life.

The presence of a dog during a portrait sitting also has the advantage of helping children stay still. In the north library, a child, seemingly a little girl in frilly petticoats, is depicted holding a pet dog on a lead. It is in fact a little boy and it was painted in 1770 by Thomas Hudson. Perhaps it was the presence of the pet dog that persuaded the child to stand still and look happy for long enough for the artist to paint him.

Many of those who work and live at Highclere today have dogs. They have been part of the estate and landscape here for several thousand years. Domesticated dogs date back to the Iron Age (circa 1430 BC) and were traditionally used for hunting, as well as playing a role in guarding and herding stock (sheep and cattle). Matt the shepherd's two collies are fascinating to watch as they help him move the sheep between fields, into barns or just separate them. Unlike today, however, the dogs of the past were expected to seek out food themselves, whether by hunting or stealing.

The 5th Earl of Carnarvon's brother Aubrey married Mary de Vesey in St James's Church, Piccadilly, in the summer of 1910. Mary wore a beautiful white chiffon and velvet gown and her fifteen bridesmaids wore flame-coloured chiffon over gold satin and carried bunches of myrtle. Aubrey gave his wife a beautiful ring and a pair of Irish Wolfhounds, and afterwards they left to spend the first week of their honeymoon at

Highclere Castle. At times, Aubrey had twice as many dogs as we do and of all types and sizes. I, at least, have managed to limit myself to two breeds.

The 5th Earl adored his little terrier dog Susie. Originally, he had given her to his son, but when Susie then had to stay at Highclere during the First World War, she became devoted to Lord Carnarvon, sleeping on his bed and sometimes travelling to Egypt with him. However, when he returned to the Valley of the Kings in January 1923, to continue with the exploration and conservation of the tomb of Tutankhamun discovered just two months earlier, Lord Carnarvon left Susie behind. They were going to dismantle the false wall in the first room of the tomb of the boy king, which would result in the discovery of the golden shrines and nested golden coffins.

Sadly, Lord Carnarvon was never to return to his beloved Highclere. In the centre of the media frenzy surrounding the unprecedented archaeological find, he died in Cairo in the early morning of 5 April 1923, amidst lurid tales of a curse. Back at Highclere, Susie was sleeping with the housekeeper in her bedroom. Family legend relates that, on the stroke of midnight on the day her master died, the little dog suddenly stood up, howled, turned round in circles and also died.

The 6th Earl of Carnarvon later had a series of black Labradors, all of whom, in the way of Labradors, enjoyed both the shooting field and the quality of the cooking in the Castle kitchens. Geordie recalls Prune and Custard each having a comfortable niche under the kitchen worktops. Ivy, who was the cook at the time, fed everyone equally well: the family upstairs and their dogs downstairs. The canine members of the family became a little bit too large but were very happy. After eating their own dinner, they would then also go up and thoroughly enjoy any leftovers from the dining-room table, all the while trying to look as if they were starving, which was not a successful act.

Coincidentally, Geordie's mother had a Border Terrier also called Lottie who bore many similarities to our own Lottie. Given half a chance she would be off chasing a scent through the woods. Dogs usually make their own way back home but if she was gone for too long, we would all be out calling for her. It was terribly sad when she finally died but she left many good memories.

There were possibly more dogs than Geordie might originally have anticipated, but nevertheless life was relatively settled (for him) until I thought it was time that Stella should have puppies. Trying to find a mate for her was a matter of serious study and following up leads. When the search was finally narrowed down, it was time to meet the dog, his human family, any puppies and, in this case, grand-puppies. Like any other owner, I wanted to be sure that his hips, shoulders and eyes were all good. As for his nature, choosing a sire is about watching and interacting with the dog, to ensure that the next generation is kind, intelligent, and has every chance of being as healthy and happy as possible.

Having agreed the 'marriage' and estimated the date of the next season, I then had to ensure my diary was free each side around the eleventh day. I had not found a way or time to confide such dreams to my husband so it was all done slightly on the quiet. On the day of the assignation, I had to drive about two hours north of Highclere. Unfortunately for me, Geordie wondered where I was for once. He actually tried to find me on the 'Find My' app and asked everyone he could think of. It was all rather difficult because, whilst everyone in the office knew, nobody wanted to lie to him. He said it was all very odd as I seemed to be up a track in Warwickshire.

Forewarned by the office, I rang him back to explain that I was helping a girlfriend find some furniture in a country warehouse for her new house. In the meantime, I rang her to see if she could please hide because she was supposedly with me. In any case, the deed was done, Stella was completely exhausted and slept in shock the whole way home. I didn't at this point tell Geordie what I'd done or where I'd been in case the assignation had not been successful.

Stella and I continued our life as normal and then, after about four weeks, I realised that she was indeed growing a little bit bigger, and I thought her behaviour was changing as well. Geordie was away so I thought this might be a good time to tell him, in the hope that absence might make the heart grow fonder and so on. I sent him some cute photos of Stella with love hearts around her, which he misinterpreted as sweet messages from me – though that was true in a way. In the end, a girlfriend of mine kindly blurted out the truth for me and he had a few days to collect himself before his arrival home.

Stella and I slept together for a week just before she was due to give birth, until one night she began to scrabble around and dig into the carpet. I am not sure either of us slept very well from that point. I left the curtains drawn and set up a cosy area under a dressing table, with clean towels and mats covering as much of the floor as possible. Time and matters took their own course, and some hours later a tiny shape began to leave Stella's body and enter the world. Stella was not quite sure what she had done but cleaned her precious bundle, 'talking', licking and pushing the tiny puppy with her nose. I leaned in to check it was breathing and that it looked fine. I touched her puppy carefully and moved it slightly. She looked at me with huge dark eyes, picked the puppy up to remove my hand and placed it protectively within the semi-circle of her body.

Another hour passed before the next puppy arrived, which had given the first one time to begin to suckle. Stella had so clearly fallen in love with her baby. The same process continued and, inevitably, despite my efforts to put towels under her, she would find the corner of the carpet that was not covered, but that would have to wait.

In total, six puppies appeared. Stella did a lot of talking and they began to do a lot of squeaking. I did a lot of lying down, watching, and felt very lucky to be able to witness this part of life. I am not sure there is anything in the world more magical than welcoming a litter of new puppies.

Having popped into the vet's to check that Stella and her brood were healthy, we all returned and she was settled into her own proper 'bedroom'. All the puppies were in a whelping box with large cushions outside it for both Stella and her close human family to lie on whilst the puppies slept, their tummies wonderfully round. There was also a comfortable wicker chair, plenty of water and constant room service.

For four or five days, Stella hardly left the tiny creatures. She would just pop out quickly and dash back again. As the puppies grew, their tummies could hold more milk and Stella was able to change her own routine a little. She spent time relaxing outside and even went a little further away with her other four-legged friends. Equally, we tried to maintain her security and privacy.

When puppies are born, they can neither see nor hear. Their eyes don't open until about two weeks after birth and it is a further week before their ears develop hearing. However, they can recognise scents and it is this sense, along with touch, upon which they rely. A dog's sense of smell is some 10,000 to

100,000 times more sensitive than yours or mine. Apparently, we have about 6 million olfactory receptors, but dogs have about 300 million and much more of a dog's brain is focused on scent. It was through scent that the puppies found and bonded with their mother and siblings.

All puppies instinctively pile together in a heap. They are highly social animals and want the reassurance of company. With every day that passed, the latest litter seemed to swell in size, tummy-crawling and frequently collapsing on top of each other.

All too soon and once again, it was time to find homes for them where they would be happy and loved. Of course, this latest generation had all the virtues: good-looking, loving, kind, super-intelligent. One of the puppies just sat staring up at me whenever I was there. That was Poppy and she still gazes at me with large liquid dark eyes from the first moment we meet each morning.

From observation and experience, it seems to me much kinder to keep puppies until they are ten to twelve weeks old rather than the more conventional eight or nine. They are still so very tiny when they first have to deal with separation from their mother. Gradually, though, Stella went down to seeing them twice a day and from there to just once, and then they were entirely weaned. They had to get used to her absence and so they bonded more closely with each other, to overcome this early stress.

Published research suggests that if puppies are separated from their siblings too early it can lead to problems later in their life. They learn how to roll over from each other, wrestle one another and learn that a squeak from another puppy means to stop, and that way they can all get on. It is these first formative weeks that should help ensure calmness and a mild temperament later on.

Naturally, puppies are always popular with my family, with the team here and various friends with children of all ages, which helps get them used to different situations and different people. This stands them in good stead when they go on to share other homes and lives. Even at this age, their innate recognition of emotions and feelings is far more sensitive than ours. They will turn their heads, looking and listening, aware of my body language.

There are moments of such happiness, watching the puppies go outside for the first time to explore across the lawn. Or later showing them the wildflower meadow, although they can't see very far. Such adventures exhaust them so it is all quite brief. It is Operation Puppy Wrangling when they first wiggle their way into the Castle – some cleaning up after them is always needed – and a week or so later they try to scale a couple of stairs and practise their red-carpet walk.

Choosing the right dog on the one hand and choosing the right family on the other is not straightforward. For some friends, taking on one of the puppies is a leap in the dark. We handle it all slowly, with the proviso that if it does not work out that is quite fine but the puppy comes back to me.

The Labradors in *Downton Abbey* had fictional names referring to ancient Egyptian gods, playing on the strong Highclere connection to the wonders of the ancient world. In fact, dogs were very much part of everyday life in ancient Egypt. The Egyptians had two words for dog: the first, *'iwiw'*, was an onomatopoeic reference to a barking dog; the second was *'tesem'* for a barkless dog or hunting hound. Dogs were portrayed in tomb paintings, sitting beside or under their owners' chairs. Occasionally, their name can be distinguished. For example, one can see that a royal guard dog called Abutyu received an elaborate ceremonial burial in the Giza necropolis.

The inscription is in a wall scene in the tomb of an unknown man at Giza, but it is clear this was the beloved dog of a Pharaoh who lived some time before 2280 BC.

Just like today, dogs in ancient Egypt were always named and the name written on their collars. There are a very few preserved leather collars but many depictions of them on frescoes, stelae and reliefs. They include names such as 'Brave One', 'Reliable', 'Healthy', 'Grabber', 'North Wind' and 'Good Herdsman', and whether high-born or not, all were adored dogs.

On leaving this life for the next one, the Egyptian guide for the dead was the god Anubis, who was represented either as a recumbent jackal or hound, or with a jackal or hound's head on a man's body. He was there to guard and shepherd the dead carefully into the afterlife, echoing a domesticated dog's role in everyday life.

Dogs are more than just a pet, but conversely it is all too easy to attribute human traits to them. They have their own needs, which we should remain aware of. Luckily, we are all different and enjoy different pastimes, as do dogs. We do, however, share the same love of play and, it would seem in a dog's case, specifically any game that involves a ball. If the spaniels only show half-hearted interest in ball games, the Labradors are fixated. Football, rugby, golf, tennis, squash, cricket, baseball, lacrosse, hockey, billiards or polo fill human news and lives. One of my latest puppies, Isla, can find balls lost in the gardens for years and loves a canine version of tennis or football in which all the balls rapidly become the worse for wear whilst she smiles relentlessly throughout. Her sister Poppy tends to take the ball from her, her aunt Freya is very polite and will largely ignore it, sometimes her mother will retrieve it for her, whilst Finse, their grandmother, is undeterred by her age and keen to snaffle any ball she can.

Each of the dogs has found where they like to sleep – their home if you like – but after supper Isla and Poppy think it is time to share sofas. Poppy will launch herself at Geordie convinced he wants nothing more than to pet her, whilst Isla will lie around my shoulders on the back of the sofa and we all see how long we last before they find the TV an unconvincing pastime.

At the end of every day, whatever the weather, the dogs and I head out across the grass for a last walk in the dark. After a few yards my eyes adjust, my feet automatically finding their way after treading the same ground night after night. Looking up at the stars, following the planets through the seasons, seeing the dark silhouettes of the cedar trees etched against the star-embroidered sky, must be one of the most humbling and peaceful moments of the day. Owls swoop out of the cluster of trees behind the old church where a priest first celebrated Mass some 1,200 years ago, when there was no light except rushlights, the stars and moon. The night is a void into which we have thrown our dreams and fears for untold centuries.

As ever, the dogs bring me back down to earth, my old friends nosing me for a quick hug and the others returning from time to time to check that I am following where they lead. The friendship given by this gaggle of family dogs is part of my sense of belonging here at Highclere, and it is a similar story for so many others walking under the stars in other parts of the world.

I am not sure Geordie can quite believe we have eight dogs nowadays and sometimes I too wonder how on earth it happened. But they make our journey here so much richer – to the point where I sometimes think they have a clearer idea of where they are going than we do in our more muddled lives. If Geordie is away in London, some do on occasion try to hop onto a large comfy basket otherwise called my bed. Having drifted off, they seem to dream just as we do – perhaps they are chasing balls or have found a very promising bin to empty as they make funny little yipping sounds in their sleep.

The dogs undoubtedly make our lives richer and more present. They make us strike up conversations and they bring us together. For all the visitors' excitement when they arrive at 'Downton Abbey', the question I am most often asked is, 'Where are the dogs?' The answer is: safely away from the food.

CHAPTER FIVE

May: The Secret Gardens

'If you look the right way, you can see that the whole world is a garden'
— The Secret Garden, Frances Hodgson Burnett

A weathered sign stands tall amongst a rambling collection of pale-leaved hydrangeas and buddleias. Beneath are blowsy white paeonies, tulips, nodding white campanulas and geraniums. Wordsworth celebrated the fact that 'May is on the lawn / A quickening hope, a freshening glee' – everything grows so hastily in this month that no gardener can keep up with its enthusiasm.

The garden sign points towards a black ironwork gate set in a mottled old brick wall, and when you are close enough you can see the words 'Secret Garden', faded but still etched into the greying wood.

Run your fingers idly along a shelf in any good bookshop and you may well find a copy of the book *The Secret Garden* by Frances Hodgson Burnett. Written in 1911, it draws you into a story about hidden creaky doors found in high garden walls, the discovery and rebirth of a garden, and the two main protagonists' corresponding return to better mental and physical health. The happy scenes it describes of the children in the garden have stayed with me since I first read it as a child myself. Magically, the original film of the book, which starred Maggie Smith as Mrs Medlock, was partly filmed in this garden at Highclere. Dreamy gardens make perfect places to escape into and every garden helps to make a home a real haven. Everything comes together in a garden.

Turn from our weathered sign and, pausing to glance at the long scented white tendrils of wisteria that clothe the garden wall to either side, push open the old frost gate. An overgrown metal arch frames the entrance, whilst to left and right a vivid green grass path leads between deep winding serpentine borders of flowers and shrubs.

Originally designed by Jim Russell for Geordie's grandfather, the 6th Earl, this 'garden' once finished in a dead end on both sides. You couldn't even walk round it in a circle and it always made me feel faintly trapped. At one end, however, I could just about crawl into a dark mass of softwood trees whose branches threatened to whack me in the face as I pushed further in. What then became apparent was that this marked the beginning of what had once been an avenue, although only a few magnificent beech trees remained.

I had once read that 80 per cent of National Trust members join purely to see its gardens. Two World Wars and changing times had led to Geordie's grandfather reducing the gardening team at Highclere to just two and following a plan of minimal garden maintenance. Geordie's parents continued to maintain what was left but also created a white border behind a yew hedge instead of a cutting garden. It was, however, a small garden walk compared to the rather large house.

Research in the Castle archives and endless (happy) reading led to the realisation that this whole area was once a designed wilderness. Geordie's ancestor Robert Herbert lived here for the first half of the eighteenth century and in the gardening vogue of the time created formal gardens with parterres near the house. He built twelve follies, planted a number of magnificent avenues of beech and, to amuse his guests and himself, created a wilderness adorned with classical and ancient statues to the south-east of his home. It was possibly laid out with help from the much-admired eighteenth-century garden designer Stephen Switzer, with whom Robert worked at Wilton House, a renowned historic house in Wiltshire owned by his elder brother, the 9th Earl of Pembroke. The latter was an inveterate traveller and collector, often leaving the management of his house and gardens to his brother.

Addicted to parading in the finest clothes in the best circles, Robert Herbert devoted a lifetime to improving what was then called Highclere Place House in order for it to win acclaim as the perfect gentleman's seat. He built on land he had inherited from his grandfather. At that time, Highclere was a handsome L-shaped brick house of some antiquity, set in the centre of a pleasing estate. His grandfather had already planted some allées and begun 'garden work', which Robert continued apace.

Thanks to his social ambitions, he was particularly concerned with improving the landscape around the house; creating an enviable 'Arcadia' with walks, parterres and grand avenues. To the south-east a diagonal beech avenue led to a mount adorned with a rotunda whilst, nearer to the house, serpentine walks meandered through pleasure gardens in which 'Eminences', often enhanced with a statue, were scattered. Never satisfied with what he had achieved so far, he was always contriving some new project. By 1733, he had just completed a charming Octagon to complement the Rotunda in the Great Wilderness and was now considering a 'theatre in the woods', which would extend his walks, rides and viewing points.

A secret glade in Rookery Pit, an old chalk pit to the east of the house, seemed a perfect place to become a pleasure dell in the manner of the quarry garden that had been created at Wilton. Switzer, author of the popular garden tome *Ichnographia Rustica*, often advised his clients to create these little gardens set a mile or two from the main house to act as pleasant 'surprises' on rides out, not to mention providing the perfect setting for illicit assignations. Jeremiah Milles, Robert's friend and erstwhile fellow student, described the new area thus:

> At some distance from this in a little copse is a beautifull pitt, with a Tuscan Temple standing over the brink of it. Mr Herbert showed his taste in this improvement, which was nothing else but a deep chalk pitt surrounded with a little scrub wood. He cleared & levelled the bottom of the pitt, & then turfed it over so that it appears like the Arena of an Amphitheater. One side over this arena is 40 feet perpendicular heighth out of which the bushes & briars grow in a very agreable wildness. The Tuscan Temple which is of wood, is an oblong square, & has 4 pillars in front supporting a triangular pediment. Opposite to this on the other side of the pitt is a seat, with a slope before it down to the arena, behind & all around it is a wood, thro' which there are serpentine walks.

A century later, the Etruscan temple described above was moved to a new location and now sits gazing towards an exceptional Arcadian view of fields, soft slopes and woodland. Behind it, Geordie and I have added a new garden area facing west in memory of his mother – Lady Jeanie's Garden thus faces towards the USA and Wyoming, her beloved childhood home. It is planted in the soft blues, whites and pinks that she preferred, with some perennials that have architectural foliage to give shape, whilst just below it a wisteria grows up a wooden pergola.

Highclere was not built on the same scale as some of the huge Palladian country houses. Their draughty rooms were cold and difficult to live in, and so small garden follies became increasingly attractive options as they were cosy by contrast and provided an escape from over-formality. Nevertheless, with his smaller house and grand garden plans, Robert was hoping to have the best of both worlds.

In all aspects, this was an era of literary and classical allusion and Robert referenced more than most. Along with his brothers, he had been educated under the auspices of the Reverend Isaac Milles, the father of Jeremiah, who had been given the living of Highclere by Robert's grandfather. A much-admired classicist, Milles's influence was so highly regarded that Lord Pembroke had recommended the clergyman's eldest son (Thomas) to Queen Anne for the Bishopric of Waterford and Lismore in Ireland.

With this scholarly background for inspiration, Robert happily mixed pagan gods of fields and nature with druids and ancient Britons and set them beside Roman and Greek gods. One of his main influences was the renowned poet and celebrity Alexander Pope, many of whose works Robert had added to the library at Highclere. Although he is now better known as a poet, Pope was also very interested in garden design, going so far as to claim that 'gardening is more antique and nearer God's work than poetry'. He worked extensively on his own garden at Twickenham where, amongst other artifices, he created a grotto.

Pope's influence was reasonably widespread and no less a person than Jonathan Swift described him as the 'master' and 'contriver' of the garden style that was more naturalistic than the endless symmetrical hedges and clipped parterres of the previously fashionable French style. Pope would 'Consult the genius of the place in all', as he put it in one of his poems. As the eighteenth century progressed, landscape and gardens were thought of in increasingly poetic and painterly terms, and the finest style of landscape was considered to be that in which artistic composition was translated not onto canvas but into the three-dimensional form of plants and trees, light and shade, enhanced by eye-catching ruins and classically inspired temples.

Pope knew the Herberts and briefly stayed at Highclere. He also visited their neighbours, the de Lisle sisters, in nearby Crux Easton, in order to admire their famous seashell grotto. Sadly, nothing remains of this now but at the time it was quite an edifice. The front elevation was built of flint, the interior studded with shells, scoriae of iron ore and other natural substances, and it contained a seat for each sister, with a niche for the presiding 'magician'. Pope described the scene in his 'Inscription on a GROTTO of Shells at CRUX-EASTON, the Work of Nine young Ladies':

> *Here shunning idleness at once and praise,*
> *This radiant pile nine rural sisters raise;*
> *The glitt'ring emblem of each spotless dame,*
> *Clear as her soul, and shining as her frame;*
> *Beauty which Nature only can impart,*
> *And such a polish as disgraces Art;*
> *But Fate dispos'd them in this humble sort,*
> *And hid in desarts what wou'd charm a Court.*

An inscription, dated 25 August 1733, also held to have been composed, extempore, by Pope is titled: 'On seeing

MAY: THE SECRET GARDENS

the LADIES Crux-Easton Walk in the WOODS by the GROTTO':

> *Authors the world and their dull brains have trac'd*
> *To fix the ground where paradise was plac'd;*
> *Mind not their learned whims and idle talk;*
> *Here, here's the place where these bright angels walk.*

Robert Herbert and the de Lisle family enjoyed a longstanding relationship. In 1735, Robert presented the living at Burghclere (a parish adjoining Highclere) to Dr Thomas de Lisle who remained rector there until his death. Margaret, the youngest de Lisle sister, possessed a talent for painting and two of her portraits, depicting Sir Richard and Lady Kingsmill, who lived at Highclere before the estate was bought by Robert's grandfather, can still be seen here at the Castle today.

Despite all his landscaping, Robert was never quite satisfied with his efforts, always feeling that he lacked sufficient eyecatchers, the features that would make his garden – and thus himself – outstanding in the area of garden design. In the quest to earn the same level of acclaim as Pope's Thameside garden at Twickenham, he never stopped adding to his plans or showing off his latest improvements to friends and acquaintances. He especially enjoyed creating picnics and al fresco entertainments and outings, believing that they showed his creation in the best possible light.

During the course of the assorted circular walks on offer, various 'stands' would mark places where visitors could pause to admire a particular view or effect. Sometimes rustic benches were permanently installed at these points, and on other occasions chairs and tripod tables would be carefully placed for a nuncheon (now called luncheon), with food appearing from baskets. This often took the form of a cold collation: cooked ham and chicken, even a small venison pie, followed by a syllabub or an ice cream from the dairy. Alternatively, *piqueniques* – a French term which conveyed the idea of small dishes to 'pick' or 'peck' at, whilst the rhyming addition 'nique' suggested a 'thing of little importance', a mere bagatelle – became a popular choice. Even then, it seems, they appreciated that food eaten outside often tastes better than it does inside.

By the end of his life in 1769, Robert Herbert had witnessed the accession of three Hanoverian kings: George I, George II, and finally, in 1760, George III. He had built even more 'eyecatchers', developed longer rides and walks, and given the topography at Highclere some beautiful retreats. Using the Rotunda as a clock face, he led the visitor's eyes and footsteps to the follies Heaven's Gate (1737) and Dan's Lodge, the theatrical temple in Rookery Pit, the Temple of Diana, Jackdaws Castle (1743), and finally a walk around Milford Lake with its villa at one end. His friend Jeremiah Milles wrote in his diaries:

> Mr Herbert's house ... lies at the bottom of Sidedown Hill, from whence an avenue of beeches leads to it, it is near half a mile long. This house, which was a very good one in the ancient taste, has been so much alter'd and improved by the present worthy Possessor that it is for its size one of the most beautifull and elegant houses in England. It has besides a good old Gothic front, which faces the stables, two other modern ones, the Principal one towards the hill, the other towards the garden which is laid out in grass.

Despite the fact that the eighteenth-century design elements were an important part of Highclere's garden history, they were almost entirely lost but old maps as well as letters from visitors at that time were invaluable resources as we began to reinstate them.

Once granted a forestry licence to take down the softwoods I had so laboriously clambered through, it was possible to distinguish the original outline of the wilderness, though work on reinstating it could not begin immediately. The money received for the softwoods just about paid for the deer and rabbit fence around the perimeter of the newly rediscovered area, which would ensure the shrubs and saplings we now planted would have a chance of growing successfully.

During this stage the whole area was cordoned off and looked like nothing more than a rather sad, muddy and abandoned eyesore. To be honest, John was very unimpressed by my endeavours and rather thought I should have left well alone.

Before it was cut down, the softwood plantation had screened the views of the park fields from the Castle to the south. This meant that John and I felt able to book both a wedding in the Castle and a corporate event in the parkland, which we had thought would be obscured from each other due to the thickness of the foliage. One day he was happily admiring the view from his office when he realised to his horror that, now the softwoods were no more, rather too many bright white tents were visible stretching right across the field in front of the Castle lawns.

He was not at all happy that the Arcadian idyll sold to the bridal party was now contradicted by the tent city that had suddenly sprung up. I realised I had got it wrong once more, but there was no way I could stand the trees up again and nor did I want to. I remarked to John that, hopefully, the bride and groom would just be gazing at each other, all the guests' eyes would be on them, and soon the sun would set and night would cover the tents. It was the best sales line I could think of.

The reinstatement of Robert Herbert's beech avenue was the next project and it was marked out to be planted in the same spacing as it had been in 1730. We then moved semi-mature beeches from elsewhere on the estate with a modern tree spade, cutting each tree back by one-third in the dormancy of winter, before placing it in a generous planting pit, backfilled with some soil improver and lots of water. We waited and in spring all the trees began to green up. Given the shock of relocation, they did not progress for a little while but, over the next few years, they noticeably began to feel well rooted and to assume their role in the avenue. Being Highclere, we had inadvertently moved one copper beech into place amongst the green and, dithering momentarily about what to do, decided it was typical of the place and so it remains.

Some of those first summer months were quite hot and Geordie was to be found several times each week dragging a heavy long hose from the new standpipe we had put in to water the trees, determined they would not die. Two years later, we relocated another forty at the far end of the avenue, to bring it up to the Mount and Panhandle marked on the old maps. There is still a mound marking the denouement on which Robert Herbert would have built a temple of some sort; a classical building to catch the eye and one from which there would be further views into nature. Sadly, though, the temple itself is long gone.

Meanwhile, I had walked in winding arcs through the muddy wilderness followed by a tractor, which was my way of marking out the paths through the future imagined wooded glades for our visitors and friends to enjoy. My aimless circling

MAY: THE SECRET GARDENS

walks would then be de-stumped to ensure there were no trip hazards. The task seemed never-ending but, to paraphrase *Alice's Adventures in Wonderland*, 'I don't see how we can ever finish, if we don't ever begin.'

Thinking about Vivaldi's violin concerti 'The Four Seasons' and wondering if perhaps we could plan a performance to be held here in the garden, I then had the idea that it might be fun if the planting plan could reflect the theme of the music – it could drift across an area dedicated to each season, beginning with spring in the east to autumnal planting in the west, before a walnut walk led towards the setting sun.

Vivaldi depicted each season with detailed precision, drawing upon the four sonnets he composed for 'Spring', 'Summer', 'Autumn' and 'Winter'. The poetry described the dramatic content of the music: from different singing birds, to a shepherd and his barking dog, buzzing flies, storms, drunken dancers, hunting parties, frozen landscapes, and finally warm winter fires. Gardening may be practical but it is also about reflecting the spirit of each season. Today, I think that even if we might not be able to tick the box for every one of Vivaldi's themes, we can 'check' many of them, from birds or clouds in the sky to dogs, distant shepherds and sheep. We have even poured drinks and tried the occasional dance.

The plans forming in my mind were all very well, but in reality it remained a huge area with little to recommend it. Twelve oak trees were also transplanted to the central area from elsewhere at Highclere to provide a little height and grandeur in the midst of the mud, but grass seed was the next project. I co-opted my son Edward, who was about six or seven years old at the time, to help me scatter seed from a basket. Even at that age he was not impressed by my amateur approach, but luckily the farm manager happened to drive past and, feeling rather sorry for us, offered to do it using a quadbike and trailer. That was hugely efficient help and a great relief.

Walking through the new area in the winter, frost crunching underfoot, my number-six sister Georgie and her friend James and I were trying to think what to call this new–old addition. It was both wilderness and arboretum but James suggested the name the Wood of Goodwill, so that was it. Robert Herbert's pleasure gardens were enjoying a rebirth and a new name. In some ways, it is a very modern garden, established in old depleted ground which now has new light and space in which to recover. Furthermore, the planting blends from more cultivated human-framed areas into the wilder landscape – it transitions to a wilderness and beyond. This part of the garden is a conscious balancing act, moving from neat and tidy beds into a lighter collaboration with nature, and then out into the wider and wilder parkland.

Gardens retain memories of people, places and time. From slow beginnings, the Wood of Goodwill is now filled with horticultural gifts from friends and by trees planted to commemorate people who used once to work here or for those who still do. A grassy path winds through the summer plantings and is dedicated to musician and performer Kit Hesketh-Harvey, who brought joy through song and dance to so many of us. It is both a tribute to his love of pilgrimage and to colour – the colourful clothes and language that would make his audience cry with laughter. The yellows and purples of gaudy lupins fill borders with mad colour and orange montbretia crowd together under an acer sapling. Corners of the large natural areas are dug out and planted with *Philadelphus* 'Lemoinei' for the summer, and *Cornus kousa* and *Acer davidii* (Père David's Maple), named for the missionary priest who discovered it in China, to reflect Kit's deeply Christian heart.

Pat and Mike Withers chose an acer, and we planted other trees for Stan Anstey the brickie and Albert Saxton, clerk of works, all of whom worked here for many decades. I planted a tree for Nora Sutcliffe who was secretary to my father-in-law and then Geordie and me for forty-two years altogether. I will plant one for Don the gardener, but I think he and I may still argue in spirit about which tree it should be. Geordie's friends have given him trees for various birthdays, and my friends such as Smiles and my sisters have planted trees to mark my birthdays or their weddings. Trees were also planted by Sophie and Jean Louis de Potesta to celebrate their friendship with us; and by Sally Popplewell to mark a New Year's party. The Clout family planted a tree in honour of Highclere's contribution to their relatives: Almina saved the life of Charles Clout during the First World War and introduced him to her secretary, Mary, whom he later married.

If the trees offer air, space, peace, support and some shelter from sunshine or rain, it is perhaps the tiny bulbs emerging from the wintry earth that bring us the most pleasure. They are a result of Geordie's 'time-lapse' planting, in which bulbs provide colour and shape in the garden from the earliest months to late summer. In the past two decades we have planted over 250,000 of them, including snowdrops and croci, daffodils, camassia, chionodoxa, yellow-species tulips, fritillarias and alliums. Bulb catalogues are always lying about everywhere, Geordie's indecipherable writing and pen marks scattered through the margins. I try to request a few specific choices but, in true husbandly fashion, I doubt he hears a word.

I am always so thrilled to see the first snowdrops appear

and, whilst I want to enjoy each day, I am impatient for the arrival of the determined crocus: clumps of misty lavender, delicately veined with white, and others in the deepest purple that flaunt bright yellow stamens. It is always so lovely to start seeing colour in the garden again. The most well known of spring bulbs, though, must be the daffodil – such positive, light-affirming yellows, which reflect the sun and are a welcome sight amongst the sparse brown-limbed shrubs and trees. They are symbols of creativity, energy, resilience, forgiveness and vitality. We have scattered many varieties throughout the wilder areas, from brash double-headed orange-yellows to purest white ones and scented narcissi. Varieties that welcome us early and others that extend towards cherry-blossom time. Their huge advantage is that they grow anywhere and are not eaten by deer or rodents.

Jim Russell used several flowering cherries for height and colour in the design of the Secret Garden and we have extended these arching, freely blossoming trees along the other side of the beech hedge, spilling out into the Wood of Goodwill. The Japanese Embassy in London very kindly offered us twenty-one young trees, slim and willowy but full of delicate blossom and the hope of warmer weather to come.

Flowering cherry trees are part of Japan's history, culture and identity. For centuries in Japan, spring has been marked by the practice of Hanami, holding feasts, picnics and parties underneath the blooming *sakura* (cherry blossom). Some ancient trees are sacred in Japan, the fleeting joy of their blossom in full beauty each spring symbolising the ephemeral nature of life. The delicate layered flowers are usually pink or white, with single, double and semi-double forms, and can have anything from five petals to well over a hundred. In Housman's words: 'Loveliest of trees, the cherry now is hung with bloom along the bough', and in May they seem to throw all modesty to the winds just to share the excitement of their colour and growth. Cherry trees may bloom fleetingly but they embody hope and renewal. Another ten days, though, and their glory will be fading. As Shakespeare put it:

> *Rough winds do shake the darling buds of May,*
> *And summer's lease hath all too short a date . . .*

All gardeners know that seasons must pass, reinforcing our sense of the transience and fragility of life. Much of the background 'chatter' in our homes is about the weather, the life-cycle of the seasons and the pace of the earth. More prosaically, cherry trees are also an important source of food for birds, insects and mammals.

If the white cherry trees are dipping their blossom-laden branches to shoulder-height, beneath them the long, veined leaves of tulips are still standing up straight, a delicate pale green, and the swelling flower buds just waiting for a little sunshine to set them blooming through the curving borders. May is just so busy in the gardens.

Leaving by a weighted wooden gate to enter the sparse tufted expanse of meadow, the Labradors race off, tumbling each other over, reluctant to relinquish any tennis ball they find hidden in the grass. Over the coming months, these acres will develop into a dense mass of wildflowers, but just now only the softest-coloured primroses can be seen as the tiny gathered lampshades of the cowslips are still wondering whether to make an appearance.

If the older inhabitants of Highclere and elsewhere left no records for us, they did at least leave their thoughts and culture in the names and lore surrounding these tiny spring flowers. Primroses on the doorstep would ensure fairies bless the house and protect everyone. If you pick a cowslip on May Day, it will unlock a wish for you.

Later on, the cowslips give way to chalk downland wildflowers, which we seeded nearly twenty years ago. Over time, the mix has developed and diversified. Old species with their associated legends and traditions are now back in our lives. Meadowsweet, with its frothy cluster of scented flowers, was invoked by our forefathers to conjure up the fairest and most beautiful maiden anyone had ever seen, and like many native wildflowers was thought to possess magical healing properties as well. Lady's bedstraw covers the meadow later in the year and was traditionally believed to have stuffed the mattress on which Mary lay whilst giving birth to Jesus. Yarrow was used by Achilles to heal his soldiers' wounds on the battlefield. Humans and wildflowers have a long association, whether the plants are gathered for food, for their scent, or for the light and life they bring into the home. The folklore of wildflowers allows us still to hear the voices of our ancestors.

Along the edge of the meadow are more cherry trees. Less protected from May breezes, they tend to lose their blossom early, tiny confetti tossed in the wind before drifting underfoot.

At the far end of the Wood of Goodwill, beyond the Walnut Walk, is a flat, sheltered area ringed in hazel within which we made and planted a circular rose arbour. I am not sure I could choose an absolute favourite flower or tree but, like so many others, I am always drawn to roses and my favourite scents are based around them. It lies within the fenced gardens and we planted it in memory of my mother.

We chose roses named for the novels and plays she loved. Beginning with Thomas Hardy, Emily Brontë and Jane

Austen, we then moved on to Shakespearean characters or phrases: 'Sceptr'd Isle' (*Richard II*), 'Othello' and 'Prospero', or else names that encourage leading a good life such as 'Compassion' and 'Tranquillity'. Finally, we added in a few stalwart favourites such as 'Comtesse de Chambord', 'Fantin-Latour' and 'Roseraie de l'Haÿ'.

Throughout many civilisations, roses have captured the imagination and appeared in poetry and dreams. Dante's *Divine Comedy* culminates in the image of the sunlit rose blossoming beneath the sun of God, but beyond their cultural significance, most roses are simply grown for their beauty and fragrance.

As well as the rose arbour, we have planted a multitude of roses – in beds, as hedging, against walls, and clambering up trees. For the most part we think of them as belonging to the summer: unfolding petals of blush colours lighting up corners, or passionate strikingly red cups adding richness to a summer scene, but they can also enhance a winter garden. Some of them, especially the dog rose (*Rosa canina*) and *Rosa rugosa*, bear wonderful hips in the autumn; rich in vitamin C, they are good for us, as well as being an excellent source of winter sustenance for birds. May in the garden is filled with their promise.

Along the edges of the meadow grows the hawthorn, which has ancient associations with May Day, the point in the country calendar when spring becomes summer. Hawthorn flowers traditionally adorned May Day garlands as well as the wreath of the Green Man, a pagan figure associated with nature and seasonal renewal. You are not supposed to bring hawthorn into the house but can use the haws in jellies or salads, and in folklore it was in this tree that fairies were said to live. In fact, the site of Westminster Abbey was once called

Thorney Island after the sacred stand of thorn trees that grew there.

Now there is a range of paths to take through the gardens. One route leads back past some large old juniper bushes towards the Monks' Garden. It is a rather curious fact that Highclere's Secret Garden lies outside the ancient walled garden rather than in it whereas most secret gardens are enclosed. Such gardens are deeply embedded in our consciousness: they are the gardens of legend, such as the Hanging Gardens of Babylon, a Wonder of the World, or the paradise described as the Garden of Eden. There, Adam and Eve were gardeners, not just passive admirers of the setting, although in their garden blossom and apples appeared at the same time. In Milton's *Paradise Lost* some of the most lyrical lines remind us of the beauty of the world, despite the fact that many gardens and estates at the time were decaying thanks to the Civil War and Cromwell's Puritans. In Highclere, the old Monks' Garden was in steep decline until the arrival of Geordie's direct forebear in 1677 inaugurated its renaissance.

The Monks' Garden at Highclere has been here for around 1,000 years, which is pretty amazing. Originally an orchard and herb garden, it was transformed around 1780 into an Italian-style garden. Nine arches were created in what was once a wall to reference the nine classical muses. Family and guests could wander through further arches of clipped yew and admire topiary and classical statues.

Today, it remains a good place for a leisurely stroll. Although the yew arches are still there, some of the clipped yew hedges are now rather large. They grew unchecked throughout the World Wars of the twentieth century when growing vegetables took priority over topiary given the limited manpower available. Sadly, any statues are long gone but Geordie and I have contributed a bird bath in the centre of the circular rosebed.

Around the old walls of the garden, we still grow medlars, figs and crab apples – a nod to the medieval orchards of the past. Covered in dazzling blossoms in May, crab apples are the original wild apple trees – fossils of which have been found dating back 45 million years. In more recent Anglo-Saxon times, crab apple trees were a familiar feature in every orchard as well as along the edges of woodlands and are still often found growing in hedgerows.

Their ubiquity is referenced in many family surnames such as 'Crabbe treow', probably shortened today to Crabbe, and in the names of villages – Crabbtree, Lower Crabbe. In folklore, they are a symbol of fertility and associated with love and marriage. They are also much loved by foragers and the small, hard fruits make a delicious jewel-coloured jelly. Crab apples are rather tart eaten raw but the jelly is easy to make as the fruit has a high pectin content.

Highclere's crab apples are trained laterally along a wall, but left to grow vertically they can reach a height of around ten metres. They have a greyish-brown flecked bark and a wide canopy of gnarled, twisted branches, which can include spines on the twigs. In fact, its 'crabbed' appearance is probably what gave the tree its common name. The branches are often encrusted with lichen as well as being successful hosts for mistletoe.

Their official Latin name is very different – *Malus sylvestris*. *Malus*, the Latin adjective meaning 'evil', is a homonym for another Latin word meaning 'apple', borrowed from the Greek μῆλον. 'Mal' is the root of many English words of ill omen (maltreat, malice), whilst in legal terms 'malus' is a financial penalty incurred by a trader or banker when an investment or deal results in a loss. Thus, the Latin terminology has burdened this little tree with all the negative implications of Adam's fall in the Garden of Eden, despite the fact that theologians believe the forbidden fruit was not actually an apple.

An established crab apple tree needs little maintenance, although we do prune them annually given where they are planted. In springtime, they have an abundance of blossom which lasts for a long time, hence the species' robustness, and it contributes to wildlife and insects as bees come in search of early nectar. In summer, the crab apples offer dappled shade, followed by fruits in autumn. Despite this, they are not as popular as they used to be, which is a shame. All of us should plant a tree if we can and a crab apple, with its compact form and year-round interest, certainly repays the effort. The well-known Victorian illustrator Cicely Mary Barker, who created some very popular children's books, described them as:

> *Crab-apples, Crab-apples, out in the wood,*
> *Little and bitter, yet little and good!*

Behind the Monks' Garden are Victorian glasshouses, cold frames, a vinery, peach house, carnation house and orangery. There are various gates or wooden poles with 'No Entry' signs on them so, of course, this is where everyone wants to explore. Beyond the public areas are well-worn paths leading through old garden doors that have warped over time so that they no longer fit their frames.

Much has been repaired, but this is a somewhat loose term given how little there was left actually to work with here. Most of the structures had to be more or less rebuilt from the first course of bricks upwards. In any other situation, such buildings would simply have been demolished and a modern replacement installed. However, they are part of the heritage of Highclere Castle so we try to assess each project in turn, prioritise them and look into the future. They are all still used to grow and prepare plants for the Castle, such as orchids, geraniums, lemons, and tiny oranges to go to the distillers for Highclere Castle Gin, and are full of bedding plants ready to go out into the herbaceous borders. If only it would stop raining . . .

At one point, the orangery was part of the Georgian house but it had to be dismantled to make way for Sir Charles Barry's new building plans. Archives from 1850 refer to a 'conservatory with 24 tubs containing orange trees, camellias and lemon trees', so it was obviously well used and well loved. In a laudable effort at recycling, Lord and Lady Carnarvon decided to try to reuse the orangery elsewhere but, as usual, there was the matter of the budget. Barry wrote to Lord Carnarvon on 2 June 1842: 'An Estimate has been forwarded to me by Mr Jackson for the removal of the Conservatory, but as it was in a gross sum I have referred it back to the Clerk of the Works to examine and procure for me all the requisite particulars.'

Despite this rather ominous note, the move was accomplished, although again there are comments on the issue of leaking roofs, both in the orangery and the other conservatories after the relocation, alongside small sketch-plans of sections and the layout of heating pipes. The orangery survived well into the twentieth century when, in 1939, once again the wooden framework had to be renewed. In the last few years, Geordie and I have, in our turn, had to undertake a great deal of restoration and have renewed much of the structure.

Before the nineteenth century, glass buildings would have

been objects of awe to the majority of people. Glass was heavily taxed, making such buildings impossibly expensive for any but the wealthiest of the aristocracy. With the Industrial Revolution and the removal of Window Tax, the Victorians' fascination with flora and fauna led to a proliferation of various kinds of glass constructions, conservatories, orangeries and vineries, of which the grandest were seen on estates such as Highclere. The Castle even had a 'heathery' at one point as the archives from 1845 refer to it as not being sufficiently weatherproof.

The ultimate status symbol, however, was a glass fernery, which aimed to mimic the heat and humidity of the tropics. The Dutch may have had tulip fever in the seventeenth century but the Victorians had fern mania: in their homes, their art, their fabrics and their literature. It even had an official name – Pteridomania. Highclere had one of course – added onto the back of the orangery, facing north. It was also in a sad state but is once more restored.

Leaving the Monks' Garden through a brick arched gateway clad in *Clematis armandi*, the gravel path winds up towards the very familiar oblique angle from which you begin to glimpse the golden stones of the Castle, framed to perfection by two large cedars. Walking towards the Castle lawns, the gardens are left behind and the setting relies on the expansive views and perspectives offered by Capability Brown's parkland, rolling north towards the distant Oxford spires or to the wooded hills behind, with their vivid acid-green May foliage.

In fact, it was only because Brown had designed a brand-new, huge, sloping walled garden a mile to the north-west of the Castle, to be used for extensive vegetable beds and orchards, that the functional role of the Monks' Garden was abandoned. Further greenhouses were built all around the new kitchen garden: a melon house, a pineapple house, and others in which to grow tomatoes, peppers, peaches, apricots and so on. Greenhouses were always a luxury, though are far rarer these days, as now we can pop down to a supermarket to find a wealth of readily available food options.

Old maps and records show that beyond the productive walled gardens Brown laid out, there was a *ferme ornée* (ornamental farm) – the dairy herd was based near the walled garden as it would provide excellent compost later and it was easy for the fresh milk to be delivered to the kitchens. The pigs, however, were kept behind the orchards on the high downland. Pigs are effectively recyclers, enjoying the peelings, the spoiled remains from orchard trees, the bounty of woodland edges as well as grains from the arable side. Our British Lop pigs are playing their part, just as their predecessors did.

As with the other gardens at Highclere, this whole area began to disintegrate after the Second World War. It was too labour-intensive and wasn't really needed any more. However, we have reinvented Capability Brown's old walled kitchen garden. Push open the slate-blue door set inconspicuously in one corner of the high wall and you enter a new world: in front of you are neat lines of vines – Chardonnay and Pinot Grigio. Immaculately wired and tied in, the lines of vines are still crossed in each direction by the old eighteenth-century paths, whilst the tall surrounding walls offer some frost protection, augmented by candles to ward off sharp May frosts.

The chalk geology of the Champagne region of France dips under the English Channel to reappear along the Hampshire downlands, so the tap roots of our new vines should reach deep into the chalk and return with a wealth of minerals and taste, to help produce delicious grapes for the best sparkling wines. Chalk handles water well and vines do not like being waterlogged. Whilst we cannot call our sparkling wine Champagne, we have named it 'Château Highclere' for fun, and all of us look forward to trying it in two years' time whilst sharing the sentiments of Lily Bollinger, who said, 'I drink Champagne when I'm happy and when I'm sad. Sometimes I drink it when I'm alone. When I have company, I consider it obligatory. I trifle with it if I'm not hungry and drink it when I am. Otherwise, I never touch it – unless I'm thirsty.'

Despite the chalk geology in which we place so much faith, around the east lawns of the Castle, most unexpectedly, a mass of diverse azaleas offers May colour. Azaleas need ericaceous soil, not the lime soil of chalk, and so these beds are entirely man-made. The 2nd Earl of Carnarvon wanted to grow azaleas and rhododendrons so, undaunted, he employed men with horses and carts to dig out this area and refill the holes with the acidic soil beloved of such plants. It allowed the creation of a so-called American Garden and shrubberies, which developed into an extensive mass of beds and formal walks that began near the library windows and extended across to the classical temple. The 2nd Earl, his brother William Herbert, his head gardener James Carton and private secretary James Gowen, were very keen plantsmen. They created new hybrids, consumed by the eternal goal of finding something better, and left us all with *Azalea altaclerensis* (now *Rhododendron* 'Altaclerense'), which is named from a Latinised form of Highclere, as is the holly *Ilex x altaclerensis*.

From a once-prized garden, there were only few beds remaining by the time Geordie and I were walking across broad green lawns towards the pillared folly known as Jackdaws Castle. Over the last decade, I have spent quite a few winter afternoons removing the brambles and bringing back some of this lost garden of azaleas and specimen trees that were hidden at the far end of the lawns. Now, in early May, blooms of yellow, red, peach and pink, orange, white and mauve shroud the shrubs, leaving only a few leaves to be seen. Gloriously clashing and scented, they are in fact rare Ghent azaleas introduced from North America in 1734. The species *Azalea pontica* (or *Rhododendron luteum* as it is now known, with yellow and highly scented flowers) dates to 1806 whilst azalea hybrids here include 'Ignea Nova', 'Coccinea Speciosa', 'Narcissiflora' and 'Gloria Mundi'. Later in the year, when the summer is dry, it is possible to see the shape of the old beds in the parched grass and every so often we plant another oval bed with azalea species and hybrids, recognising and revitalising past elements of the gardens.

Highclere's gardens are not all traditional herbaceous borders, although there are some. There are walled gardens and a white garden, a rose arbour but not a formal rose garden. There are wild areas, though it is not all wild, and there are spring bulbs but it is not just a spring garden. Some areas are mown and some are not. There is an arboretum but it is a very personal woodland – there are exotic trees but also British natives. It is perfectly imperfect and just a beloved series of pleasure gardens, representing both the history of the location and Geordie's and my own style.

Ten years ago, standing by myself outside a tent on the gala evening of the Chelsea Flower Show in London, waiting for my husband to reappear, two confident ladies nearby asked me where I had come from. I replied I lived near Newbury and they probed further. 'Highclere,' I replied. 'Just south of Newbury.' One remarked, 'Oh, yes, of course. If I remember, Highclere doesn't have any gardens, does it?' Feeling squashed,

I quietly replied, 'Perhaps the gardens may have changed over time.' The lady smiled, knowing far better, and turned away. I was of no interest.

In some ways she was right, but such comments only spurred me on to further obsessive planting. I was soon out with wheelbarrow, gloves, fork, some new shrubs, a Thermos of coffee, tennis racquet and ball for the dogs, and my phone so I could listen to music – Vivaldi. Actually I garden because I enjoy it, scrabbling around in the mud, taking my gloves off, completely focused on what I am doing in the now.

Many gardens follow rigid rules about plant placement and colour combinations, and their default is to be kept neat and manicured at all times. Highclere's gardens will never win any prizes, they are too idiosyncratic for that. They are neither tidy nor perfect, but they do set out to be relatable, to establish connections with the viewer. I rather think everyone and every plant deserves a second chance; it is amazing what can unexpectedly take root and how a new life can bloom.

Apart from the gardens, Highclere is defined by its overall sense of place, imparted by the setting, the prospects and the trees. The 1,000-acre parkland planned by Capability Brown is on an extraordinary scale, creating distant horizons and closer contexts, with long winding drives to astonish with a succession of new views. It is bounded by serpentine woods, with collections of specimen trees artfully planted to accentuate the lie of the land or frame a vista of unfolding pastures.

Capability Brown's signature addition to every landscape he created was water, and Dunsmere Lake was excavated from two smaller ponds to fashion a surprisingly long, wide, winding landscape feature. Water, as is recognised by ecologists today, offers wildlife welcome new habitats, encouraging more diverse flora and fauna. Dunsmere is both a reservoir and a precious reserve for humans and other creatures alike.

At Highclere Brown had immediately realised that he was working within an old medieval park, which originally would have been 'timbered' with a mixture of oaks, beech, elm, ash, rowan, box, alder, lime, crab apple, birch, poplar, whitebeam, aspen and yew, as well as blackthorn, holly, juniper, pine and pear.

Highclere's original settlers had taken the long view which allowed for trees of a multiplicity of ages – some were 100 years old, some 300 years old and others survived for more than 500 years: nature's veterans. Together they created a mosaic habitat. Grazing animals, such as cattle in the spring or pigs in the autumn, contributed dung to encourage invertebrate and fungal diversity, forming a complex diverse ecosystem. In medieval times Highclere's land was characterised by pasture woodland, but over succeeding centuries the requirements of shipbuilders and the need for pit props for mining led to a less curated approach.

From the beginning of our stewardship, we have invested love, time and money in the gardens and grounds. In some ways, they are an obsession, whether it is deciphering their history, finding unusual cultivars, using scents to draw people after an elusive perfume, bright colours to attract interest – or to remind those who visit to stop and stare at a beautifully composed masterpiece of planting that it is in fact the wildflower meadow.

Robert Herbert created gardens to enjoy with his friends nearly 300 years ago and it seems entirely magical that, once again, some of his winding walks have been rediscovered and the lost paths, 'rooms', glades, views and dells reawakened by Geordie and myself. We all know that, as the ancient proverb goes, 'A society grows great when old men plant trees whose shade they know they shall never sit in.' Gardens and gardening are good for us. It is all about landscape painting and getting dirty, and is therefore thoroughly approved of by our four-legged friends.

Every gardener is working with the seasons and every gardener is thwarted by them, but Highclere's gardens endure, full of imagination, dreams of a future yet to be realised and precious memories of what once was.

CHAPTER SIX

June: 'I Went to a Marvellous Party'

'Let's pop Champagne and dance on the table'
— a favourite phrase of Team Highclere's

It is June and for houses such as Highclere, this month is all about the social season: galas, dances, racing at Royal Ascot and garden parties.

Soigné, amusing and endlessly talented, Noël Coward epitomised the glamour and flamboyance of the 1930s, effortlessly striking a pose in theatres, cabarets and society events, whether to deliver a poem, song or witty riposte. He was a multi-talented entertainer: a composer, novelist, singer, dancer, comedian, stage producer, film director and TV star. Of his many poems, there are some which, fifty years later, I still memorise to entertain friends with in my best inter-war BBC accent, including of course the well-known 'I Went to a Marvellous Party'.

Geordie's grandfather the 6th Earl of Carnarvon, known to all as Porchey, loved parties and was particularly good both at hosting them and being the light and life of any event. As a raconteur, he had a penchant for amusing verses and fantastic stories. He seemed to engineer his way into all the best parties and knew everyone from Ian Fleming and Noël Coward to Bert (Duke of) Marlborough. Once, leaving one of Noël's parties with the actress and dancer Tilly Losch, whom he was courting at the time, Porchey was rather taken aback to be severely scolded by her. She gravely informed him that Noël Coward was an exceptional artist and Porchey really should not have whistled along to the Master's piano-playing, but rather have remained awed, respectful and quiet. Such sentiments were not part of Lord Carnarvon's psychology. Besides which, he was quite hurt as he'd thought his whistling was rather good. Porchey would later wed Miss Losch, but they did not share a similar sense of humour nor a long marriage.

Porchey was also part of Ian Fleming's circle, joining him frequently for cards, bridge and golf, and visited him often at Goldeneye, his house in Jamaica. Fleming had bought an estate on the northern coast in 1946 to escape drab and dreary post-war Britain and there he hosted high society and Hollywood alike. Noël Coward built his own house Firefly nearby and famously hosted notorious naked pool parties. The three men saw a good deal of each other when they were there, and Noël Coward was the only person who called the 6th Earl 'Porchey Dolling'; in his turn Porchey acclaimed him as 'a warm-hearted genius'. However, whilst Porchey loved to party, it was his mother Almina who threw them on an extraordinary scale.

In 1911, for example, she hosted no fewer than three enormous parties at the Castle within just a few months. On New Year's Eve, she gave her annual children's party for 500 children in the community with a local band performing alongside London entertainers. Just twelve days later, she hosted a ball, again for 500 local people, but this time Meier's Viennese Orchestra supplied the dance music with no fewer than twenty dances on the programme. The Castle was beautifully illuminated by electric light and the carriage drives lined by lanterns. Lady Carnarvon formally greeted her guests but

JUNE: 'I WENT TO A MARVELLOUS PARTY'

Lord Carnarvon came down only briefly before retiring due to ill health – he had endured a terrible car accident the previous year in which he had nearly died. Slowly recovering, he still had dreadful migraines. Instead, Almina was supported by her mother, her brother-in-law Aubrey and his wife, and her husband's sisters. Despite his absence, the party didn't end until 6 a.m. the next morning. Then, a few months later, to celebrate the Coronation of King George V, she organised a picnic underneath and around the spreading cedar trees in the park for 5,000 people, all seated at long wooden tables.

Almina had excellent credentials for giving marvellous parties. Her father, Alfred de Rothschild, delighted in hosting celebrations both large and small at his country residence Halton House and in his London house, Seamore Place. More was more and too much of everything could be perfectly wonderful.

Halton House in Buckinghamshire was a brand-new mansion, designed in an extravagant French style to be both a home and a house in which he could welcome guests and host spectacular parties. Splendid rooms flanked a central saloon, with smaller, more intimate rooms built 'enfilade' and all decorated with French silk tapestries, huge Chinese vases and classical statues. It was incredibly luxurious and warm and comfortable. Mr Alfred possessed an extraordinary collection of art and furniture, ranging from tables stamped by Joseph Baumhauer and Claude-Charles Saunier to Greuze's *Le Baiser Envoyé*, exceptional pieces of Sèvres porcelain, a garniture of three vases by Dodin and Louis XVI candelabra.

He was fastidious about his dress and equally meticulous about every detail that would ensure perfect comfort and elegance for himself and his guests. Staying at Halton House was like staying in a fairy-tale château and, with the latest hot-air heating systems and electric lighting, it was considered by some the height of *luxe* and fashion, although others like Lady Balfour considered the house 'terribly vulgar'. With a mix of witty, entertaining and often cosmopolitan guests, ranging from ambassadors to opera singers, including Dame Nellie Melba, Alfred hosted parties for eminent statesmen such as Lord Kitchener, art connoisseurs and royalty. He had his own private orchestra, which he would conduct with a diamond-encrusted baton. Coincidentally, Halton House has been used as a key location for the very successful Netflix series *Bridgerton*, which is ironic given that Almina's subsequent home, Highclere, is most famous now for its role in *Downton Abbey*.

The Carnarvons' winter months in Egypt were similarly marked by a series of splendid parties, interspersed between their more scholarly endeavours. One such, remembered for years afterwards by the guests, was a magical dinner party held in the Temple of Karnak in Luxor. For most of these years, neither Lord Carnarvon nor his wife appeared troubled by minor details such as cost. Carriages were organised to collect all the guests and deliver them to the temple where their hosts waited to greet them, standing by the monumental entrance built by Pharaoh Ramses III.

Karnak is the largest and oldest temple complex in the world and 3,000 years ago, at the height of its splendour with bright colours and paintings, must have inspired awe. It was, as its original name 'Ipet-Isut' denoted, 'The Most Select of Places'. Lord and Lady Carnarvon relished its atmosphere of ancient faded grandeur. To the right of the forecourt was a torch-lit path leading to the site of the dinner. The staff had all been 'borrowed' from the Winter Palace Hotel, but on this evening had abandoned their hotel uniforms and were immaculately dressed in ancient Egyptian-inspired costumes. Standing between the immense faded pillars and extraordinary architecture, in a scene reminiscent of Verdi's opera *Aida*, the Carnarvons welcomed their guests to long tables draped in white linen cloths, with polished silverware and candelabra, the dinner laid out as if for an English banquet, a full moon lighting the surreal scene.

All the great and the good of Egyptian archaeology were there, including Professor and Mrs Maspero, the various archaeologists from the Metropolitan House, and Howard Carter, with whom Lord Carnarvon had worked on the west bank of the Nile since 1908. They were served a veritable banquet of delicious hot food, each course paired with excellent wines. Maspero, sitting to the right of Lady Carnarvon, led the conversation, which was inevitably mainly about Karnak. Georges Legrain (a French Egyptologist) had found some very fine statues and stelae over the last three years referencing a little-known Pharaoh called Tutankhamun, who may in fact have created the great colonnade here at Karnak even if Horemheb superimposed his own name.

After dinner the guests were invited into the Hypostyle Hall, also illuminated for them, before they all wandered through to the Sacred Lake, a still-gleaming expanse of water that had been created by Thutmose III 3,400 years before this assembly of guests stood there. By the time Lord Carnarvon finally suggested that the carriages would be waiting to take everyone home, all evidence of the dinner party had been whisked away as if it had never happened.

A decade later in December 1922, following the discovery of the tomb of the boy Pharaoh Tutankhamun, Lord Carnarvon once again threw a marvellous party, though this time at the Winter Place Hotel itself. The guest list on this occasion included members of the press, the Chief of Police and other local dignitaries, as well as all the archaeologists from the teams working in Luxor at the time. The gardens were lit by candles and torches, waiters moved about with delicious trays of food and drinks through the assembled throngs, and everyone cheered Lord Carnarvon when he stood on the balcony overlooking the gardens to say a few words and thank his team of *reises*, men and boys, and, of course, Howard Carter.

If Almina planned some of the parties with her husband's involvement, she also excelled at spontaneous 'get-togethers' on a scale I would find challenging today. In 1920, she was with her daughter Evelyn in London for the summer season. They had been to another wonderful party and, finding all the 'ton' to be in town, Lady Carnarvon decided to invite some 500 guests to an impromptu evening reception and dance just three days later. She didn't inform her husband, though – he did not like big parties.

The following day was a Friday and Lord Carnarvon always caught the 6 p.m. train from London so he could spend the weekend in Highclere. Evelyn, finely tuned to her father's moods, could tell that he sensed something was afoot, likely exacerbated by her mother's light-footed and increasingly exasperated anxiety to see him on his way. She was repeatedly asking Roberts the butler whether His Lordship had departed yet. Eventually, he did leave to catch his train but Roberts had to report to his mistress that, unfortunately, His Lordship had walked past the back stairs just as ten dozen lobsters were being brought in by the footmen. The ball was a total success and when Almina arrived at Highclere the following day, Carnarvon's only reaction was to ask her with a smile whether she was not very tired. A wise man knows how to pick his battles.

JUNE: 'I WENT TO A MARVELLOUS PARTY'

The 5th Earl was not unused to big social occasions, whatever his feelings about them. His father the 4th Earl hosted many political weekends and larger parties to welcome overseas guests. Whilst they seem a little more sedate compared to the parties given by his daughter-in-law, nevertheless, they had their own innovations. Some involved fireworks or a novel event – at a large weekend reception for local families this was the arrival of a cow, decorated with a necklace of flowers, which was led onto the lawn outside the library. The milk produced was there and then made into a syllabub, to the huge enjoyment of the children. Add in a marching band and old English country dances, with which his son (later the 5th Earl) and his sisters all joined in, and the afternoon gave much pleasure to all. Lady Carnarvon had engaged a conjuror who entertained guests in the saloon and later there was a buffet served from the dining room.

There is no doubt that the Castle is a superb home in which to welcome guests, whether for garden parties, house parties or a more casual and low-key evening, and I hope Geordie and I have continued to honour this heritage.

For our own parties, one central guest providing 'so much variety watching society', and gently teasing the great and the good, was our wonderful friend Kit Hesketh-Harvey, mentioned in the previous chapter. He was always the life and soul of any evening with his witty repartee, exquisite pronunciation, perfect pitch, glorious voice and immaculate timing – he was a truly extraordinary man. With an embarrassment of talents, he wrote and both directed and produced, and his cabaret acts were brimming with his often sarcastic, sometimes sardonic, and always funny songwriting.

Back when we were simply Highclere and had not yet become Downton Abbey, I received a phone call from Kit.

Joan Rivers was in town and wanted to come down to see the Castle. She duly arrived and we proceeded to explore the state rooms, some of the bedrooms, and then went downstairs to explore the Egyptian exhibition. Standing looking at the replica mummy lying in front of the Rishi coffin, Kit said to Joan, 'If I were you, I wouldn't spend much time here or Fiona won't know which one is the mummy.' His manner allowed him to just about get away with what was an outrageous statement, but then Joan was not one to mince her words either and her language was always colourful.

During a later visit, after Shirley MacLaine had played her part in *Downton Abbey*, it emerged that Joan was not in the best of moods with Shirley. Joan had been thinking of selling her house in LA and Shirley had come round to view it. According to Joan, Miss MacLaine arrived and began a dust inventory, running her fingers along the top of the doors and paintings, commenting disparagingly on Joan's ability to manage a house well. Furious, Joan told her to leave.

'Did Shirley sign your visitors book?' she asked me. I replied she had not. 'Good! Get me the book and *I* will sign it.' Joan then took great delight in scrawling various unrepeatable epithets about Shirley and signed off with a flourish.

Returning every year to perform in her sold-out Albert Hall one-woman show, Joan would take time out to visit us. She often travelled with Cindy Adams and Judge Judy. It was always a joy to see her: kind, funny, brave, and oh, so sharp. My abiding memory is of her standing silently between the saloon and the dining room, absorbing her surroundings. I was not of her world, and it seemed as if, finding herself in my world, she had to let her head stop buzzing for a while.

As with so many who pursue an artistic career, Kit

JUNE: 'I WENT TO A MARVELLOUS PARTY'

sacrificed mere mortal concerns in the pursuit of his art and spent what turned out to be his last Christmas at Highclere with my sisters and me. He didn't have much time in between his pantomime performances, but after Christmas Day lunch, still dressed in one of his extravagant dressing gowns, he for once became the audience whilst we became the performers, directors of music and photography. We replicated – after a fashion – the iconic scene from the film *Love Actually* where the prime minister, played by Hugh Grant, dances down the stairs of 10 Downing Street to a Pointer Sisters soundtrack. Geordie played Hugh and was followed down the stairs by a selection of enthusiastic wiggling nieces. Kit was doubled over with laughter and that is the picture of him I like to remember. He returned later in January, exhausted and devastated that his former brother-in-law, actor Julian Sands, was missing on a snow-covered mountain range near Los Angeles. We did our best to buoy him up, and he had some exciting new projects on the horizon. Sadly, however, he died of a heart attack shortly afterwards

In 2017, Kit was included in a special dinner party to celebrate the inimitable skills of Mary Berry, part of a TV series she was making with the BBC. Filming took place over two weeks and for all of us, upstairs and downstairs, it was a treat to welcome Mary to Highclere.

The dinner was a mixture of good food, good company and old friends, sharing stories and having a laugh. Mary set the menu, which she claimed was easy given the time of year – sheep have grazed the park and land here for centuries so lamb was an obvious choice. Likewise, I have always loved gooseberry fool and have included the recipe for it in one of my own books. My mother used to make it with generous amounts of cream and Mary (I wish I had paid more attention!) added elderflower cordial to her recipe, which gave it a delicious tang.

The dinner took place in the dining room and, after the meal, Kit stood up and sang a song about how much we all love Mary Berry. It was quintessential Kit and most amusing, although I am not sure viewers were lucky enough to hear it because, as usual, quite a lot of the filming remained on the cutting-room floor. Even better, Mary and I got to cook together in my kitchen amongst our spaniels, where we discovered that my little Evie looked almost the same as Mary's spaniel, Darcy.

There is not enough time during filming to worry about how one might look or sound, but I took my lead from Mary who is unflappable and always on point, knowing that one needs to follow direction and keep to time – every filming day runs to a schedule. In retrospect, I feel both honoured and a bit scared to think I was trying to cook on-camera with a national treasure. One of my first cookbooks, given to me by a girlfriend, Smiles, was Mary Berry's AGA cookbook. We shared a flat and held many dinner parties at university, although I confess, I often left her to play to her strengths in cooking whilst I played to mine: readying myself to greet our guests! I would reappear, relaxed and refreshed, and to mitigate Smiles's understandable crossness, would rapidly pour her a large glass of wine. She invariably served up a miraculous supper to students more used to modest 'toast and . . .' menus. I learned many cooking skills from her over the years, which have been invaluable, and we still party together.

The word 'party' originates from the old French word meaning 'a part or a section', which seems a little contrary. The word still has several meanings, but for most it evokes the idea

JUNE: 'I WENT TO A MARVELLOUS PARTY'

of simply having a good time surrounded by friends. The most famous parties in the world are often over-the-top, extravagant spectacles organised by teams of professionals who ensure that nothing goes wrong and everything appears seamless.

However, I find the best parties are not necessarily perfect, and extravagance doesn't always equate to fun. Unexpected guests, incidents or misunderstandings, can make for memorable or downright hilarious evenings.

Whilst I loved studying at St Andrews University, I fear my parents believed my main degree was in partying. I've found that essential party ingredients involve a good mix of guests, great food, plentiful drink and cocktails, and the entertainment can, more often than not, make itself. Diana Cooper, the famous actress and socialite from yesteryear, who stayed many times at Highclere, always said that the best menu for a successful party was too much to drink and a chocolate pudding!

According to the worlds of TV and cinema, historically those who lived in big houses such as Highclere led lives of elegance and restraint: characters tend to be shown drifting from room to room in beautiful frocks, lingering over idle dinners, or sitting on sofas carefully balancing dainty cups of tea. They have to face few troubles except those they create for themselves.

As ever, there is an element of truth in these portrayals, given the brilliantly vivid descriptions of the interwar period between 1922 and 1939 written by the novelist Evelyn Waugh amongst others. *Brideshead Revisited* is indeed worth revisiting. Curiously enough, Waugh married into the Carnarvon family – first, briefly, to 'She-Evelyn', the daughter of the 5th Earl's elder sister, Winifred, and secondly, to Laura, daughter of the 5th Earl's brother Aubrey.

From reading biographies of Waugh, it seems he was always searching for a family both in fiction as well as in real life. Through his marriages, he knew Highclere and commented in letters to Nancy Mitford that if something, the weekend or an entertainment, was particularly good, it was 'very Highclere'. Living in a different century, entertaining is certainly a part of our lives, but it is not the whole of them. These days, at its heart, Highclere is a business. It has bills to pay just as those who work here have mortgages, responsibilities and dependants who need looking after.

Where does a party begin? With an invitation, of course. It is very important to let people know what to expect – timings, dress code, format and so on. However, even before that you need to decide on the guest list, which is an art form in itself. You need to make sure you have enough people who you know will jolly everyone else along and gladly sing for their supper. A good mixture of old friends who know the form and new friends to introduce, with family occasionally filling gaps!

Great parties are not always lavish ones. Don't lose sight of the fact that the important thing is not to worry about getting everything right, but to have fun and never make the mistake of getting lost in the complexities of style over substance. Decorations can be helpful – a well-dressed table is enjoyed by everyone, but it need be no more than that.

Equally, it is important to be part of your own party. Don't make it so complicated that you spend all your time in the background or rushing around to the point where you never want to host an event again. As guests arrive, make sure parking directions are clear, be on hand to greet them, give them a glass of something delicious and steer them towards someone to talk to so they can get past the awful panicked first thought of: do I know anyone here? In essence, a successful party is a combination of a careful guest list, exciting invitations, good food and drink, and a confident host or hostess.

I always think that an evening at Highclere has three components. First, the arrival, with initial introductions, drinks and canapés. The second, and likely longest, part is the dinner, which generally in the Castle is more formal in the dining room. Placement of guests around the table can be tricky, so it's always important to seat together people who will likely bounce off each other conversationally, or perhaps place a more reserved guest with someone sympathetic or who is more of a listener, and above all try to avoid contentious clashes.

In the third and final part, guests adjourn to the library with coffee, tea or brandy, for deeper or continued conversations and a more relaxed postscript to the evening.

In contrast, summer parties can wind informally through the gardens as long as there is a wet-weather plan. On a warm evening, the east lawns by the glorious cedars of Lebanon are wonderful for a post-dinner brandy or liqueur with convivial friends.

As any party winds down, it becomes what I think of as the cosy part of the evening; most of the guests have gone, leaving just the house party to mull over the event; time for my sisters and me to talk nonsense between ourselves and laugh our way to bed, eventually.

It doesn't matter who you are or what you are attending, everyone's worst moments are the same. Funnily enough, I don't think they particularly change with age and experience either, though one may learn to disguise them better. Not knowing who to talk to, having an awkward conversation with someone you barely know, looking at your watch and wondering when it would be OK to leave or simply not having enough to eat or drink.

One always hopes for the highs and dreads the lows, but sometimes a near-disaster can be the making of an evening. There was one particular party at Highclere that perfectly summed this up for me and will never be forgotten.

It began with elegance and sophistication and a wonderful guest list. Graceful in pale gold chiffon, alongside her equally dapper husband, Katie (a good friend) drifted down the oak stairs into the saloon, delighted to find Luis (Highclere's butler, who is not as tall as Mr Carson, but very adept at cocktails) ready with a silver tray of drinks. A gaggle of other similarly sophisticated guests were already there, their hostess running slightly late . . . but very soon I was delighted to be sipping a Champagne cocktail with my friends.

At that point, Luis quietly approached with a problem. Matthew, one of his team, had informed him that there were sheep on the main drive. I asked how many, thinking it would just be a few inquisitive lambs who had found a gap under a gate. 'Hundreds.' Not so good . . .

There was absolutely nothing to be done except deal with the problem. Taking a deep breath, I informed the assembled party, glittering in silks and velvets, of the issue and rather tentatively asked if anyone would be willing to come and help me deal with the sheep. To my astonishment, three of my beautifully dressed guests offered. I suggested they brought their cocktails with them, and we all glided out of the saloon, carefully carrying our glasses, and climbed into the little golf buggy that I, by chance, had borrowed for the weekend. There was a very convenient glass-holder for me and we set off for the crossroads pursued some twenty minutes later by Luis and Matthew, still in their tails, in a 4 x 4 car.

There were indeed hundreds of sheep. They were everywhere. After dropping off Katie, my Louboutin-shod girlfriend,

JUNE: 'I WENT TO A MARVELLOUS PARTY'

on the tarmac at the crossroads with my other friend's mother, known as Mrs Smiles, Keven, who wore more practical flat shoes to go with his immaculate evening attire, ventured across the grass to be in charge of gates. Meanwhile, I trundled off in the golf buggy to the furthest-distant escapees, to begin my best sheepdog impression and start the process of rounding them up.

Driving carefully in long loops to encourage forward progress, and tooting as I went, I crowded hundreds of ewes and lambs towards my glamorous guests, waiting with outstretched arms, Champagne cocktail glasses still in hand, but with no opportunity to take even the smallest sip. Meanwhile, Luis and Matthew parked across the road on the other side to prevent any splinter movement.

But what a success we were. Clearly, we were marvellous sheep wranglers and quite a number of the flock thankfully peeled off into the field and were promptly shut in by Keven. It was undoubtedly the wrong field but that seemed the least of our problems.

A toast was in order but our lips had barely touched our glasses when Luis announced that a further group of sheep had headed down a narrow track towards the Temple of Diana. We now needed to go cross-country, around the shoulder of a hill, to head them off. After pausing prudently to sip our drinks and reduce the possibility of spillage, we set off again. The hill was slightly steeper than I realised, and we all had to lean forward into the incline to help keep our buggy stable and not tip it over, but thankfully we made it. Once more relying on Keven to be the opener of gates, we circled back round to corral the woolly stragglers and toot-toot our way back down. Luis and Matthew were on traffic duty in front of a gateway, with Luis shouting directions, although I am not convinced the sheep spoke Portuguese.

I was very happy to see Matt the shepherd and Harriet, plus Bonnie and Clyde, their excellent collies, when they arrived to take over – Geordie had sensibly called them. I apologised for putting them in the wrong field, Katie was very concerned about bringing sheep poo into the Castle on the heels of her lovely shoes, Mrs Smiles thought my driving was 'interesting' and Keven said it was all such fun that he'd been delighted to help.

When we returned to the Castle the cocktails had all gone and Geordie wished to go straight into supper . . . I felt remarkably pleased that we had taken our glasses with us. The rest of the evening felt a little ordinary by comparison.

One of my favourite extraordinary nights of the year is at the end of January: Burns Night. 'And we'll tak a cup o' kindness yet, For auld lang syne!'

Shakespeare might be said to belong to England, Victor Hugo to France, Goethe to Germany, Dante to Italy and Yeats to Ireland. The list could go on and on but out of all the poets and authors in the English-speaking world, it is Robbie Burns from Ayrshire in Scotland whose words are sung on New Year's Eve, and his birthday on 25 January is the only one that is celebrated every year both in and far beyond the shores of Scotland.

Being partly of Scottish heritage, and a graduate of St Andrews, I of course persuaded Geordie that we should hold a Burns Night party at Highclere. It has proved to be a high point of the annual calendar, though I am only allowed by my entertainment-diary 'moderators' to hold it biannually.

The evening has a degree of ritual about it. First of all, I never tell everyone what exactly we are going to be doing, and, secondly, we welcome everyone with a bagpiper at the front door and a large cocktail for courage. We have to dance for our dinner, and we launch into some energetic reeling, at times with more enthusiasm than flair, but it's quite an icebreaker. It all starts with the Dashing White Sergeant, which is a progressive and relatively simple reel that repeats, so by the time you've finished, you'll have figured out where you're supposed to be and are consequently starting to get the hang of it!

I have worked out that we can comfortably fit four 'eightsomes' into the saloon, but if we squish up a little, five is possible. There is some argument about who might actually know what they are doing. In order to ensure that the dance is at least mostly successful, I have a number of girlfriends who are stalwart 'reelers', and they can be relied upon to take the lead and teach the reels in each group. My lovely friend Sarah also doubles up by giving one of the traditional Burns Night speeches.

Sometimes, however, despite the teachers, reeling does take a bit of practice. One year, amongst our guests we had a famous footballer who naturally was very light on his feet but who had never reeled before. He was paired with another girlfriend, Sally, who was patiently trying to walk him through the grand chain without, it must be said, a great deal of success. She turned to her partner and suggested he should imagine he had a football at his feet. Instant success and the dance went on.

After dancing, we process into the dining room to the sounds of the piper. Dinner with friends is really the heart of the evening. We begin with a little amuse-bouche of haggis with 'neeps and tatties', before enjoying the traditional soup and main course, and ending with Lord Carnarvon's boozy bramble pudding. Between each course is either a poem or a speech, the first of which is always the 'Ode to the Haggis', whilst the second is 'Toast to the Lassies', a talk more about Burns himself as the romantic poet, a farmer's son who was always broke and never travelled far from home.

Burns's education was minimal. He failed to make a living as a farmer, had a short and discouraging stint as a tax collector before briefly joining the army and then succumbing to illness. He died, destitute and in debt, at just thirty-seven years of age, but at least was buried with full military honours. What he was good at was wine, women and partying, and so, despite his rather dismal traditional career, in his memory, Burns Night celebrates a life lived to the full that produced the glorious romantic odes to the beauty of fair wives and girlfriends that made him famous all over Scotland, and indeed the world.

The tradition of Burns Night was started by the man himself in 1780, at the age of twenty-one, when he and his brother Gilbert, along with some other young lads, founded the Tarbolton Bachelors' Club as a 'diversion to relieve the wearied man worn down by the necessary labours of life'.

As its first president, Burns helped draw up the membership rules, one of which required that: 'Every man proper for a member of this Society, must have a frank, honest, open heart; above anything dirty or mean; and must be a professed lover of one or more of the female sex.' He himself would most certainly be counted in the latter camp, with many lovers to whom he wrote poems professing his affections.

Later, Burns would publish a volume of the poems that he had written over a span of some years – the famous Kilmarnock Edition of 1786. Despite the difficulties presented by the colloquial language he used, Burns's style is marked by spontaneity, directness and sincerity. His agrarian life gave him a close connection with nature, which can be seen in many of his poems such as 'To a Mouse' or 'To a Mountain Daisy', and he collected and preserved folk songs from all over Scotland. As a storyteller-poet, Burns has few peers; is there a better short ghost story than 'Tam o' Shanter'?

In 1999, following Devolution, the new Scottish Parliament was opened with a sung version of his poem 'A Man's a Man for A' That', with its themes of equality and universal brotherhood. Undoubtedly, though, his most famous work is 'Auld Lang Syne', sung here at Highclere and all around the world to welcome in the New Year and which celebrates goodwill, good times and friendship:

> *Should auld acquaintance be forgot,*
> *And never brought to mind?*
> *Should auld acquaintance be forgot,*
> *And days of auld lang syne?*

The tradition of singing the song with crossed hands linked is such a strong symbol of unity and fellowship that it is not surprising it has universal appeal.

As well as holding our own, hopefully 'marvellous parties', Geordie and I have been asked to some very special ones. Is there any greater honour than being asked to stay with Queen Elizabeth II and Prince Philip at Windsor Castle? One invitation was to stay during Ascot Week, which is in June and has always been rather a special time for my husband. Geordie is a keen racegoer, both as an owner and a lover of thoroughbreds, much like Her Majesty and his own father who was the late Queen's racing manager.

Driving up to the correct gate of Windsor Castle, we momentarily panicked that we were early or late or in the wrong place. The credentials of both car and occupants were checked by police and security. Our car was remarkably clean, polished and tidy, inside and out. Driving through, we followed directions before drawing up under the portico where the doors were opened for us and we were ushered in. I had packed with great care as kindly efficient Windsor staff were on hand to unpack guests' suitcases, so everything had to be well organised.

We needed to be prepared to change clothes several times a day, ready for the next event. Our visit began with afternoon tea followed by dinner. The next morning before racing, Geordie and I were invited to go riding with the Queen in Windsor Great Park. Geordie rode a wonderful horse, which at one point had been ridden by President Reagan, and I rode a rather handsome black gelding. For once in my life, I was properly dressed for riding in a smart hacking jacket and, in my case, a reinforced riding hat, whilst the Queen simply wore her trademark headscarf.

My main riding task was to ensure my horse did not overtake Her Majesty's but stayed quietly behind as directed. When we got back and dismounted, the Queen gave me a carrot for my mount. I realised I had not been paying close enough attention when I found myself looking at four almost identical black hindquarters and had a moment of complete panic: I couldn't remember which had been my horse. Walking between two of them on the principle that it gave me a slightly higher chance of getting it right, I turned to the one on my left, whereupon Her Majesty called out that mine was the one on the right. Attempting to conceal how flustered I was, I muttered something about wishing to share out the treat, but I'm quite sure Her Majesty knew I couldn't tell which was my horse. Graciously, she said nothing further.

Then after a light lunch, it was off to the races. We were

incredibly fortunate to be in a Royal carriage rather than the cars. I will never forget the distinctive smell of the carriages and horses, and it was a tremendous privilege and honour to be included in the carriage drive ahead of the first race. Everything in the Royal household is so elegantly choreographed. You know exactly where you will be sitting and who else is going to be there, so you can prepare some topics of conversation in readiness. Surrounded by magnificent paintings, flowers and footmen, every lunch or evening event was beautiful.

Despite feeling nervous, I enjoyed the link between the heritage of Windsor Castle and our own home. During Bishop William of Wykeham's tenure at Highclere (1360–1404), he had also been architectural adviser and clerk of works to King Edward III. During this time, he completed the reconstruction of the stone cloister in the Upper Ward at Windsor. An inner gatehouse with cylindrical towers was built and, on the north side of the quadrangle, the Royal apartments we were now visiting. At that time, the rooms and chambers were for King Edward III and his Queen, Philippa of Hainault, and they were arranged around a series of internal courts. Hence the name the Winchester Tower – Wykeham was Bishop of Winchester. It is said that the words *'Hoc fecit Wykeham'* were placed upon it. These might be read as 'Wykeham made this', but instead were interpreted as 'This was the making of Wykeham'.

We were not staying in that particular tower but had a room in another one, which always seemed at a slightly awkward distance from wherever we needed to be. I have clear memories of running in haste along a corridor and, before rounding a corner, stopping to bend down and put on my evening shoes, then sallying forth in a rather more stately fashion.

Geordie and I were also asked to the Queen's Golden Jubilee Rout, held at the Ritz Hotel. Needless to say, the overwhelming question at that point was what to wear. With the help of a dressmaker, I designed a red velvet dress with a high neck and low back, similar to one I had admired in a magazine and which I thought would suit me. As Audrey Hepburn said, 'Life is a party – dress for it!' The Rout was an incomparable party with delicious cocktails and a favourite band, all planned by Lady Elizabeth Anson.

Being around racing and racehorses always gives a person plenty of splendid excuses to throw parties. In 1983, Geordie's father's horse, Little Wolf, won the prestigious Gold Cup at Ascot, so naturally he threw a party at the Savoy Hotel to celebrate. He invited most members of the Royal Family, and they duly arrived for an excellent knees-up. One guest later related that during cocktails before dinner, he had been sitting next to Geordie's grandfather, the 6th Earl, who was by then eighty-six years old. Her Majesty the late Queen was making her way through the guests. Old Lord Carnarvon turned to the guest and said, 'Can you tell me when the old girl gets near so I can stand up!' The Queen was within earshot and replied in her very recognisable clipped voice, 'The old girl is right here but please stay in your chair!' And moved past. It was indeed a marvellous party.

As well as giving and attending parties in our private lives, we also hold various parties for our visitors. We have hosted Champagne carolling in the Castle at Christmas, online virtual cocktail parties during the Covid pandemic, and of course garden parties and concerts in the summer.

Imagine the sun is shining, the rolling parkland perfect in stippled hues of green, distant white sheep settled in the shade of majestic branching trees, the long drive winding

JUNE: 'I WENT TO A MARVELLOUS PARTY'

up towards the house, whilst glimpses of turrets and towers hove in and out of view. This is the arrival scenario for guests invited to attend our annual late-summer garden party. Is the *Downton Abbey* theme tune playing in cars and taxis as they arrive? I do hope so!

Ironically, despite the predictable vagaries of the British climate, we have a fixation with creating outside events. Fingers crossed, almost every year so far, luck has remained on our side. If the sun does not always shine, the weather has at least mostly stayed dry.

A garden party, to my mind, must have a marquee – and we usually have three. Two for dining and one for dancing. We frequently arrange a traditional carousel, a throwback to childhood memories of excitedly riding horses in the Mary Poppins style, although sadly these don't leave the carousel. Nearby, Sarah (normally seen in the gift shop) both teaches and comperes croquet, and to the front of the Castle, a policeman on stilts helps to entertain the queue waiting to enter the house. Many guests choose to dress up and wear elaborate costumes, hats and gloves. There are prizes for those who do dress up, and everyone has to dance!

The Charleston, a dance synonymous with the *Downton Abbey* era, is a great ice-breaker with which to start the party, and we have some helpful teachers who effortlessly trip the light fantastic, showing us how it's done, before taking us through our steps. It's impossible not to be happy and smiling whilst dancing the Charleston. The ragtime jazz and syncopated rhythms get even the most reluctant guests tapping their feet.

Across the lawns, Highclere's little Citroën van serves cocktails and coffee. Inspired by Napoleon's desk, which sits in the music room in the Castle, we have called her 'Joséphine', pronounced, of course, with a very French 'J'. When we first got her, Luis and his banqueting team spent some time establishing exactly how to secure a shelf inside this most compact and bijou of vans. A piece of wood was acquired and a fixing team assembled – Luis, Matthew and Jorge, with Fred and Mahesh on standby. I'm sure there's a joke that begins: 'How many men does it take to fix a shelf?' John G helpfully provided many possible endings, including noting that Lewis Hamilton's tyre-change time of three and a half seconds put the Highclere 'pit crew' in the slow lane, coming in at thirteen and a half hours by comparison. As the Noël Coward song says, 'I couldn't have liked it more.'

We also have that extraordinary British institution – morris dancers. They wear bells on their legs and dance and dance whilst waving sticks, swords or handkerchiefs in time with traditional folk music. Once a key part of May Day celebrations, fortunately for us, they seem happy to join us whatever the month.

Apparently, despite their popularity in the UK, the history of garden parties dates back to France in the late seventeenth century when the French nobility introduced the concept of a *fête champêtre* or rural party. The creation of Versailles initially began with work on its park and gardens. Landscaped with follies, temples and pavilions to accommodate such celebrations, the gardens remain as much a wonder of the world as the palace itself.

The English soon followed suit though on a very much smaller scale. However, as we have seen, inspired by these trends from abroad, people like Geordie's ancestor, Robert Herbert, built assorted temples and grottos, created wildernesses and woodland walks and garden glades with statues and follies in which to host their own garden parties. These

JUNE: 'I WENT TO A MARVELLOUS PARTY'

were perfect places for musical performances or to act as settings for plays, and idyllic locations for picnics.

A century later, Queen Victoria and Prince Albert would host the grandest of garden parties at Buckingham Palace, inviting all of society. This tradition continues today with three garden parties held each summer at the palace in London and one at Holyrood House in Edinburgh.

The American novelist Henry James stayed at Highclere, and I often remember the opening line from his novel *The Portrait of a Lady*: 'Summer afternoon – summer afternoon; to me those have always been the two most beautiful words in the English language.' Nothing is more English than an afternoon tea party: pots of tea, scones, cakes and finger sandwiches, with the occasional errant Labrador on a speculative 'tidying up' mission. Our summer events season culminates every August in the Battle Proms concert with wonderful 'Last Night of the Proms' music and fireworks. We welcome friends, who bring their friends, and friends of friends, such that 8,000 of our friends arrive to set up picnics on the grass in front of the Castle. We have held the Highclere Battle Proms for well over twenty years now, and are still at it, come rain or shine, undaunted by the vagaries of the British weather.

The Proms are a glorious mixture of cavalry-charge displays more reminiscent of the nineteenth century than today, combined with rousing classical music and singing, some evoking the 1940s and wartime Britain. The sound most evocative of this period must surely be that of the Spitfire's Merlin engine, and as the plane circles overhead, 8,000 people listen in silence as it climbs, rolls and performs a fly-past whilst we wave it on its way.

We do not often organise fireworks here because they are not enjoyed by most animals, but occasionally we might finish an event with a display, lighting up the darkness with colours and shapes fantastical. Ultimately, whatever form they take, parties provide a joyful lightness to our lives, creating memories and moments to treasure. There are times to be serious and times to work hard, but the times to be frivolous and carefree make life and living more valued.

To return to where we started and Noël Coward:

I went to a marvellous party,
We played the most wonderful game,
Maureen disappeared
And came back in a beard
And we all had to guess at her name!
We talked about growing old gracefully
And Elsie who's seventy-four
Said, 'A, it's a question of being sincere,
And B, if you're supple you've nothing to fear.'
Then she swung upside down from a glass chandelier.
I couldn't have liked it more.

CHAPTER SEVEN
July: Nature and Nurture

'One touch of nature makes the whole world kin'
— *Troilus and Cressida*, William Shakespeare

July is the busiest harvest month and as ever I was keen to film the farm in action for our social media. I'd asked Simon where the combine harvester was working that day. He told me it was past the Steppes (the field otherwise known as Twenty-one Acres) but perhaps best accessed from the track where the wild garlic grew. I felt a little panicked as I can never remember all the gateways and fields despite having been here for years. However, rather than appear a complete twit, I nodded, smiled and set off with Caitlin in my faithful little blue Land Rover Defender called Mabel.

I'd hoped I might be able to spot the combine since it was large, high and brightly coloured, and there should a plume of dust rising from where it was working, plus if I did end up in the wrong place or go round in circles, Mabel and I can normally get ourselves out. Needless to say, we bumped round in circles entering and exiting fields but, given I had provisioned both of us with water, coffee and a little piece of caramel shortbread, we were not unduly worried. Caitlin loves all snacks and is very positive but never has any sense of direction.

Eventually, we caught sight of the combine through a gate, which Caitlin swung on in order to try and open it as it was jammed – it was clearly not the gate Simon and his farm team were using. Nevertheless, we made it through and pulled up at the top of the field, marked by long lines of straw lying thickly across the prickly cut stems. Having made it there, I was definitely going to hitch a ride. When Tom, driving the combine, saw me, he paused so I could clamber up, leaving Caitlin in charge of the shortbread.

Tom then asked me if I would like to drive? 'Of course,' I replied, 'that would be great.' We swapped places in the cab of the huge green and yellow machine and he briefed me on raising and lowering the vastly wide and unwieldy head in front of us, how to control the speed and how to turn. Then it was my go.

Luckily, I only had a small audience. Beginning very slowly, I lowered the header rotor and we were off. We started forward rather bumpily as I tried to steer and line up the next section of crop to harvest, but after a while, I became less tense and managed to maintain a speed of 3.2 kph.

The aim is to pass over each tramline of crop just the once and yet miss nothing. 'If you can look into the seeds of time, And say which grain will grow and which will not, Speak then unto me,' says Banquo in *Macbeth*. He was, of course, musing metaphorically about future possibilities, but the reality is that farm mechanisation and data analysis has meant we can now maximise success when sowing and growing real crops. Modern research means we can better identify which seeds will grow according to the soil type and conditions, even if unfolding weather conditions may, later on, make a nonsense of the data.

These machines are extraordinary as they make harvesting

so efficient. Modern combines can cut and process up to fifty tonnes of grain per hour, as well as giving the driver all sorts of information on yield and grain moisture. Being connected to satellite GPS systems you can also see a yield map of the field as the harvest progresses. Having tracked several times back and forth, we then had to pause whilst Jake drove alongside with tractor and trailer and we could transfer our overbrimming grain to him, watching the steady stream of gold running through the auger into the hopper.

Farming is the oldest industry in the world, but tractors and combine harvesters have only been around for the last hundred years, although in that time they have changed the earth. For millennia, most of the global population was involved in cultivating the land using horses or bullocks – it was both slow and labour-intensive work, which involved most of the families in any community. Today, it seems like a nostalgic dream to imagine the shire horses hitched to a plough, followed by the farmer feeling its balance, knowing instinctively when to bear down on the handles or lean right or left, lightly steering the mouldboard and share through the earth of the field.

Farming began with people just dragging sticks through the land to break it up and then scattering seeds. This developed into using an open shallow plough to push soil to one side, before a new model was eventually developed that cut a long slice in the soil and inverted it, turning the grass over into the earth to rot down and thereby aerate the soil.

During Anglo-Saxon times at Highclere, every tenant had to make his own plough in order to be entitled to till the land, and the remains of their techniques can still be discerned in the ridge and furrow system preserved in the parkland and downland around the Castle. The majority of Anglo-Saxon people grew most of what they ate and ate most of what they grew. Livestock and arable farming were indispensable to one another. Arable crops depended on the manure and labour of animals, which in turn fed on the products of arable land, as well as the land lying fallow. The word for field 1,200 years ago was 'acre' and that was also what a man and a horse could plough in a day.

Ploughing was so central to life that it had its own church day. Traditionally, Plough Monday was the first Monday in January after Epiphany and represented the return to work for agricultural communities. In the fifteenth century, the priest in the ancient church at Highclere lit candles – 'plough lights' – to bless the farmworkers as their working year began once more.

Ploughs changed little until the eighteenth century when the first factory ploughs were produced. The Rotherham swing plough of 1730 was followed by Robert Ransome's plough of 1789. A third Englishman, James Small, improved the design still further, before John Deere in the USA introduced a steel plough in 1837, which allowed ploughing to take place on land that had proved too challenging until that point.

Ploughs pulled by a horse would invert ten centimetres of soil but the modern plough drawn behind a tractor will invert twenty or twenty-five. Today, ploughing is sometimes even deeper as the topsoil is compacted and damaged by the weight of the heavy machinery.

Nowadays there is some debate about whether to plough at all. Regenerative farming is so called as it avoids ploughing altogether, given that the process damages soil structure, earthworms and beneficial fungal hyphae, as well as increasing carbon loss and leaving plants without roots. Regenerative agriculture drills straight into the soil without removing

JULY: NATURE AND NURTURE

vegetation but may well lead to the use of more herbicides to remove weeds that would otherwise compete with the crops, which may in turn impact on other plants.

Every generation makes changes and Highclere has been operating a no-till and direct-drill approach in some fields for many years now in order to avoid damaging the soil structure. This works well with some crops such as rapeseed, which grows high and generously thereby smothering any weeds attempting to grow in its place. However, rapeseed has its own risks in that the cabbage-stem flea beetle can destroy the entire crop, whilst the chemical seed treatment used to combat this for many years is now banned in the UK to avoid damage to key insect populations such as bees.

Providing sufficient food for the population depends on a combination of good weather conditions, a favourable climate, and good husbandry in relation both to the soil provided by nature and the actions of previous farmers, often over generations. There are good years and bad; famines and subsequent conflict have caused societal collapse throughout history. Scarcity of food always exacerbates strife whilst a plentiful supply allows people to concentrate on other things. For example, in ancient times, understanding the Nile with its seasonal floods and resulting fertile land allowed the long-lasting and extraordinary ancient Egyptian civilisation to develop and flourish.

Many of our ancestors, whether from ancient Egypt or families living around Highclere in Jane Austen's time, would have known how to grind flour from wheat to make bread, whereas for many of us today, bread is simply something wrapped in plastic on a shiny shelf in a supermarket. It has become all too easy to take our food supply for granted.

It was the English economist Thomas Malthus who

identified that population increases geometrically (i.e. 2, 4, 8, 16, 32, 64), whereas food-supply increase is linear (i.e. 1, 2, 3, 4, 5, 6), thus identifying the issue of 'never the twain shall meet'. Humans have been depleting natural resources since time began, whether mining fossil fuels for energy, altering river courses, building dams or cutting down trees to make space for more arable land, but the pace of the depredation has been growing exponentially.

In more recent years, we have also been trying to grow crops more efficiently. This has largely been achieved through the Haber-Bosch process invented in the early years of the twentieth century, which converted atmospheric nitrogen to ammonia and led to the large-scale synthesis of nitrogen fertiliser. From 1950 to 1992, the world's grain output rose from 692 million tonnes produced on 690 million hectares of cropland to 1.9 billion tonnes produced out of 700 million hectares.

In order both to reduce use of nitrogen fertiliser and cut carbon emissions – as most ammonium nitrate is still made using fossil-fuel-derived natural gas – we have been increasing the amount of what are known as legume crops, such as beans and peas, which have the amazing property of being able to 'fix' atmospheric nitrogen in the soil in a symbiotic partnership with soil rhizobia. This happens in the root nodules and can fix from sixteen to twenty kilos per acre of nitrogen, so that once the bean or pea crop is harvested, this is left to be used by the next crop, reducing the need for artificial bagged nitrogen in these fields the following year.

We also now mix fermented molasses with the nitrogen applications as this feeds the beneficial bacteria that help more nitrogen to be fixed naturally in the soil. Furthermore, when applying nitrogen, we use a satellite GPS system to ensure

JULY: NATURE AND NURTURE

accurate application where most needed, as our yield-mapping data knows the harvest output from the previous year.

In spring 2025 we planted 116 acres of spring beans and sixty-one acres of vining peas, which are to be used as seed by the large frozen-pea manufacturers in East Anglia.

With technological advances and a misplaced sense of superiority, we often take rather too much from the land and rarely allow the earth time to recover. The fact is that our life on earth is not a partnership with but a dependence on the natural world, and there are endless complex natural processes which interconnect us all.

This is not the first era, nor the first generation, to feel there is cause for concern about the fragility of that relationship. The English poet John Clare (1793–1864) passionately described a world he felt was passing, although he uses a vocabulary we are also losing in a way, simply because we forget to observe things around us closely.

> *To see the beetles their wild mazes run*
> *With jetty jackets glittering in the sun.*
>
> *Now summer is in flower and nature's hum*
> *Is never silent . . .*

Were we to unplug ourselves from technology and sit quietly, we too could hear the soft noise of the breeze gently rustling through swaying stems, whilst the insects' wings whisper the sounds of summer in the broad sweeps of wild grass and flowers which edge the fields of grain.

Highclere has been part of what are known as Higher Level Stewardship schemes for many years, and we are transitioning into an even more comprehensive scheme that aims to protect and enhance the natural world. Today, we have 1,000 acres of our parkland and chalk downland included in a low-input preservation scheme. This includes significant Areas of Special Scientific Interest where rare species of flora and fauna grow, enhancing biodiversity. Around our arable fields we have created fifty-four acres of wildflower headlands and forty-two acres of species-rich grassland. There are twelve acres of winter wild-bird crop and we spread six tonnes of wild-bird feed each winter. A further fifteen acres of rough flinty ground is devoted to encouraging stone curlews and lapwings, which are endangered species in the UK.

Barn owls are one of nature's miracles of flight. They are precision predators, but although their numbers have been falling over recent years, we have had success at Highclere in encouraging more nests and chicks by placing barn-owl boxes in key locations. Further nest boxes for another predator, the kestrel, also housed new chicks in spring 2024.

Birds circle overhead whilst the sun plays tag with the clouds. This is the magic part of the cycle of the year: the wonder as golden acres, grown from seeds sown during winter and matured in the warmth of the summer sun, are transformed into grain. Highclere's wheat goes for flour (it's the hope anyway but by no means certain, as the market conditions for bread-making regarding protein levels and dough quality are stringent), the oats for horse feeds (and these need to be high bushel weight and bright with no dust!) and the barley for distilling malt whisky in Scotland (which also has to meet a tough specification in order to qualify).

Humans have been cultivating grain for over 12,000 years and it is the basis for much of our history. However, our fields today look very different from those of the past. Were you to stand in a medieval field, you would see stands of bread wheat of varying heights, mixed crop 'melanges' of barley and oats, or even oats grown with peas and turnips, and they would have been a riot of colour from both arable mixes and annual weeds.

Over the last twelve years, Geordie and I have gradually restored the barn at Manor Farm, Old Burghclere, which is the longest-surviving medieval barn in this part of the world – no small undertaking as it is inspirational in its size.

Originally built to store the harvest, it remains a familiar landmark after hundreds of years, even if it is no longer ideal to serve its current purpose of housing modern combine harvesters and tractors, which do tend to be somewhat larger than a bullock cart.

Records show that oats are grown in the same fields on the estate today as they were 500 years ago and they are still an important part of our farming business. It is one of the few areas in which we can add value for our end-user customers: trainers and breeders in the world of racehorses, polo ponies and top eventers. Horses cannot digest oats straight off the combine as the husks are too hard, so we have invested in some traditional machines which grade, clip, polish or bruise the grains, depending on what is best for each client. As humans, we know we should eat well rather than buy manufactured and reconstituted food, and it is the same for our four-legged friends.

Oats are a natural food essential for slow digestion, with high dietary fibres and phytochemicals contributing to their nutritional value. Horses chew them effectively, maximising their goodness. To this base a horse owner can add, for example, alfalfa, which contributes minerals such as calcium, zinc and copper, and digestibility attributes that help to regulate the acidity in a horse's gut. Oats themselves are a good source of the mineral phosphorus and provide protein, fibre and B vitamins.

Given horses need calcium (a key mineral not present in oats) we have created a new product, Oatalin, which combines oats, for their fibre content and energy, micronised linseed, which promotes healthy skin and strong hooves through its high concentration of Omega-3 fatty acids, and alfalfa pellets, which have a high protein content and contribute additional minerals. Horse feed needs to change according to season and what the horses do – the whole science of it is absolutely fascinating. At the very least, just like humans, good food will make horses happier, and therefore safer if you are riding them and faster if you are racing them. Just as so much has changed over the last decades in terms of how we eat, this has changed for horses too. Once they would just have been fed hay and oats as needed, with perhaps a bran mash, rather than the compound, processed manufactured nuts of today.

———

The journey from choosing which mares to send to which stallions, and then some years later deciding which races would best suit their progeny, is a passion for Geordie as it is for so many other horse breeders. It is all about patience, detail and a great deal of optimism.

Apart from my rather eccentric but beloved riding horses, Geordie and I have continued in his late father's footsteps (if on a much smaller scale) with a few broodmares. There is something rather amazing about researching a stallion, with all his particular attributes, bloodline and traits, to mate with your mare and hopefully produce a foal that will at least win a humble race or two, even if it never progresses to the glory of a key race at Royal Ascot or Newmarket. If you get your mare in foal (which is not guaranteed), you then have an eleven-month wait before hopefully she produces a bonny, fit and healthy foal with four strong legs.

The last few days before the foal arrives can involve quite a lot of waiting up at night, as it is important to be around to act as 'midwife' when your mare finally goes into labour, so that you can maybe help bring this miracle of life into the world and certainly prevent disaster if it threatens. My husband's current thoroughbred star is a beautiful filly called Pink Lily who, whilst not at the top of the racing tree, has won six times for him and been in the first three another nine times. She is a flaming chestnut with an extraordinary determination to get herself in front towards the end of a race and so obviously enjoys her moment of glory at tracks like Goodwood or Bath.

However, her arrival into the world on a very cold night in early March 2020 was not so easy. She was the first foal for her mum Mellow and, when she was born, Lily was not very keen to get up and suckle her first milk, which is of course vital to sustain life and growth in all mammals. Geordie can remember spending much of the night coaxing her to stand up and manoeuvring her into the best place by her mother to get that first drink of colostrum, with all its important antibodies and nutrients. It was worthwhile as Pink Lily has given the family so much excitement and amusement on the track, as well as being a brilliant colourful advert for our excellent-quality horse-feeds business.

All the foals and yearlings here enjoy the rolling chalk downland pasture at Highclere and eat and live well before they are sent away to 'school' – in our case, Richard Hannon's yard.

Fillies such as Lyric Fantasy, Niche, Lemon Souffle and many more were celebrated winners when they returned from the racetrack to his stables. On my pa-in-law's recommendation, the late Queen sent several of her horses to Richard as well. When he retired, one of his sons, Richard Hannon Jr, took on the mantle from his father and has since achieved over 1,600 winners.

Owning racehorses means that you dream of breeding an animal with the perfect combination of speed and athleticism whilst having to remain always full of hope that the next offspring will be even more successful. Up to now, Geordie's and my role has simply been to ensure that the young horses are as relaxed, happy and well fed as possible, that they are not fussing and remain willing to try. Food and digestion are entirely key to their racing life in Richard's yard, as they grow and develop, physically and mentally.

July also marks the winter barley harvest. This grain used to be more widely cultivated than wheat, not least because it is more adaptable to a greater climate range and ripens in a shorter time than any other cereal, which may prove useful in future climate-change conditions. We grow winter barley to sell for animal feed, but it is the spring version, grown for distilling and requiring low nitrogen levels for malting, that in a good year provides the best gross margin for the farmer. It is not perhaps widely known that the chalk downs around Hampshire and Wiltshire have ideal soils for growing the malt for Scotch whisky via the production of spring barley.

Just as in the past, Highclere practises long rotations, growing spring beans or peas to restore nitrogen to the soil, before sowing a cereal crop for the following year. Turnips are planted as a good winter forage crop for lambs and sheep to graze, often after oats. The sheep naturally fertilise the fields on the chalk slopes and are part of our crop rotation. They have been here for over a millennium – they were mentioned in the Anglo-Saxon charter relating to Highclere in 749 AD and part of the valley within the estate that was granted to the Bishops of Winchester was called Scipdell (a valley in which sheep were kept).

Sheep remained highly valued until perhaps the modern day. Six hundred years ago, sheep were ubiquitous and a widely understood commodity. The basis of vast fortunes, everyone who had land, from peasants to nobles, raised sheep. Almost 63 per cent of the Crown's total income came from the tax on wool, and by the late 1500s a law was passed that all Englishmen except nobles had to wear a woollen cap to church on Sundays as part of a government plan to support the wool industry. By the time the First Folio of Shakespeare's plays was published in 1623, wool still contributed a significant proportion of England's GDP and was the driving force of the economy. There were quite literally millions of sheep in the UK and they were an established part of the national consciousness. It is therefore perhaps not surprising that the old wives' tale to help you get to sleep involved counting sheep. Even today, it seems a rather monotonous task, but I am not sure when I was young, if I ever worried about what each sheep looked like, I just imagined vague white blobs. As British trade expanded and cotton became more important, the importance of sheep to the economy declined, but sheep and their lambs are still considered a quintessential part of the English countryside.

There is plenty of grass at Highclere and allowing sheep

to roam means fewer mechanical measures are needed to keep down scrub. The gardening team leaves some areas of the farm to remain only lightly maintained as an 'Arcadian parkland', with long-distance views and natural brakes of trees, which is what makes the eighteenth-century landscape around the Castle so beautiful.

Every year in early summer the shearing gang arrives to work their way through our entire flock of 1,400 ewes: each thick woolly coat is taken off in a matter of minutes before the shearer moves on to the next animal, without a break. It is a highly streamlined and organised process. The sheep are brought down from the large park fields and gathered into temporary catching pens before being caught individually by the shearer. The ewes always look rather surprised as they are turned upside down for the two or three minutes the process takes, after which they find their feet, shake themselves down and leap away as if years have been lifted from them.

Sheep need to be shorn because their fleeces otherwise become too thick and heavy. Each fleece can weigh between four and eight pounds, so shearing also allows the sheep to cool off during hot weather when heat-stroke can occur. Of course, in the UK, we often fail to see a real summer, but each year both we and the sheep live in hope. All the fields in the park have plenty of shade in terms of the cover offered by trees, but more often than not, the canopy is used as a shield against the rain.

Until recently, we used to be paid about fifty pence a fleece, but today we have found a higher-margin use for wool, which is once more being recognised for its sustainability. For example, it can be used as lower-carbon, more sustainable roof or wall insulation in comparison to petroleum-based solutions; more obviously for carpets, warm sweaters and

JULY: NATURE AND NURTURE

knitting, or even, as at Highclere, used to stuff mattresses. We send our fleeces to a Yorkshire factory which cleans and cards the wool before sending it to a forward-thinking company in the USA that specialises in quality bedding. Luckily for us, using Highclere wool adds considerable value to their product.

The days after shearing are rather noisy with ewes and lambs constantly calling to each other. The lambs partly recognise their mother by smell. From birth ewes are always licking and sniffing their lambs, nursing them many times a day. Shearing therefore mutes part of the recognition process – not that the lambs really need their mothers any more. They are more than able to graze for themselves by now. After a week, the fields full of sheep settle down again and, as far as passing visitors are concerned, they look like distant white bubbles of whiteness contrasting perfectly with the broad green parkland.

Of course, in earlier times there would not have been such broad green fields. One element of the Anglo-Saxon or medieval landscape would have been the wood-pasture system, which mixed wild and domesticated animals in low-density grazing around trees.

The Anglo-Saxons built with timber and considered wooded areas both spiritually important and life-giving. The landscape in southern England and around Highclere at that time was characterised by a blend of woodland and grassland dotted with scattered trees, often ancient, which created a mosaic of habitats supporting diverse biological communities. Venerable trees within wood-pastures are particularly valuable to wildlife as well as to humans, both of whom selectively cleared the areas around. Pannage, the feeding of pigs in the autumn on acorns or beech masts, both turned over the ground and prevented scrub from encroaching. Just to the east of the Castle is the area called Penwood – 'Panne' wood – which would once have been such wood-pasture. Pigs are particularly flexible in their diet, allowing them to be reared on poorer land than other livestock. The cycle of swine fattening on acorns followed by slaughter was so important within the medieval agricultural cycle that it became the standard calendar depiction for the winter months. The system not only worked well in oak woodlands because of the ready supply of acorns but also, due to the herbage in the grasslands underneath the trees, opened up the field to sunlight, benefiting both the grass and the light-loving trees.

Over time, such wood-pasture has been infilled, becoming just woodland in which the ground vegetation consists only of plants that tolerate shade. Sometimes, though, it has been 'improved' into grassland studded with spreading trees, which does have merit. Wood-pasture, however, was a mosaic habitat, which are tremendously diverse and of exceptional ecological value.

Despite changing times, Highclere's landscape remains diverse. Behind the walled kitchen garden are various wooded areas long-overgrown with brambles and scrub. A park field grazed by sheep and lambs lies alongside and sometimes the lambs escaped from it and, like all sheep sometimes manage to do, tangled themselves up disastrously. Somehow, we needed to find a way to clear it back. Simon and I decided that the answer was pigs: we would buy and rear some to help clear our own overgrown area.

Thus, Thelma and Louise arrived, and if, to start with, they seemed to make no impression on the mess and intertwined brambles, over a few months it was transformational both to the scrub and to the soil. The pigs are an old endangered breed – British Lop – friendly and good at living outside.

JULY: NATURE AND NURTURE

There have of course been pigs at Highclere before. The 5th Earl had an award-winning herd of Old Berkshires. His father was also a keen pig breeder, but their main concern was how many piglets they could produce and how well they could be fattened up. I am rather more interested in integrating pigs back into the cycle of farming, rather than the human fattening cycle, and in letting them roam naturally without the constraint of breeding in confined places.

We borrowed a boar called Ernie for a month in order to look forward to some piglets in the spring. The gestation period is very short: they were due to arrive in three months, three weeks and three days from when Ernie mated with their dams, which of course we were not quite sure about, so the precision of the gestation cycle was somewhat lost. We bought two pig huts – good shelter, full of straw. We now have Lady Mary, Lady Sibyl and Lady Edith. (They are part of the actress line. Arthur, who arrived as part of a *Countryfile* TV show, is from the Cornish line.) Two of the ladies are still here. Adam Henson (well known to many UK viewers from *Countryfile*) has taken Edith and we have kept Mary and Sibyl and later added Violet and Cora. It is very much a shared-crèche approach as pigs are highly social and intelligent animals. In folklore, they are often said to bring fertility, life and abundance. What is so sweet is how the piglets play, clambering over logs, nipping each other, and burrowing their noses in the mud just like their mothers do. They are also very social animals: bonding, making nests and relaxing in the sun together.

Pigs play their part in Highclere's fictional alter ego as well. In season four of *Downton Abbey*, Lord Grantham sets off to America, reminding Mary on his departure to enjoy her new endeavour – raising pigs. Lady Mary and her beau Charles

Blake end up refilling water troughs and getting extremely muddy – dressed, of course, all the while in full black tie.

Pigs have starred on-film at Highclere Castle in other productions too. When Highclere was Totleigh Towers in the *Jeeves and Wooster* TV series, one of the main storylines was the competition between Sir Watkyn Bassett, who lived at Totleigh Towers (Highclere Castle), Lord Emsworth, resident of Blandings Castle, with his beloved prize-winning sow, the Empress of Blandings, and Emsworth's arch-rival Sir Gregory Parsloe, who owned a sow called the Pride of Matchingham and who was always up to dastardly tricks.

Today, most people enjoy our English woodlands for the joy of walking through them: the dappled shade in the spring and summer and the delight of kicking through the fallen leaves in the autumn. This is nothing new. The Anglo-Saxons had many more words for wood than we use today: *graf*, *hangar* (sloping wood), *bearu*, *holt*, *hyrst* (copse), *sceaga* (thicket), *strod* (marshy land with brushwood), *wald* or *gemaen*, which suggests a common wood, *hris* (small branches), as well as *lind* (lime tree), *timbran* (hard timber), *treow* (tree), *bearu* (grove), *weald* (wooded area) – it is a long list. In addition, much of everyday Anglo-Saxon life was described using words derived from the many uses of wood, e.g. *yðbord* (ship), *hleobord* (shield – protecting board). Finally, in the UK, we have a long history of naming each and every area of woodland, no matter if it is just a copse, because it matters.

Despite our long association with them, our knowledge of trees is less ingrained today and tends to revolve around what they do for us. But if you pause and take the time to actually look at a tree, it is a thing of beauty in itself. Looking at its bark, you can lose yourself in its crevices – in an old tree, they are deep and ragged, reflecting the battles the tree has

JULY: NATURE AND NURTURE

fought to survive as the trunk thickens. Trees are implicitly a metaphor for life itself. Even when turned into timber, the wood is still a living material, which changes as it ages in our homes, whilst fallen trees left in woodland rot down to replenish new life. Trees and plants make us feel better; they come into our houses when decoratively in flower, and as timber they panel our walls and provide roofs and furniture.

Highclere today remains more wooded than many other estates, with a total area of 1,100 acres, including both commercial and amenity woodland. Even so, this is rather less than before the medieval period when vast swathes of timber were used by the bishops for their building projects and an increasing amount of open grazing was needed for the large flocks of sheep on the chalk downland. At other times, timber was needed for shipbuilding, for example, and there was a wave of heavy felling during the Seven Years War of 1756–63. Those in government in the eighteenth century were acutely aware of the reduction in woodland and a government comment in 1788 descried a 'perpetual struggle of jarring interests'. *Plus ça change, plus c'est la même chose,* you could say when you think of the urgent discussions today about how to grow food well and to find the space to increase the wooded area of the UK. Conscious of the lack of forestry in this country, successive governments over the last century have promoted the establishment of large-scale forestry plantations but that is not the whole answer, as they are even-aged and typically a softwood monoculture which, over ensuing rotations, can result in loss of soil nutrients and suitable habitats for wildlife.

Tree-planting today is often undertaken in the belief that it will recreate a habitat that previously took centuries to achieve and was the result of many different actions or interventions. Ancient woodlands need veteran trees, which means we need to leave middle-aged trees to grow older – not necessarily easy to achieve as trees have far longer lifespans than humans, let alone governments.

At the present time, Highclere and other similar estates are being encouraged to plant trees and we have converted over twenty-two acres of steep arable land at Crux Easton into new mixed broadleaf and softwood woodland, including some fruit trees. Over the last two years, we have probably planted some 27,000 trees and in the process created new shelter belts on the open chalk downland.

Walking down Lime Avenue on the south-eastern edge of the Castle, there is something about the pale, elegant canopy of leaves overhead that promotes calm. It was planted to celebrate the birth of the 6th Earl in 1899 and in maturity is one of the wonders of Highclere. The trees are now up to fifty feet tall and in early spring produce a fresh green canopy of truly impressive proportions. If you take an early-morning walk or jog along this avenue, it can only lead to feeling better and thinking more clearly. The distant smell of lime or linden tree (*Tilia cordata*) flowers at this time of year is almost intoxicating, and if we think the smell is sublime, so do the bees. Once a few of them have alighted on such an excellent source of nectar, they return to the hive and do a 'waggle dance' to signal to their nest mates where the best nectar or pollen can be found using their own version of GPS. Bees are vital for the pollination of our crops and flowers and lime-tree-based honey is a source of natural sweetness not to be missed.

Whilst much of our human life in developed countries today is based upon use of technology and an urban lifestyle, we know we feel better when we are out and about in nature. Evolutionary preferences are held deep within us. When I ride an Arab mare, she always begins to dance as we leave a wooded track and head out into a broader landscape. There is an innate instinct in her that there might be a scary animal lying along a branch at the edge of the wood, although I can vouch that, so far, I have never seen one.

Likewise, we instinctively know nature is good for us, although I rather think we need nature more than it needs us. Without a healthy natural world, it would be hard to sustain the life we take for granted on our beautiful green planet. Looking to the south, out of the second-floor windows of the Castle, you can see the shapes and drifts of past generations of Carnarvon family landscaping as you watch the light playing upon the seasonal colours of the trees, some more ancient than modern, hymns to our countryside. Panning along the contours of Siddown Hill, with the extraordinary folly Heaven's Gate at the summit, different colours blend into harmonious shapes and shades. Somehow, it's incredibly relaxing as views and light catch and hold the gaze.

Whilst walking their rutted tracks, it's evident that woods have their own character. Perhaps it comes from their sense of continuity, the fact that trees have been growing here for generations in human terms, or perhaps from the oxygen they produce: clean, cool air with fewer pollutants. The trees have their own communities: their root structures are twice as large as the canopies that we see and they have their own ecosystem too. Fungi filaments tap into the roots, absorbing nutrients. They transmit information through chemical compounds and electrical impulses, preparing as far as they are able for times of stress. The practice of thinning trees can ensure that those selected to remain become more robust over the course of their lives; curiously, older trees grow faster than young ones and are therefore more productive.

Highclere's fields and woods, hedgerows, lakes, meadows and downlands, give us beauty and space in which to listen to those with whom we share the natural world. I am not the first to think this and will not be the last. As Alfred, Lord Tennyson wrote in 'The Lady of Shalott':

> *On either side of the river lie*
> *Long fields of barley and of rye*
> *That clothe the wold and meet the sky;*
> *And through the field the road runs by*
> *To many-towered Camelot.*

This can be interpreted in two ways – Camelot the place and Camelot the symbol of perfect peace and happiness.

The trees and plants in our pastoral landscape give us so much during their lifetime – food, clean air, shade, pleasure – and are still able to contribute to the circle of life even after their death, giving back even as they decompose, their nutrients recycled by fungi primarily followed by myriad insects, larvae, bacteria, slugs, snails, millipedes, springtails, earthworms and beetles. Death leads to renewal, a replenishment of nutrients.

It is not, however, a passive paradise. Food must be grown, woods managed, animals looked after, and every day is challenging. When Geordie's father left the army after the Second World War, he was twenty-four years old. He then went to Cirencester Agricultural College (as it was known) and won a prize as an outstanding student before returning to farm at Highclere. The family has been farming here ever since. It is rare that an estate of this size is farmed 'in hand' without farms being let to tenants, but the tenant farmers had all retired or moved on by the time the 7th Earl was demobbed

JULY: NATURE AND NURTURE

and he wanted to get the estate making a productive income again, whilst staying in overall control of the land.

We have continued his ethos and farm Highclere entirely ourselves despite all the challenges from the weather, changes in farming technology, and the often-varied government policy towards farmers. We are still growing winter and spring crops, producing around 2,250 lambs per year and ensuring that agriculture is an integral part of this historic and enduring landscape. Farming is a risk business with planting in the autumn more like venture capital than investment in a more standard manufacturing or retail operation. The weather can be extreme and commodity prices can fluctuate as much as bookmakers' odds at the racetrack. Governments continually move the goalposts and are not reliable friends, which makes staying in farming more a way of life and a desire to be a good steward of the land as much as it is a business. Whilst the nostalgic, rose-tinted view of rural life never did match the harsh reality of previous centuries, it is still extraordinarily demanding today. July requires that every moment of good weather is used to best advantage, whilst winter is the time to catch up with maintenance and, if you are very lucky, take a holiday. As ever these days, technical competence is key.

Today the land, buildings and woodlands of the estate are all tended with an ever-increasing understanding of the balance with nature we need to find. Climate change threatens the core of our food supply as well as our security in all directions, whereas ironically, the concept of change, so hard to accept for humans, comes more easily to the natural world. For instance, new and intensive cultivation of some areas in order to allow us to leave other, previously cultivated ones completely untouched, so as to offer a refuge to wildlife. Recent history seems to be showing us the consequences to the environment of 'hollowing' out nature, even if this country is just a very small part of the global picture.

For visitors who come here in search of time out, I believe that Highclere is inspiring: a marvellous compromise between untrammelled nature, man's vision of what nature could be, and productive farmland.

Or as John Clare so aptly put it:

I found the poems in the fields,
And only wrote them down.

CHAPTER EIGHT

August: Mr Darcy

'I cannot fix on the hour, or the spot, or the look, or the words, which laid the foundation. It is too long ago. I was in the middle before I knew that I had begun'

– *Pride and Prejudice*, Jane Austen

On a perfect summer's day, Jane Austen's Mr Darcy (Colin Firth), wearing a wet white shirt, emerged from a winding lake to stride back to his house, Pemberley in Derbyshire (Chatsworth). It made television history – certainly in the UK. There by chance on a walk and a tour was Miss Eliza Bennet. He hurried across to see her, the dismissive first impressions of her made at the beginning of their acquaintance now entirely revised. There is less pride and prejudice on both sides, although it is perhaps a moot point whether Miss Eliza's favour was enhanced more by Colin Firth in a wet shirt or by the sight of Mr Darcy's extremely beautiful house and rolling parkland.

One of the most beloved English classics, Jane Austen's *Pride and Prejudice* was completed by August 1797. The setting of each house and estate forms the backdrop to the story as well as prompting the reader about who exactly these characters are and their respective social standings. The Pemberley Estate is Arcadia – the stuff of dreams – in its grandeur and beauty, and also in terms of the dizzy social standing of its owner.

The very word 'estate' suggests privilege, history, ancestral land, lineage and grandeur. From Mr Darcy at Pemberley and the disintegrating lives in *Brideshead Revisited*, to *Rebecca*, *Howards End*, *Summer Lightning*, *The Remains of the Day* and, of course, *Downton Abbey*, there is boundless interest, both in fiction and real life, in the continuation or else the decline and fall of these old houses. The American novelist Henry James, who stayed twice at the Castle, wrote:

> Of all the great things that the English have invented and made part of the credit of the national character, the most perfect, the most characteristic, the only one they have mastered completely in all its details, so that it becomes a compendious illustration of their social genius and their manners, is the well-appointed, well-administered, well-filled country house.

I have always hoped that Highclere exceeded his expectations.

What made these houses sustainable was that, as they were hopefully passed down intact over generations to a direct heir or a relative, they could be supported by their surrounding estates: the agricultural revenues from growing food, whether grain or dairy, sheep or pasture. There were also the rents from tenant farms, houses and cottages. In fact, the dowries accompanying new brides were often invested in a parcel of land that supported a dairy herd – it was a good revenue. There may have been quarries producing aggregates for use by the estate and for sale, whilst trees have always been invaluable, both for their versatile commercial use and their beauty in the landscape. The fact that these tracts of land were managed as a whole rather than piecemeal has led over centuries to what we now view as the quintessential look of the English countryside; the farmland, dells and groves celebrated for their peacefulness and the views and prospects they offer.

However, the advance of global industrialisation, war and changing social expectations of the twentieth century, irretrievably broke down the old way of life for many great houses and estates. By 1945, when Evelyn Waugh published *Brideshead Revisited*, many of them were already, or soon would be, abandoned, with much of their fabric and chattels auctioned off. The purpose of these houses and estates was no longer clear. Some of the largest ones became institutions or museums and as a result still stand, encapsulating a particular moment in architectural terms or in interior design or else the heyday of landscaping, but the quid pro quo of this survival mechanism is that they are isolated from their original purpose and there is no possibility of further evolution. Of course, neither agriculture nor forestry is in general a good source of income in Britain today, so estates nowadays tend to raise revenue outside these traditional areas. Some are sold off completely and revitalised by new wealth, but even new money only lasts so long without an obvious long-term raison d'être. Finally, there are some places like Highclere, which are still owned by the original family and which try to find a new path in the modern world.

The irony is that such estates often only represent wealth to the owner at their point of sale. It is income that is paramount. A visitor once turned to me outside the Castle as he was admiring the building and said, 'Aren't you fortunate to have so many windows?' I wasn't entirely sure what he meant, whether he was talking aesthetics or merely the size of the house, and I was feeling a bit low about the seemingly endless repair bill, so replied: 'Thank you, but not a single window has yet returned even ten pounds.'

In fact, I found a reference from Lord Carnarvon's agent in 1845, noting that Sir Charles Barry:

> ... keeps the windows for the most part without change but not all; makes a porch at the north entrance which projection he carries up to the top of the house, but the mixed gothic effect is attained by string courses ... All the chimneys are carried into the Loggia and all brought out in picturesque gothic forms ... [It] must not be disguised that it must of necessity be more expensive ...

Sadly, Geordie has not yet appeared from the lake wearing a wet shirt and is always irritated by the mention of the perfect Mr Darcy. Jane Austen sensibly leaves her characters at the altar, but it is after the marriage service that the work really begins: to learn the compromises and the demands of a life together or whilst sharing a stately home with many other people.

Highclere's estate might well be nominally recognisable from Jane Austen's time – sweeping parkland, beautiful trees, sheep safely grazing, a large and harmonious house, curving lake and distant inspiring views – but beneath the surface it is very different.

Arrive through the front gates and follow the narrow road into the estate – it is the correct width for horses and carriage but not for modern delivery lorries. Every time I drive in, I still find it unbelievably special and think I am incredibly lucky. However, I am also consciously noticing that the side of the road is disintegrating just there and will need repairing before it gets any worse. I am now well versed in such repairs and can relate that Highclere has nine miles of private tarmac road. Luckily, somehow we found David Wilson who is on my speed-dial and arrives very early for meetings. John and Geordie both have favourite road projects in their sights so we all argue about priorities – they do both love smooth tarmac. David always starts, 'For you, Lady C, it's a good price. And, tell you what, I'll throw in some scalpings for free' – but his total quote nevertheless unfailingly makes me turn quite pale. We then begin a delightful debate where I try and get him to improve the quote or include digging out some ditches or filling in more potholes, and we sort of get there. It is the usual rule of thumb that 'a stitch in time saves nine' as he always points out to me. John and Geordie have learned to ask me to forward the quote, which is often verbal, but we seem to muddle along.

Driving on the tarmac road over a speed bump – my addition – and past Shuttlecock Corner, where the road camber goes the wrong way and many of our staff end up in the field, I pass endless fences and quite a few gates. I am always on the lookout for broken straining posts or dropped gates. When I first met Geordie there were lots of so-called Hampshire gates, which are a wire-based way of opening and closing a field entrance, and too often he left me to struggle with them. Given I find them completely unwieldy, over time we have acquired more of the usual twelve-foot-wide barred wooden gates, which are so much easier and to my mind look nicer. Of course, they cost more and may sometimes need rehanging. The sheep fencing used to have barbed wire along the top but gradually this has been softened in the middle of the park. It is much better with just a single strand of wire or, in some fields, a wooden rail.

Part of the delight of Highclere for wildlife is the lack of fences within the park so there is freedom to roam, whilst the unfurling undulating expanses offer far-reaching views for visitors. Nevertheless, there are about twenty miles of fencing around the circumference and within plenty of the fields beyond. Horses need better fences than sheep, though as we have seen these do have a penchant for escaping at the most inconvenient time. Horses have the knack for somehow finding the smallest weak point in a large fenced field, putting their hooves through and getting stuck, which may well be expensive in terms of vets as well as painful for the animal. Combining equine and sheep fences is rather more costly but has the advantage of being long-lasting and more elegant than barbed wire. Also, as we are open to the public, first impressions do matter.

The park is studded with veteran oaks offering much biodiversity – over 2,300 species are known to find an ancient oak an attractive habitat and that doesn't include all of the fungi, and it is aways sensible to continue to plant young trees that will grow into veterans in 400 years' time. When young, however, they need tree guards to protect them from sheep and deer.

We try to clear up some of the fallen limbs in the open parkland but leave them lying in the surrounding woodlands as useful wildlife habitats. The farm also kindly cuts down nettles and thistles from the central grassland, although they thrive at the fence lines where they help to create cover and are food for aphids, for example.

Some of the cedar trees on the drive to the Castle have grown so majestic that the forester has suggested we employ a tree surgeon to reduce the canopy weight a little to help with their long-term survival. There is less water in

Lebanon where they originate so they tend, sensibly, not to grow so tall in their native land. Their very success here exposes them to damage in high winds, to cracking in frost, or splitting under the weight of snow or a canopy sodden by continuous rain.

We keep the wide verges in the park tidy as it adds to the stately atmosphere when driving up the hill towards the Castle. There are a number of these, as well as areas where the sheep don't safely graze, so it is non-stop mowing from May and throughout the summer as the inevitable rain and shine of the English summer means the grass grows with a vengeance.

The challenge entailed in running a historic house and estate today only came to the fore for me after my father-in-law died. As for every family at that point in time, there is emotional turmoil as well as many practical exigencies to face and, of course, many brown envelopes to sort out and plans to consider for the future.

Those responsible for Historic England, Natural England, general architects, historic architects, those interested in water or trees, historic monuments, historic interiors, archive conservation and chattel conservation, all had contributions and suggestions to make as to what we should do first – and everyone and everything required money. Having conversed with Geordie at length it was clear that he was not like the original Mr Darcy, even if he was my Mr Darcy, and that there was no obvious pot of gold at his disposal. Often we would both wake at night – our son Eddie was in any case only two years old – make a cup of tea and then begin to contemplate what the best way forward was so as to preserve all the historic elements for the long term. Of course, this meant compromise and shelving projects on areas we would have loved to fix, but you have to make a choice when resources are limited. The roof needs fixing as a first priority before moving on to more interesting restoration projects.

The family's home and estate were built and rebuilt, shaped and cherished, throughout many centuries and it represents a collective custodianship both of the land and of 'things'; a joint heritage of art and architecture and a historic way of life. Highclere is an eclectic mix of the remains of Bronze Age tumuli in the landscape to the south, Egyptian archaeological treasures in the exhibition in the cellars, Corinthian-columned temples and follies in the parkland and Victorian revival Jacobethan architecture in the Castle itself. The stone carvings are rich in symbolism that repays closer study yet the weathering effect of time on stone is beautiful and interesting in its own right. For the custodians it's a question of striking a balance between centuries of interest and imperfections with the need to ensure that the fabric of the house endures.

On a practical level, this meant that there was an endless programme of repairs to begin and, as for many other families embarking on their role as custodians, there was little money in the kitty. The deemed value of Highclere to Historic England is the unique continuity of habitation for 4,000 years within the bounds of an estate, so it is about not selling land or cottages but keeping the entity intact – that is part of our remit with them – whilst opening to the public. This, in my view, is best done by telling stories to our visitors and sharing the beauty of the Castle and surroundings with them.

In order to comply with all the restoration requirements, we needed time. I listened to a speech by Torstein Hagen, CEO and President of Viking Cruises. A friend and I enjoyed his analysis of data, as accurate data informs every decision, but he also spoke about time. Time is precious for every single one of us and it is always running out. In business terms, I remember my father saying good businesses survive tough times given financial time. Time spent listening, time spent learning, is never enough, and early on we inscribed a sundial in the garden with those famous lines: 'There is a time for everything, and a season for every activity under the heavens.'

From Highclere's point of view, time was also of the essence. Most importantly, we needed to start repairing the roof. Most things are achievable if they are broken down into distinct tasks. Geordie knew the Castle far better than I, so his first project was the leaded lights and roof over the saloon in 2003. During winter rain, the saloon was decorated by buckets and towels in too many places; water tended to come in at one corner of the roof and reappear inside at the opposite diagonal, hence buckets on the floor at intervals around the saloon floor space. Thousands of new tiles and almost five tonnes of new lead flashing were helped on their way up by a large crane, which sat somewhat expensively outside the front of the Castle. This project was followed two years later by the renewal of a large section of roof, chimneys and render towards the south part, as from the heavens above Highclere there comes much rain.

I was rapidly learning how much damage water ingress can do. In fact, like many homeowners, I soon learned to dread water altogether. The Victorians were very clever in all their roof-drainage schemes, but if these become blocked with debris or flaking stone, or the lead flashing is rotten or not connected well around the large glass lights, water always finds its way inside, which is what this new round of roof work really needed to sort out.

In the meantime, the Castle was open in the summer to visitors and we were continuing to build our wedding and corporate business. That ensured the money kept coming in and, if I clambered up a faded yellow ladder on the roof, I could see where it was going out. It was a seamless process! Soon enough, the next architect's certificate for the contractors would materialise.

I really don't like heights: I don't like Ferris wheels, roller-coasters, hot-air balloons, although strangely as a child I did very much like climbing (low) trees, adventure playgrounds and swinging on ropes. In order to understand what we were trying to achieve, I thought I needed to clamber up this rather narrow thirty-foot-long ladder, with flaking paint, which led from outside a door on the top bedroom floor to the first point of roof access. Without looking down, up I went to see what was going on. The architect Peter Brownhill was my guide and had proffered a smart yellow hard hat before I began.

He enthusiastically pointed out what they were doing. I don't think he was aware I am averse to heights and I didn't want to let on and seem pathetic, so when he asked if I would like to clamber up another ladder, which was possibly a little bit too close to the front elevation of the Castle but did lead to a higher part of the roof, I said yes. I didn't mean to agree, but found that I had. Gritting my teeth, I made it up and didn't look down. I look at that ladder sometimes today and feel perfectly ill to think I went up it.

It was nevertheless incredibly useful. This was an architect-run project, following various competitive quotes, in which they were also re-rendering many of the chimneys, stabilising stonework, re-pointing and replacing lead, wooden rooflights and slates. Naturally, every single slate was by no means standard and everything had to be specially made or brought in, usually by crane. The costs were eye-watering but it was entirely fascinating. Later on, I asked Peter for a map of the roof and it remains a prized possession. I did also ask if there was another way down – please.

Water is a recurring theme at Highclere. Rain either makes its way through blown stone, plaster or rotten wood into a building, or else water bubbles up into fields signifying a burst pipe or a spontaneously occurring spring. Water in the wrong place always leads to more expenditure and always in quantity. I remain in awe of Victorian engineering. It worked so well but, sadly, it was also executed a long time ago. Originally the water for the Castle and cottages that lie downhill from the main buildings came from a large reservoir that had been built two-thirds of the way up the side of Siddown Hill. It was all quite low-tech – there was a mast and flagpole stationed above the reservoir, visible through binoculars from a south-facing bedroom on the top floor of the Castle. If the flag started to drop, it indicated a problem with the reservoir. The slope gave the water sufficient natural pressure so that when it was piped down the hill, across the park and into the Castle pipes, it would feed into the four-inch pipe, which in turn led straight up inside the Castle to the water tanks on the roof. These are, as you might expect, rather large and are now supported by iron girders.

The problem we had was that there were now tree roots growing into the reservoir, which meant that it was no longer viable. Instead, we had to take our water directly from the Southern Water reservoir at the very top of the hill, which serves many of the villages to the north and south of the estate as well.

Some of the pipes leaving our old reservoir were quite old and would need replacing, but, in any case, various pressure-reducing valves had to be installed in order to maintain a safe and consistent level of water and not 'blow' all the old joints in the pipes we were able to keep. Naturally, since then, many of these *have* blown and we have had to replace nearly all of them. We have also had to replace most of the stopcocks. In fact, I would go so far as to say that I have found stopcocks to be far more essential to my life than I ever imagined. Each time we try to turn off a stopcock in order to work on a water pipe, it is so ancient it inevitably breaks and we have to have everything on standby ready to replace it. At that point, it usually also becomes apparent that we have not turned off what we thought we had and everyone working near the repair job becomes entirely drenched.

Given the Castle has been a home for so many centuries, it is quite tricky working out how it has been put together and where the utilities run. Much of the knowledge was handed down through experience. One particular man, Albert Saxton, was clerk of works for Geordie, his father, and his grandfather the 6th Earl. When I joined Geordie's team, Albert had already been there some forty years. As a young man he had worked on the railways as a station manager at Guildford, he drove a sports car, loved his garden and cricket, and there was nothing he didn't know about how Highclere worked in terms of utilities. Sadly, by the time the pressure-reducing valve situation was developing, he had died. I was tasked by my husband with searching through the archives to see if I could find any of Albert's notes. To my absolute joy, I found two pages of his handwriting on ruled paper explaining that if I walked three paces in this direction and four paces in that, I'd find a particular stopcock and that the water pipe then ran right towards the fire hydrant and this way towards the kitchens. If you turned left and paced three steps the other way, it led to the four-inch mains pipe. It was very precise and very detailed, very

Albert. Unfortunately, at no point in the two pages of notes did it tell me where to start.

We ended up having to dig up about eight feet of tarmac to see if we could find a main. We did of course – by hitting it. Wherever we have had to dig, we also try to put in water meters as that means you can compare data and see roughly where a leak might be. One summer, John's phone was full of hundreds of photos of grass puddles as he was busy amusing himself by tracking leaking pipes.

From the Castle, the water pipes then run via the reservoir field to all the cottages. Of course, under the new modern pressure, more pipes burst and more joints went at various points and so the saga continued. I think Geordie had been dealing with it all for so long that he felt it was time for John, Luis and me to take over the research on this specialist subject.

The three of us have now achieved a Master's and, alongside more recent members of our team, Bushy and Paul Min, we can now work the fire-hydrant ring around the Castle and, if stuck, even backfill through it. I have also learned that if water coming out of the fire hydrant looks white and creamy, then it is full of air, which means we have an airlock somewhere. If it is clear then there's no air. Since most emergencies happen at night and in winter, a torch is essential for close viewing of the water.

Looking forwards, there are more stopcocks to fit in the coming years and more roofs to repair and the rendering does seem a little endless. It is never finished, despite all we have done, including part of the roof of the west wing, a large leaded roof on the north side and surrounding stonework (more render), a roof behind the kitchens, quite a few windows and several downpipes. Like Zeno's Dichotomy Paradox, we continue towards infinity taking a small step, then half as far, then half as far again and so on. Many of the trades – roofers, plumbers, water specialists and the electricians – are now on my speed-dial, but we have come a long way in terms of being much more watertight and also fire-safe, as we have upgraded our electric distribution boards, which I could also offer as a research subject. Kilowatt hours saved by the use of LEDs in much of the Castle lighting has helped on running costs and carbon saving, as well as safer lower-temperature bulbs, and no doubt we will be looking at more energy cost-saving or local power generation in future years.

This is, however, just the Castle. Behind the Castle, the U-shaped courtyard was crumbling and in need of love. Its roof was in a parlous state, which meant that much of the inside flooring was rotten and unsafe; if it had been stepped on, you would have gone through the first floor and landed twenty feet below. Exploring the side of the courtyard that did have a first floor, in order to understand how the rooms worked and what we could possibly do with them, I wondered how deep the built-in wardrobe at the back of one of them was. Opening it, I found to my surprise another door at the back of the wardrobe – I was clearly in Narnia. Stepping through, I discovered a staircase going down to the right and another door across the passageway that led to a large broken-down, magical (dangerous) space. Although the staircase was rather rotten, I nevertheless tiptoed down to open the door at the bottom – and revealed an entirely bricked-up wall.

Returning the way I came, I went round in a circle trying to imagine where this door was in terms of the layout of the estate office. It was an entirely plastered plain wall and I would never have known there was a door behind it. It was not long before we had removed the plasterboard and a solid, old, traditionally painted mustard-brown door was once more before us. The rickety staircase would be scheduled for replacement in coming months. Eventually, the floors were replaced, the roof repaired and new oak beams spliced into old. Some of the old beams were notched as if for the inclusion of windows, and the hypothesis was that they might have been repurposed from the church when it was rebuilt in the nineteenth century – but old seasoned wood is good wood.

Over time, one side of the courtyard was partly converted to tearooms whilst the central part remained offices, and there were now floors, stairs and windows, which was all quite exciting. Geordie and I cleared the rubbish of decades out of the stables and set them to rights with fresh paint and happy horses. They are once again filling the purpose for which they were designed and many visitors enjoy popping their heads in to have a look. If the farrier is working, he is the biggest attraction of the day.

During the rebuilding, we also began to strip the modern, rather hideous, glossy cream paint off the external bricks in the courtyard. Pat Withers and team had in fact painted it on originally, so we were both laughing as together we found ways of removing her handiwork. It was quite addictive, peeling off white paint in larger or smaller flakes, and a good excuse for time passed away from office desks. Without the jarring paint, you can once more read the collection of buildings forming the courtyard and your eye and mind better understand how they and the main Castle buildings relate. The mellow bricks are beautiful, combining shades of rosy mandarin and wintry earth colours, with blue-greys in between.

Fortunately, the removal of the paint also meant that we can more easily spot cracks and other problems that are developing. We could immediately see a large crack extending above a broad garage opening. It might once have had more support within the space than it does now. Like everything here, spaces, rooms and outbuildings have been endlessly recycled and adapted. These days, of course, we have surveyors and engineers to advise us and there was much pursing of lips at the sight of the widening crack that ran through the brickwork above the double doors and towards the roof. It did not change for a few years and then began to become a cause for concern. It was suggested that the long wooden beam and lintel above the wide doors was cracking (we could see the supporting post was rotten) and that we had come to the point where making do and propping up to extend its life was no longer an option.

For all the work we have done above, in and around the Castle, Historic England explained that there were many other buildings on the estate also at risk. Some of these were to be found down the long winding pitted track leading past the expansive Capability Brown lake and the Temple of Diana (in which my husband had done a great deal of work in the 1990s to completely repair the dome, which had a tree growing through it, and where much work at the base of the columns was needed, though it is a continuous repair challenge), then through overgrown rhododendrons to a broken black gate with some pillars either side, which seemed once to have been a triumphal arch but was now in a sad condition. Peering through, I could see two very dilapidated unattractive cottages to the left-hand side. They were closely surrounded by undergrowth, meaning nobody would want to live there.

There was much to research and understand before we could proceed. This was once the imposing entrance to Highclere Park, created by Geordie's ancestor the 1st Earl to mark the fact he had been granted a peerage by George III. Capability Brown's great works meant that part of the landscape and lake wound towards the north and east and therefore in the direction of London, so this gateway was named London Lodge. Entirely obscured by undergrowth were the remains of two once harmonious wings to the central arch. The whole area was swamped by the very successful common rhododendron, *Rhododendron ponticum*, which produces eye-catching purple flowers each spring but grows like an invasive weed in our climate. Needless to say, underneath the lodge and road we would later find broken culverts and drainage. Once more, with the help of Peter Brownhill and the architects, and with all the required permissions, we chose the best quote to almost completely rebuild the arch as well as the rooms to either side.

The whole project took two years and part of the journey was about restoring the work of Mrs Eleanor Coade (1733–1821), who was famous for perfecting Coade stone or Lithodipra, used for architectural decoration, moulding for neoclassical statues and garden ornaments. She did not invent Coade stone but improved the clay mix and the firing process. (The word 'Lithodipra' in Greek means 'stone fired twice'.) We have found that amongst crumbling brick her stone still remains hard, so the pattern formations can be taken down, the brick restored, and then the Coade stone replaced in fine condition.

Eleanor Coade was an unusual woman for her age: born into a prosperous merchant family with ties to Cornwall and Devon as well as London, she became a well-known businesswoman and entrepreneur who successfully ran her business for nearly fifty years, by combining artistic flair with unusually good marketing skills.

Records give an insight into her marketing techniques. She had an impressive showroom, conducted tours and printed what we today would call brochures, quoting classical authors. These 'brochures' also listed her clients, one of whom was the 1st Earl of Carnarvon who commissioned a number of ornaments in 1793 to surmount his new entrance to the park. In fact, the splendour of London Lodge is almost entirely due to Mrs Coade. 'Coade Artificial Stone Manufactory' made statues, fountains, urns, garden features, mantelpieces, commemorative and heraldic devices, and other decorative interior carvings, such as candelabra. Every eminent architect of the time, from Robert Adam to Sir John Soane, John Nash, and the brothers James and Samuel Wyatt, commissioned work from her, which can still be found today throughout Britain. She also exported to North America – for example, Philadelphia and Washington ('new Federal building friezes, keystones and chimney pieces'), as well as to South America, Russia and Poland. Mrs Coade was inspired by the classical style but also referenced the taste for Gothic as well as Egyptian works of art. In the UK, her commissions adorn the Royal Naval College at Greenwich, Buckingham Palace, St George's Chapel at Windsor and Windsor Castle itself. The great lion on Westminster Bridge is made from Coade stone and you can also find the stoneware surmounting doorways on London streets and the porticos of various great country houses.

Largely unknown today, she was a most remarkable woman, dressing sometimes as a man in order to gain business. In some ways her commissions were such successful imitations of stone that her clients did not promote the fact they were just ceramic. She always remained closely involved in the production side and never revealed complete details of the ingredients of her product or her exact firing technique.

She was not the first person to create artificial stone – the

Romans did as well – but her particular secret formula unfortunately died with her. The significant attribute of her stone was that it did not shrink when fired, which would have been achieved by incorporating pre-shrunk clay into the mixture. Mrs Coade, a devout Baptist, was a philanthropist and proponent of women's rights. She never married and after her death left her fortune to family, educational charities and women in difficult circumstances, stipulating that their husbands should have no control over the money.

As part of the achievement of bringing out once more the beauty and setting of both the lodge and drive, we also clad the little cottages in wood, straightened them and cleared back the rhododendrons. With new double-glazed windows, insulation, patios, hedges and gardens, I hope those who now live there are happy.

In the meantime, the entrance welcomes its own guests in the two lodges where visitors can stay for two or three nights. The whole project probably cost something over £750,000 and we will never get the capital expenditure back, but through finding a new role today, the entrance building should sustain itself for the future.

It is a beautiful place for guests to take time out, with a cosy sitting room, log burner and kitchen on one side, whilst if you follow the sunken lights and trip the light fantastic along the paving stones to the other, you find a very comfortable double bedroom and bathroom. With books and games to play, and lovely walks in all seasons to the Temple of Diana, we hope it is a good place from which to explore or just to chill.

When I married my Mr Darcy in 1999, I had absolutely no idea about the extent of his 'follies', which was probably a good thing. Not all follies are visible but quite a few of

Geordie's are right in front of me. It turned out that in the eighteenth century there were likely to have been at least twelve, but luckily there are now only six and, one by one, we continually try to repair, restore and consider once more what possible role they might have in today's world.

One of the most visible follies from the Castle is on the east lawn and takes the form of a classical Greek temple, somewhat surprisingly called Jackdaws Castle. It was built by one of Geordie's ancestors in 1743. There may well have been an avenue behind it favoured by these birds.

Geordie's father partly repaired Jackdaws and we have too, but it is now battling serious water ingress and thus we return once more to my old friend the rain. I have realised, from studying old sketches, that it once had a grey-tiled roof, which makes sense. It was used by Robert Herbert, Geordie's ancestor, as somewhere to have tea. I can only assume it rained 300 years ago much as it does today as, on reflection, every folly he created had wet-weather provisions. Therefore, my discussion with the architects focuses on asking Historic England to allow us to reinstate the roof. Then we need mend it only once as a roof will stop the water penetrating into architraves and plinths, and we can once more have tea there, whatever the weather. The whole project is a little depressing otherwise in terms of its long-term futility.

Dan's Lodge, originally called Andover Lodge, was built around the same time. It lies at the head of an old deer run and is a most unusual, triangular building, rather decorative in its own way, but it has been a ruin more or less since I first knew it and remains a future project. Heaven's Gate on the summit of Siddown Hill to the south of the Castle is a testament to Shakespeare's Sonnet 29. It offers views both towards heaven and, if standing underneath the arch, back to earth, to home and towards the northern hills of Oxford. Geordie has stabilised it several times but once more I suspect we will need to start at the top and at the very least remove marauding vegetation.

There is also the little Etruscan temple in the Castle gardens, which does have a roof and sits rather nicely between the old ice house and a new garden I have built in memory of my mother-in-law. We have recently restored all the external brick tiles and roof of the Etruscan Temple and, whilst standing looking up on the inside, I often wonder about the unusual Greek carvings around the back wall, which may once have been inside the Castle, but for now the building is stable so we can all enjoy it and the amazing views south across the Brownian landscape to Siddown Hill.

For all the challenges they pose, Highclere's follies are of great architectural interest in themselves. Follies were often modelled on Roman temples, representing classical virtues, and were particularly popular in eighteenth-century English landscape design because of the 'Grand Tours' around Europe undertaken by wealthy young gentlemen, who would have visited the most famous classical sites and afterwards attempted to recreate them on their own estates. Despite this, very few follies were completely without practical purpose, even if today that purpose is not entirely clear to us. Some were picnic spots, some little theatres; others served as places in which to escape the formality of a great house or as locations for illicit trysts. Mr Darcy and Eliza Bennet met at a folly as part of their emotional journey and, in the *Pride and Prejudice* TV series with Colin Firth, the folly used there looked very similar to the Temple of Diana at Highclere.

The Temple of Diana seems to be always only partially consolidated and restored, but I take my hat off to Geordie that he has chosen to spend so much money on it for years and to keep going. It is an extraordinarily elegant testament to classical architecture, carefully sited on a constructed false hill area above the majesty of Dunsmere Lake. First of all, the setting is important as historically Diana's worship may have originated at an open-air sanctuary overlooking a lake (Lake Nemi), and she is associated both with Egeria the water nymph and with Virbius (Hippolytus) the woodland god. There is water below Highclere's temple and woods behind it. Possibly first built in about 1760, it was much altered by Sir Charles Barry in the 1840s. It has a colonnade of twelve smooth columns of the Ionic order, with a modillion entablature, and is surmounted by a very elegant Italianate dome constructed on a drum, around which is a felt waterproof covering. The balustrade and urns sit above the cornice and the base has openings with plain architraves and a plinth. Every single one of these words encapsulates heritage and leads to more brown envelopes.

The largest and most daunting at-risk building to restore at Highclere was the medieval barn at Manor Farm, Old Burghclere. This most extraordinary architectural project was without doubt the biggest challenge we have yet faced, but it was also one that mattered immensely to Geordie. The barn is almost cathedral-like in its size and space, and the dendrology tests suggest it was last rebuilt in about 1438. The footprint has an unusual width as well as length and it's possible that the Bishops of Winchester, who owned Highclere for 800 years, employed carpenters who were also working on jobs in Winchester Cathedral and in Oxford colleges, which would account for the craftsmanship. It is an utterly fascinating building. It has eight bays with great oak trusses that span the width. There are king posts at either end and queen posts which link to the curved trusses, thereby creating the shape of an arch whose compressive stress gives maximum strength and support to the building. High up in the roof, every truss is notched ready for a purlin but left unused, which suggests that the foreman and carpenters changed their minds and divided the top supports into thirds rather than halves so as to use two levels of purlin support. The result is a church-like interior which maximises space.

In order to understand the project and reach the high beams, I had to clamber up and down further long ladders. Of course, once I returned to ground level, I was very careful not to walk underneath them. I suppose I am a bit superstitious but so were our predecessors – we have found at least two carved witch marks. One is clear to see near the main grain door and was intended to prevent any bad spirits from entering. They are supposed to have been so transfixed by the never-ending circle within the mark that they could not cross the threshold. The other is placed much higher up.

Hampshire Oak have, with care and time, rebuilt footings, spliced in new oak to beams or queen and king posts, re-roofed with the old tiles and, more recently, found 'new' old tiles. As far as possible, all the existing beams were kept. Over time, they have become as hard as iron but in fact are harder and more resilient. Our ancestors built well and this barn is a testament to their skill and determination to build things that would last.

The barn stored the local harvest, and with grain dry storage is key. '*Bere*' was the Anglo-Saxon word for barley and '*aern*' means an earth house, a home or a secret place, so a barn is quite literally a home for food. It was therefore entirely appropriate that the first time it was used after the restoration was for 260 farmers from the Hampshire farmers' club who joined us to feast once more in this special space.

Running an estate is all about managing the day-to-day expenditure that supports the Castle and its workings, from staff accommodation to rented cottages, the fences, gates, a bridge or two, roads, tracks, ditches, gutters and drains, not to mention an inordinate quantity of fairly dicey windows. The list always reminds me of when you land on the wrong property in Monopoly: you squint at it in disbelief but it is too late to roll the dice again.

My husband's grandfather, the 6th Earl of Carnarvon, passed on the responsibility for running the maintenance of many of the cottages and the parkland to a property management company nearly forty years ago. He was of a generation who, following the misery of the First World War, were determined to occupy themselves henceforth only in life-enhancing ways. There were then decades of what we would, these days, call bodge jobs. Rotten window frames were mended with putty and painted shut, roofs remained leaky, loos were in outside sheds and there was no damp proofing or heating. The buildings were all very basic. Over time, my husband gradually began to bring them into a more modern state. In fairness to him, the 6th Earl's era was blighted by war, boom and bust, very high taxes and then inflation after the Second World War, along with strict rent controls on all the cottages, so he did not have an easy time.

After beginning with enthusiasm and a new strategy twenty years ago, we keep going. An estate is all about community and it works best if it has different people of all ages and from all backgrounds living, working or weekending on it. I try to meet tenants and, especially if the cottage is quite close to the Castle, find out whether they like coffee, wine, dogs and horse racing.

Some of the cottages lent themselves to being refurbished

in a slightly smarter fashion – restored floor tiles, wallpaper, curtains, comfortable kitchens, good showers, outside areas for fire pits and wooden tables to share food and views with friends. Over the long term, these cottages help pay for and support the houses lived in by those who work for us, but every cottage I update expands my knowledge of insulation, pointing, French drains and septic tanks. Just as important as the inside is the outside space for hedges, bird tables, vegetable-growing, flowers and sheds. Every cottage needs a shed.

Every pound that comes in from visitors or rent usually quite literally goes straight back out again to put another brick in a wall or fix a leaking pipe. I have not been trained in CAD design so I ask Team Highclere to help me imagine how a kitchen or bathroom may look. Standing in a new bathroom, I ask James to pretend he is in the bath. I place Jo where I think the loo should be, whilst Laura stands where the shower might fit. It is a practical way of seeing the space, and then they can all pretend to wash their hands. Everyone is quite used to it now. Sometimes, someone volunteers to pretend to be in bed whilst another person sees if they can walk round said imaginary bed. We all wonder what would happen if we would like a cup of tea in the morning – how far away is that? If the answer is too far then we need to find a better solution. Where is someone going to sit outside? Where is the sun? Where can they park their cars and where can they stack logs for a fire in a snug? To my husband's immense astonishment, there may even be a rather detailed budget and invoices marked off against quotes. There are, however, always surprises.

Geordie does tend to question me about budgets and I must confess that sometimes I do not really have one, but that is because I never know whether the ceiling will be rotten or the floor have woodworm. It is almost like asking how long a piece of string is, and that is always a problem with very old buildings that have not been taken care of quite as well as they might have been in some of their life. He experienced this himself with his careful budget for the restoration of Winchester Arch, which was originally the main entrance to Highclere. It did not take long for his own estimation of 650 new bricks to expand to 1,650 bricks. As usual, more work was needed to the pediment on the top than anticipated and so on, but it was properly done and will now last a few more generations.

With cottages, gates, lodges and castles come keys. When Robert Taylor arrived as a footman at Highclere in 1937, one of the first entries in his diaries described following Smith the butler, keys jangling, the full length of the bottom corridor of the Castle to be shown the china cupboards. This was the set for breakfast; the Bretby set for tea; the Chesterfield silver for dinner; and so on. He was then given the keys, but that was just one cupboard and one set of (quite important) keys. The system he observed with them remains the same: if you use a key, put it back.

Hilariously, I am renowned for losing my own keys, but try to have a plan when it comes to other buildings and other people's keys. Nevertheless, rarely a day goes by when you don't hear one of the Highclere team on the radio asking if anyone has seen the key to something or somewhere. Given the quantity of them, we are slowly moving towards using keypads on various doors and gates. I am in charge of choosing the codes for these which, as a historian, I often base on battles, sometimes treaties and occasionally the accession of a king, not necessarily in any particular order. I once found some guides staring at a keypad desperately trying to remember whether the code for it was the date of the Battle of Crécy or Edington, Bosworth or Waterloo, the Treaty of Berwick or Vienna, for example. Actually, it was the year of the award of the earldom to the 1st Earl of Carnarvon. They nodded wisely and I moved on, crying with laughter, mainly because earlier I had opened the door already and it was on the latch.

Anton Chekhov described his play *The Cherry Orchard* as a comedy with some elements of farce, but more often it is treated as a tragedy. The main protagonists, an aristocratic Russian landowner called Madame Ranevskaya and her brother Gayev, carelessly assume that something will turn up to solve their financial problems and do nothing themselves, despite warnings from the entrepreneurial Lopakhin that they must act. Gayev is a talkative eccentric, addicted to billiards and thus leisure, which renders him helpless in the face of change. He lacks the drive or doesn't understand the real-world mechanisms necessary to realise his aims. At Highclere by contrast it is essential that we do not rely on luck (although good fortune is always welcome) but always plan ahead, so far as is possible, for every contingency. There is not just the greatness of past triumphs to be seen in houses such as Highclere. Echoes of each loss, failure and everyday endeavour are preserved within its fabric.

When I pledged to love Geordie in the Savoy Chapel in 1999, I had no idea of the journey ahead of us. It is immense, sometimes completely overwhelming. It can lead to smiles and equally to tears, but these emotions are always mixed with a sense of what a privilege it is to have been entrusted with the stewardship of this very special place. Gladly, we work together to ensure its continued survival – a matter of taking small steps each day rather than panicking about the longer view. As the late Queen Elizabeth II said in her Christmas broadcast in 2019, 'It's worth remembering that it is often the small steps, not the giant leaps, that bring about the most lasting change.'

CHAPTER NINE

September: What It Takes

'The best way to predict the future is to create it'
— Abraham Lincoln

In September, all our senses are attuned to the approaching autumn – to an implicit sense of time passing as the month unfolds, with leaves edged bronze in the chill mornings and the twittering birds contemplating their imminent departure for warmer climates. It is both nostalgic and a time of transformation.

In September 2019, Geordie and I flew to New York for the premiere of the first *Downton Abbey* film. Rather like the changing season, both of us were caught up in the excitement and anticipation of the new film and what it might mean for Highclere. We had met the American businessman Stephen Schwarzman and his wife Christine a few times and they kindly asked us to the launch party for Steve's much-awaited book, *What It Takes*, recalling episodes from his extraordinary career in investment along with anecdotes, insights and reflections.

My overwhelming memory of the party is Geordie's suggestion that we walk from our hotel to their apartment. He may have been saving money . . . it was not my choice as, for once, I was wearing some proper high heels and it was a bit further than we had anticipated. Sure enough, a few blocks along, my feet ached so much that I actually had to take my shoes off and trip warily along the pavements. I think Geordie realised then he needed an upgrade from Geordie version 2.1 to at least version 4.1.

Nearly there and pausing just out of sight, my shoes went back on and we swanned in. It was a very special evening and Steve gave a short speech commenting on how challenging it was both to write and market his book. It is a book to consider and return to often.

Steve and Christine have stayed with us at Highclere both in summer and winter, the latter being a flying visit en route from Davos. It was a fun evening with Scottish reeling (my favourite) and a little haggis as well as other food options pertaining to Geordie's love of the Scottish Highlands, such as his favourite boozy bramble pudding.

When I walked into the dining room for breakfast the next morning, Steve was already at the table. I so enjoy breakfast after a more formal evening, everyone sitting where they want, wandering over to collect more scrambled eggs or coffee and the inconsequential chatter of friends catching up.

He called out for me to come and sit by him, saying he had a few things to share with me. I imagine everyone wants to learn from an acknowledged éminence grise – undoubtedly Steve and other financial seers such as Warren Buffett have mastered the art of investing. I expect the rest of us all hope we'll one day receive some straightforward advice on how to do it from someone infallible – like being told the answer to the ultimate meaning of life is forty-two, according to *The Hitchhiker's Guide to the Galaxy*.

Steve told me I needed to find a geometric rather than an arithmetic revenue stream to bring in money to sustain Highclere. He did not tell me how to do it, just that was what

I needed to do. The conversation moved on but those few words stayed with me.

By 2019, our business model at Highclere had changed. We hosted fewer weddings and had, both by circumstance and strategy, moved away from corporate events. In contrast, we had begun to create more events ourselves, around the seasons and various themes, many of which related to the idea of fictional dramas and real storytelling from a long-established historic home. My main objective was to try and develop a schedule of events and tours throughout the year, so that in every month there would be revenue coming in, because, like any other business, as sure as the sun rises in the east and God made little apples, every day, every week and every month at Highclere money goes out. The priority was at least not to lose money so that, at a minimum, outgoings would be matched by income. We organised car rallies to raise cash for the Air Ambulance, which soon became a little large for us to manage; welcomed a country fair that has towards 20,000 visitors in late May, and a firework concert which hosts 8,000 people most years. The latter two events still take place twenty years later, are still a great success and so have become well-established features of the Castle diary.

Even so, we continually have to market ourselves. It takes time to create a brand of any sort, but I am particularly proud of the way we have adapted to the growing opportunities that social media provides, in particular with our Instagram account. Instagram gives small businesses a reach into the world that was never possible before this century and our efforts with it are definitely a nod to Stephen's advice about geometric progression.

Highclere's Instagram Reels have become more ambitious and fun, with recreations of a visit from Barbie, Winnie the Pooh, many Labrador escapades or any other bright ideas that often involve input from Team Highclere. I might be seen crawling downstairs holding up Winnie and Eeyore, whilst Hannah is hidden in a bath with a Barbie doll peeking over the top and Father Christmas is trying out various chimneys on the roof. Every so often I have donned a sheet to play a ghost, bumping into walls as I do my best impressions, Caitlin giggling behind the mobile-phone lens, whilst I always hope I don't upset any real ghosts . . .

The Castle office inbox is a frequent resource in our 'market research' as it can offer new perspectives. People write in looking for tours and dates to visit, which allows us to shape our diaries and events to what will make them happy.

Highclere is brick and stone, beautiful, historic but inanimate. It is the people who have lived here, and those who still do, upstairs and downstairs, that are the source of real fascination. From the beginning, Geordie and I have tried to explore ways of bringing people to Highclere because they love it and the stories it tells and want to be part of it. In order to offer highlights each year and create a buzz, we have several large community gatherings such as the late May Country Fair and early August Battle Proms, along with, from time to time, a large-scale charity event.

From our earliest days, Highclere had developed a good business hosting weddings as well as corporate events within the Castle and family fun days in the grounds. Tours and group visits in contrast were a smaller part of the business. Geordie and his parents had applied for a licence to hold civil ceremonies as soon as it was permitted by legislation and, despite a few bumps along the way, the business was building, although we had probably reached the maximum number of weddings we could welcome per year and wear and tear was increasing within the building.

SEPTEMBER: WHAT IT TAKES

Geordie and I worked at the sharp end, helping to move furniture at midnight, working shifts to be up early the next morning, lending a hand with polishing glasses for weddings or tying bows on chairs. The revenues were strong, however, and allowed us to keep paying for the work on the roof above the saloon and other key restoration projects around the Castle.

In March 2003, clutching a mug of tea at 4 a.m. in the morning, Geordie and I listened anxiously to the BBC World Service as the Iraq War began. It is always far easier to start a war than to end one. These years would have a long-term impact on many lives and also on the world economy. It has never really stopped . . .

Corporate business events were put on hold and confidence and trust declined. Highclere may have its own peculiar challenges to face, but it is still also dependent on others' sentiments and force majeure. Nevertheless, we continued to search for the next new client, the next board meeting, conference or wedding. It was a relentless business model as it is for many others in our position. Park events were easier on both Team Highclere and the Castle. A Vodafone concert was booked for June in 2003, which required a set and temporary marquee for some 10,000 guests, and to our delight Lulu, Bryan Adams and Robbie Williams took to the stage. Not that we knew it then, but this was one of the last large-scale corporate events we held in the grounds near the Castle.

Fame was then achieved with the wedding of Katie Price and Peter Andre in September 2005, a pink Cinderella coach, fifty-two pages in *OK!* magazine, two helicopters (one from *Hello!* and one from *OK!*) arguing for airspace overhead, as well as photographers hiding in various bushes. The security team hired by the client for the occasion patrolled around the gardens most industriously, but it was my dogs who barked at a prone figure disguised in the ha-ha. It was all very intense, with innumerable photographs taken. Despite it being a lovely, warm late-summer day, all the Castle windows were shut for privacy and so many of the guests found it very hot inside the rooms, until they all made their way along a walkway to the wedding breakfast in a marquee across the lawns.

Like other country houses, we frequently welcome location scouts for movies, TV or adverts. One memorable music video filmed at Highclere was with John Legend. It was called 'Heaven' – but heaven only knows why it took two days to make. It was filmed outside as well as inside and it was a total joy to hear John Legend's honeyed voice fill the saloon. One element of it was filmed in the library, with a beautiful girl lying on a richly coloured fabric-covered table in front of the fireplace.

As usual, some of us were hanging around waiting for something to happen, which is the way of life on every film set. John G and Diana the housekeeper were chatting in the main library, standing by a table next to the French windows opposite the fireplace. Suddenly the director shouted, 'Silence, action!' and John whispered to Diana, 'Quick, let's get down.' They both dropped to their hands and knees and tried to stay discreetly out of sight under a table. There was a pause and then the American director called out: 'I can see asses. Whose asses are under that table?' Like a pair of caught-out schoolchildren, John G and Diana had to stand up guiltily, brush themselves down and casually remove themselves from view. I was spluttering with laughter but keeping carefully out of the camera line.

One evening a decade later, I was sitting next to a friend who is a Blenheim trustee when they mentioned that a material amount of the palace's visitor profits were generated

Simon Andrews (Farm Manager) and Lord Carnarvon

(*From left to right*) Sam Burch, Harry Moss and Laura Miller with Ginger, Mellow and Didi

Lady Fiona with Lady Mary

(*Left*) Where sheep may safely graze, in this case looking up to the Iron Age fort on Beacon Hill

The farming team

Feeding the chickens

London Lodge. From near ruin to restored eighteenth-century entrance lodge where visitors can stay today

The medieval barn following a decade of restoration

There are a lot of roofs

(*Left*) Heroes at Highclere, 2018

(*Below*) Our Highclere Castle gin partners Regina and Adam von Gootkin at our New York gin launch

The Hanky Panky

HRH The Prince of Wales (*centre*) at a shooting party in December 1895

The Royal party attending Highclere Church in 1949. HRH Princess Elizabeth leads the party with the 6th Earl of Carnarvon, whilst her sister Princess Margaret walks with HRH Prince Philip and Geordie's father

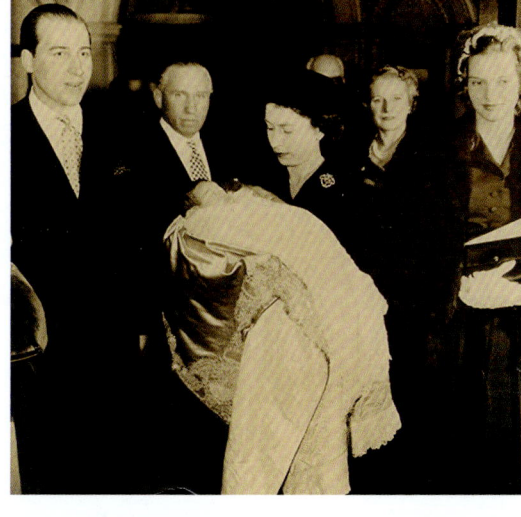

The late Queen Elizabeth II, holding the future Earl of Carnarvon – her godson – in her arms, with his parents and grandparents either side

Horses and ponies have played a central role in the lives of both the Royal family and the Carnarvons

Time out in the library at Highclere Castle

The 5th Earl of Carnarvon and his beloved terrier, Susie. He had set his camera on a timer but neither he nor Susie were perfectly in position

Halloween Highclere style

From Halloween to Christmas at Highclere

Christmas tours and carols – a much-loved celebration for many visitors each year

Sally Popplewell, Chief Christmas Elf

Gerald Dickens – great-great-grandson of Charles Dickens – performing *A Christmas Carol*

SEPTEMBER: WHAT IT TAKES

at Christmas. It was only a casual throwaway comment but it made me think. We held a few events in December to raise money for charities, but not much more than that. My parents-in-law had never opened the Castle at that time of year.

Ed Victor, the legendary literary agent, suggested I write a book about Christmas, with the Castle as a wonderful Victorian backdrop to the illustrations. So I did, and then thought through what Christmas means to so many of us and tried to reflect this through an assortment of proposed December tours – from carols to seasonal favourite food, decorations, Christmas trees, Charles Dickens, Father Christmas and Champagne receptions. That first year I entirely overdid the 'variations on a theme' and we were all truly exhausted. Thereafter, with more experience and time, we have learned to plan decorations and themes two years ahead and now focus on just six seasonal events. In fact, every year we are thrilled to welcome back many guests who like to begin their personal journey towards Christmas with a visit to Highclere. It is a tribute to the hospitality of Luis and his banqueting team, as well as the efforts of the kitchen, all the car parkers and John G's amusing and fact-filled introductions.

All of these endeavours are nevertheless an arithmetic model for adding to our revenue and not the geometric progression urged by Steve Schwarzman, and whilst they have brought in cash to repair and restore – to literally put another brick in the wall – they cannot be the whole story.

Highclere is taking a similar approach to many stately homes, all of us trying to find a USP around which to base the marketing of our present and future endeavours. Goodwood is famous for its tremendous festivals or revivals of speed, coping with vast numbers of attendees. Badminton has its horse trials – and now filming – as does Burghley, which is also open to the public. Blenheim is a magnificent palace, England's Versailles and birthplace of Sir Winston Churchill. It holds many different events on a unique scale with massive tearooms, gift shops on-site and on the internet, a Christmas Market and so on. Scottish castles such as Cawdor focus on their history, as well as outside pursuits from fishing to hiking. There are endless different ways to welcome people in the hospitality business.

When Geordie and I took over, I'm not sure that Highclere Castle actually had a USP. The most obvious story of global interest was that of Lord Carnarvon and archaeologist Howard Carter's discovery of the tomb of the Pharaoh Tutankhamun in 1922, after it had lain undisturbed for over 3,300 years.

The scale of the attention surrounding their endeavours means this is regarded as the first global media sensation, catching the imagination of people everywhere and of all ages. It remains to date the only Pharaonic tomb discovered intact. However, nowadays it seems as if Lord Carnarvon merely occupies a footnote in history. Whilst much of the public's fascination was rightly directed towards the young Pharaoh Tutankhamun, the residual plaudits were largely awarded to Howard Carter after Lord Carnarvon tragically died in Egypt in April 1923, aged fifty-six, before the iconic golden mask of the boy king was revealed to the world. His achievements and reputation have faded into the background, though without his sponsorship and support the tomb might never have been found – he was fundamental to the story. Howard Carter wrote that the 5th Earl:

> . . . had died in the hour of his triumph, but for his untiring generosity and constant encouragement our labours could

never have been crowned with success. His judgement in ancient art has rarely been equalled. His efforts which have done so much to extend our knowledge of Egyptology will ever be honoured in history, and by me his memory will always be cherished.

The final years of work were completed by Carter and his dedicated team, funded in the 5th Earl's memory by his widow, Almina – an extraordinary legacy.

Decades later Historic England were very keen that we should find something to do with the cellars underneath the Castle, then being used for storing things that had fallen out of use, and wanted us to repurpose them in some way, preferably for tours. This was in 2005–6 when, of course, the downstairs of *Downton Abbey* had not yet even been invented. But the story of the 5th Earl's Egyptian triumph had certainly not faded from the memory of those at Highclere. Maybe we already had a suitable theme for a tour. Geordie and I therefore applied for permission to join up the cellars, which were in two separate sections, so that we had a circular exhibition path. We could see that Sir Charles Barry had drawn some dotted lines on his drawings, thinking about joining them up himself, but, rather annoyingly, had not dug through. One section represented the old staff dining room, scullery, beer cellars and storage rooms, rather like those shown on *Downton Abbey*, whilst the other had wine cellars, more storage rooms and flower rooms, with alcove cupboards and ancient doors.

Excavating under the Castle to dig out the connecting corridor was exciting but nerve-racking. Whilst tunnelling through solid brick waste left by Barry, we were never far from structural areas of the foundations and had to be very careful. For example, we found some of the chalk and flint foundations of William of Wykeham's medieval palace dating from around AD 1360 and incorporated into the later structure. In addition, larger present-day machines were found to cause dangerous vibrations and so we ended up adopting the deep-seam miners' technique of using very thin long drills to break up the old brick, which we then hacked out by hand. This generated so much red dust that it floated all the way up to the state rooms and into even higher parts of the Castle, much to Diana's chagrin. As we moved forward, we built a supportive steel cage and finally the tunnel was completed safely.

The cellars are atmospheric in their own right. We painted everything in dark colours, as a good backdrop to the displays and to provide a suitably subterranean feel to the story of Lord Carnarvon's archaeological triumph. It was and is a very fitting synergy.

Most of the 5th Earl's Egyptian collection was sold to the Metropolitan Museum in New York in 1925 to pay death duties. The remains were thrust into storage in the Castle and forgotten. They were found after the 6th Earl's death in the cupboards between the drawing room and smoking room, in a scene worthy of a movie script, by his butler Robert Taylor and the 7th Earl. The newly discovered artefacts were then displayed in a small room on crowded shelves with tiny labels and, whilst they were respected by family and visitors, I felt that we could do much better by them.

My first task was to research and then display these genuine antiquities in a newly designated exhibition space with modern, temperature-controlled, museum-class cabinets. This allowed us to lay 'the noble lady' Irtyru's painted wooden coffin horizontally, which both helped to stabilise it and

SEPTEMBER: WHAT IT TAKES

allowed us to offer a better interpretation of it. When he discovered the coffin, wrote the 5th Earl, it was so poignant to find a wreath of cornflowers placed on it by someone 3,500 years ago; an echo of love and compassion across the intervening millennia. In addition, there are also a number of other small Egyptian works of art.

The antiquities on display then lead the visitor into the story of the 5th Earl and Howard Carter, brought vividly to life by photographs and witness accounts, as the route winds through the cellars. The exhibition culminates with a display of amazing replicas of the most famous treasures that were found in Tutankhamun's tomb, so everyone can get a taste of the wonders it contained without actually having to go to Cairo to see the originals.

Many people are fascinated by ancient Egypt, it seems. By complete chance, Geordie received an email from partners in a new venture in Cornwall, asking if we would be kind enough to go down and open an exhibition about ancient Egypt they had created in the village of Dobwalls near Liskeard. Geordie said yes, and so on the appointed day, both looking quite smart, we caught a train to Cornwall. Arriving, we stepped out onto the platform. It was entirely empty in every direction – reminding me of the famous lines from 'Adlestrop' by Edward Thomas: 'No one left and no one came / On the bare platform . . .' We began to ponder what we were doing here as we looked around in vain.

We wondered if we had made a mistake? Perhaps it was the wrong day. An old dark-coloured Volvo pulled to a stop outside the station and two slightly eccentric-looking people emerged. We glanced at each other and then climbed into the car with them. They were incredibly polite and we set off to stay in a local bed and breakfast and have supper with them, before Geordie duly opened their Egyptian exhibition the following day. It was a challenging endeavour as the new museum was in a spacious building but awkwardly surrounded by traffic and double yellow lines. Nevertheless, they were devoted to celebrating all things Egyptian, and were passionate about their project and sharing their collection with local children and other visitors.

As part of our discussions with them, we realised that with their help we could create some replicas for our own exhibition at Highclere. They were both craftsmen with a whole plethora of contacts in Egypt who could also create replicas. Bizarrely, that unexpected email and the train journey to Liskeard were actually a key part of our journey towards creating our own Egyptian exhibition in the cellars. Their museum sadly closed in 2008, but our good fortune was to acquire from them a number of significant replicas such as the Middle Coffin, the innermost shrine, the famous Painted Chest and the glorious sculpture of Tutankhamun as a Harpooner, as well as many other objects, and we could also offer them commission for sourcing further items.

Stuart Beilby made us a beautiful copy of the wooden hunting box found in the first room of Tutankhamun's tomb by the 5th Earl. Geordie loved the intricate craftsmanship, showing the boy Pharaoh resplendent, driving his royal chariot, on the one side enjoying the hunt in the desert and on the other personified as a mighty Sphinx, subduing all the enemies of Egypt.

Everything we collected was stored high up in the Castle, as safely as possible. This process culminated one day in the arrival of a hearse in which was a replica mummy of Tutankhamun – so realistic that we are often asked if it came from the Valley of the Kings, which it assuredly did not. The hearse had seemed the most practical way to move 'Tutankhamun' from Cornwall to Highclere. He also stayed high up in the Castle with the other replicas. I found it all a bit spooky – I often worked alone in the cellars and did not need a skeleton, real or otherwise, there too. Once the cabinets had been completed, skeletons, coffins, chariots, lion-headed beds and the replica faces of Horus and Anubis all then had to move three floors back downstairs.

Wall paintings from Tutankhamun's tomb began to adorn what was previously the white-wine cellar due to my good luck in finding a girlfriend who was brilliant at producing paintings resembling the actual ones 3,000 miles away.

For the tour Geordie and I wanted to create a sense of being there, experiencing what it might have felt like to find and explore the tomb, rather than let the surroundings resemble a museum. In order to distil the experience so that it would be both steeped in atmosphere and enjoyable, I plunged in at the deep end, reading and researching exhibition and interpretation techniques, writing enough words in a big enough script for those wishing to study labels, but not so many as to induce queues. Geordie was well ahead of me as he had been involved in two television documentaries: *Return to the Valley of the Kings* in 1999 and *Tutankhamun: Secrets of the Boy King* in 2007. He'd spent time with film crews in the Egyptian Museum in Cairo and the Valley of the Kings in Luxor, so already had a good working knowledge of what was most likely to hold the onlooker's attention.

Egyptian civilisation spanned at least 5,000 years; a highly successful period based on skilful handling of agriculture. There is only one surviving Wonder of the World today from the seven that originally received that accolade and it is Egyptian – Khufu's pyramid at Giza, also known as the Great

Pyramid. Ancient Egyptians constructed the most extraordinary temples in Luxor, carved and transported obelisks, sculpted statues, and created myriad miraculous small works of art, of which those from Tutankhamun's time, the Eighteenth Dynasty, are the most exquisite. They produced their astonishing work even whilst believing that this was purely the world of transience before the soul moved on to the next, more glorious phase: the world of resurrection. The 5th Earl loved Egypt, both at the time in which he lived and for its ancient history and beliefs. We had rich and wonderful source material to work with when preparing the exhibition, a story full of endless fascination that we were eager to share with the Castle's visitors.

Finally ready to unveil this new project in July 2009, I gave the Egyptian Ambassador and my husband a little hammer each. A paper 'brick wall' was taped in front of the cellar entrance and, with much laughter, each man carefully tapped a hole into this then pulled aside the paper and climbed down into the exhibition area, followed by the assembled press and friends.

Whilst we had to go to the bank to borrow the money to undertake the Egyptian endeavour, it paid dividends in so many ways. It is Highclere's story, it is the story of treasure and tragedy, it is an inspirational part of school curricula in this country and others, and an important landmark in archaeology, which inspires people of all ages to take an interest in ancient Egypt. In terms of its benefit to Highclere, of the visitors who come to the Castle, 60 per cent are able to go down to 'Egypt' on the busier public opening days and 100 per cent on the guided tours, so it has proved to be a very popular add-on to the normal Castle visit.

SEPTEMBER: WHAT IT TAKES

It seemed sensible to write a book about our exhibition and the story behind it. Wondering where to start, I was pottering in a bookshop one day waiting to collect my son from school when I found an attractive square-format book. It was about something entirely different but I liked the shape. For one thing, it was not too big and that filled me with hope we might be able to pull off this project. I wrote an outline for the book, and then the text and captions, collecting up old photographs from the archives and persuading Geordie to be in-house photographer as every artefact we had needed to be photographed and reproduced. In the meantime, Duncan, our computer support and graphics expert, turned his hand to design and layout. We sent it off to the printers in Twickenham whom we still use today – the public's fascination with Egypt seemingly never dies. Our hope remains that the Highclere exhibition will act as a portal, encouraging Egyptian tourism, the study of Egyptology, and imaginative engagement with an extraordinary story.

After we had opened the Egyptian exhibition and begun to engage with a marketing strategy ranging from schools to those who love to travel, we became aware that *Downton Abbey* was now beginning to dominate not just the television schedules but all our marketing efforts. At this point therefore we decided to sit quietly on our 'cellar' achievement which, in the meantime, continued to give many visitors much pleasure and would go on to become a focus of interest at Highclere once more in 2022, that being the centenary of the discovery of the tomb.

Another venture came to mind after visiting a literary festival at Blenheim, where I noticed a sign for afternoon teas that directed people upstairs for a seated experience.

As in other hospitality or retail businesses, it is harder to use upstairs space well than more accessible ground-level areas, but I realised that the upstairs space in the coach house, only recently converted from a barrel store, would be the perfect place to offer a Champagne afternoon tea served by Luis and his team. Highclere was one of the first heritage houses to sell barcoded tickets online, and extras such as afternoon tea were an obvious way to add value to the standard ticket purchase.

We needed to create a point of sale on our ticket website, put together menus, choose some oak tables and nice chairs, and then decorate the new venue *à la* Downton. Sadly, since Brexit we have had to curtail our diary for these afternoon teas somewhat as there are fewer students from Europe looking for work, which makes it harder always to staff our hospitality business to the standard we require. British students study for exams in the spring and early summer and are therefore not usually available to work here until mid-July. In the past, this employment gap was often filled by those from Europe wishing to study the language and earn some money. Nevertheless, afternoon tea remains tremendously popular and, at Christmas time, is always the first event to sell out.

By this time, the business of running Highclere was progressing well, but we were still looking for the idea that would attract – shall we say? – compound interest.

Looking back over the different things that we've done here, it does seem that so many key meetings leading to continuing relationships and mutually beneficial business have happened curiously by chance. There is a balance to be maintained between, on the one hand, taking a real risk, and on the other, stepping just outside the usual comfort zone, which can lead to new paths and add much-needed diversity to a business. None of us should ever stop learning. Things can go wrong when you try something new but usually not everything, and that lends an element of future-proofing.

One such new path began when Geordie escaped from his office and came downstairs to find me standing in the courtyard, needing a morning coffee. He told me that the office had forwarded a random email from someone in America who was interested in creating a whisky with us: they had distilling and distribution experience. Our brand was clearly evolving internationally.

Geordie thought he would ring the contact and follow up. Shortly thereafter he told me he'd suggested Adam von Gootkin should come over and we'd talk it all through. Adam and his wife Regina duly flew in from Boston, though they live in Connecticut, and drove themselves down from Heathrow to Highclere.

Adam explained that he had a family distilling business on the East Coast that dated back to the mid-1800s and which had managed to prosper throughout New England during Prohibition. He had revived the distillery brand as Onyx Spirits Company, producing an award-winning New England-style whiskey – as it is known in the United States – called Secret Stash. Now he wanted to build out a new brand and felt there was a real opportunity to develop a spirit around Highclere Castle, its USP and heritage.

Having discovered we could work together, the first idea was to consider creating a whisky. Highclere's malting barley is already bought by Scottish distilleries and so we could give some useful input there. Geordie and Adam, the tasters, and Regina, the driver, set off to visit a number of distilleries based around Edinburgh.

However, on their return, we sat down to plan an entirely different project, which needed much more research and then a financial structure. We decided that our new project should be to distil the best gin in the world: a fresh, distinctive, very English spirit based on our national heritage, and also taking advantage of the brand recognition of Highclere throughout the world. The global market for premium spirits at present is driven by a taste for uniqueness and authenticity, with consumers choosing to drink fewer, better-quality alcoholic beverages.

The oldest gin distillery in this country lies outside Birmingham – once more, an old family business – with the oldest still in England operating inside the factory. Gin is about heritage, style and taste. Beginning with the wheat-based spirit (and we grow wheat), gin draws on juniper for its distinctive taste and the derivation of its name. Gin became popular in England after the introduction of 'jenever', a Dutch and Belgian liquor, became widespread after the Glorious Revolution when William of Orange, a Prince of Holland, became King of England. Over the next fifty years there was a gin craze, which only diminished after the Gin Act of 1751 introduced draconian measures restricting its sale to merchants who paid rent and taxes. Apothecaries then saw their chance and dispensed juniper tonics and wines, which were popular cure-all remedies for coughs, colds, pains, strains, ruptures and cramps, but ended up being a little too popular and were consumed recreationally rather than for medicinal purposes.

Dutch gin was used by English soldiers for its calming effects before battle, hence the expression 'Dutch courage', and for its purported warming properties in cold weather. In the 1870s, Schweppes gave a boost to gin sales by inventing Indian Tonic Water, which included a prescribed dose of quinine to fight malaria. The drink went on to become an intrinsic part of British culture. A gin and Dubonnet cocktail was the drink of choice of the late Queen and Queen Mother alike.

Our goal was to distil a London Dry gin, which is a mark of quality control as well as a process. It creates a totally neutral base, which is then redistilled with juniper. We decided to pare back the juniper whilst adding other botanicals inspired by or from Highclere. (All botanical flavours in a London Dry must be imparted through distillation.)

For many centuries we have grown tiny oranges in the orangery by the Monks' Garden, as well as lemons and lavender by the old Georgian garden walls. To that mix we then added lime flowers as well as cardamon. In fact, there are eight botanicals in all and it took nine months of tasting and rebalancing before we got it right. We would open the latest version, pour out a small amount and slowly smell it, inhale it and, without haste, taste it. Then we would try it over a little ice. Impatient to begin marketing, Adam finally thought it was there, but Geordie and I were convinced it still had a slightly sharp aftertaste. Working with the distillery, Geordie added a few rolled oats from the farm as he and the distillers had heard this might work. It did, creating a wonderful creamy aftertaste and one of the smoothest premium gins on the market.

Choosing a bottle design was an equally detailed process. Adam had alighted on the distilling heritage of the Bishops of Winchester at Highclere. The colour purple is associated with the Church so we decided to include it. Then we thought about form. The Castle towers are square and so the bottle echoes that; the colour silver is used to create the Castle's outline and the story on the label. Adam's pièce de résistance was to create the barcode in the shape of the Castle.

We threw a wonderful purple party at Highclere in the autumn of 2019 to launch our gin, but only a few months later Covid changed everything. All of our gin team had put their lives, resources, finance and passion into the project, but the entire world had to change gear as each person and society stumbled through the crisis as best they could. Confined to home, everyone bought familiar brands and we were not familiar – yet. We were at disaster point and near failure before we had really even begun. On the positive side, we all learn faster by navigating the high seas compared to times of plain sailing.

In order to market our new venture, the American team suggested we enter into the virtual world: we should curate a virtual cocktail party. We agreed that 9 p.m. on a Friday evening would work well and that we would go live to host the cocktail party on both Instagram and Facebook. We had no idea what we were doing as we had never tried anything quite like this. However, we had two cocktails at the ready and a story to talk about. A small team had 'bubbled' with us during Covid times, consisting of Hannah who was on the laptop, Cat and Charlotte who were using mobile phones for cameras which were seemingly upside down, and Paul Mac who held up signs to count down the time. (Unfortunately, he got muddled as to whether he was counting up or down.)

Before April 2020, I was excellent at ordering a cocktail from a menu, but now I needed both to research and make them. I was drawn especially by their names: The Aviator, The Bee's Knees, The English Garden, The Bronx or The Hanky Panky. Some such as a Negroni or Martini were much easier for a 'novice' to make and both highlighted the smoothness of Highclere Castle Gin. Later on, Luis, thank goodness, returned to our aid as he is a master mixologist and a great gin storyteller, explaining the cocktails with enthusiasm and style. It was a fascinating window into the best cocktail bars, famous bartenders and references to the silver screen, from *The Great Gatsby* to James Bond.

Every other Friday we would find a different place in the Castle to hold our latest cocktail party, with supplies of two or three different cocktails and usually some of the Labradors in attendance. In July 2020, we were more ambitious. We were now allowed outside as long as there were no more than two or three couples present, and my Arab pony Phoebe elegantly picked her way around a table and past a drinks table to sample some fruit for the cocktails. Miraculously, she arrived on-set, helped herself to a few berries, didn't knock anything over and then gently stepped away, thus triumphantly ending our final virtual-cocktail episode of 2020, which was watched by 80,000 people. We achieved fame in the pages of *People* magazine as a result. Today, people still come up and say they enjoyed dressing up for their evenings with us, even though we were several thousand miles apart. From time to time, we continue to stream live in order to mark special occasions, with dogs, a Shetland pony or Father Christmas, depending on the time of year.

Highclere Castle Gin is the first gin to earn a perfect score of 100 points from the Major League Spirits Association and has received over 200 gold and platinum awards – we believe we have created one of the best gins in the world. Whilst there are many successful businessmen who set great store by being the best, I have simply found that passion and common sense, civility and hard work, usually lead to things working out. I think that over the following two years we could claim that Highclere Castle Gin became a geometric revenue endeavour. The distilling trade has its own specific problems but creating a new brand of alcohol is about keeping calm and carrying on in unity – and never giving up.

Highclere Castle Gin is now sold in twenty-two states in the USA and will soon be in Canada as well as having a growing presence in Europe. The joy of this project for us is that it has been a journey integrating so many Highclere products: citrus, lavender and oats. Alcoholic spirit, like our food, comes from the land and there is something almost sacred about creating a spirit from the terroir of Highclere and then sharing this with our great friends from Connecticut, who have been the energetic force behind the whole idea and understand how to use modern distribution and marketing techniques to sell a brand based around an ancient place.

Remembering London in February 2020, it now seems almost like another world. I had been invited to an exhibition about ancient Egypt at the Saatchi Gallery by Sloane Square. It was, as ever, magical to be looking at extraordinary works of art from an ancient civilisation, and it was a peaceful and enjoyable interlude. I was then asked if I would like to go and sit in a chair and have a virtual-reality experience. Whilst I thought 'not really', out of politeness I said, 'Yes, that would be very kind,' and went upstairs to sit down and put on a VR headset for five minutes. Virtually experiencing the desert and the approach to the tombs where the exhibits were found was just fantastic and, ironically, the thing I remember most clearly about the exhibition. It stayed with me but the world then somersaulted into Covid and other things took priority. Every business went into survival mode, focusing on how it could re-invent or translate its enterprises to deal with this new remote or online-only world. Highclere is built on heritage and hospitality and, like every other such business, it had to close. Covid created an immediate crisis in terms of emotional as well as financial cost and not every business survived the impact of zero cash flow and the consequent inability to refinance at speed.

The pandemic brought into focus what really mattered to all of us, and friendship and togetherness would probably have been top of the list for most people. After being brought up on A. A. Milne's books about Winnie the Pooh, many of his thoughts were uppermost, such as 'A day without a friend is like a pot without a single drop of honey left inside', which is so well put, whilst 'A friend is someone who helps you up when you're down, and if they can't, they lay down beside you and listen' is another of my favourites.

Today's more earnest advisers might consider that friendships provide us with many mental, social and health benefits, which, combined with the sense of welcoming guests into my home, of sharing, of the sense of looking for sunshine, hugs and laughter, I decided could be built on to create something called Friends of Highclere. Most of us are curious about how others live and therefore going behind the scenes and through the doors that say 'No Access' or 'Private' is just fun.

By chance I had met some photographers and video-makers who had just acquired a 360-degree camera, which can record an entire scene in every direction via multiple overlapping fisheye lenses. The resulting video is then viewed via a virtual-reality (VR) headset. Undoubtedly specialist, they generate a large amount of data, which then takes significant time to develop. Learning to film and present with a 360-degree camera is different. You cannot edit or join things together; each video is just one take and everyone else apart from me has to hide. Plus, of course, the camera can see everywhere. Sometimes there would be squawks as Hannah G was hiding behind a flowerbed and found nettles, or one of the Highclere team pottered into view, and we had to start all over again. The result offers time out to enjoy the music room, for example, with its beautiful painted ceiling, or to wind your way upstairs to the old maids' rooms – magical spaces that are otherwise hard to share with people given how remote they are from the main rooms of the Castle. Not everyone will wish to put on a VR headset, of course, so we filmed 2D videos as well.

A new website was needed and from the start it was subscription-only. It is all about staying in touch and so Friends on Friday came into being as a catch-up, streamed from a different room every week. Book Club happens once every month and is both streamed or Friends are welcome here, in person, as my friend for free – hopefully, they will share some Champagne with me and something to eat. We invite some wonderful authors into the library, sitting with me on the famous red sofas and usually competing for space with one or two Labradors.

If Book Club is both streamed and real, then the garden parties, Christmas parties and afternoon tea in the dining room only happen 'in the flesh', so to speak, bringing friends together in reality. The heart of Highclere is about community and the heart of Friends is the same.

Whether you're a Friend of Highclere or an admirer of *Downton Abbey* or Highclere Castle, the library is always a favourite room – 6,500 books ranging from histories, novels, poetry, travel books, atlases, Bibles, biographies, books about botany or architecture, collections of speeches by the 4th Earl of Carnarvon plus some books that I myself have written rather more recently.

Whilst *Downton* sallied forth globally, there was no further direct financial advantage for Highclere so we needed to work quite hard ourselves in order to try and associate *Downton* with Highclere in public perception. I thought therefore I would write a book – apparently there's one in each of us.

In return for helping Peter Fincham with an episode of ITV's *Countrywise* about the real Downton Abbey, he kindly introduced me to some publishers, one of whom sent me a bunch of flowers so I chose them. With a little research assistance from my husband, I wrote in short order a book called *Lady Almina and the Real Downton Abbey*, based on the life and achievements of the 5th Countess of Carnarvon.

Almina's story was extraordinary: her guiding ethos was to help others. The way she welcomed grievously unwell strangers into her home to make them better, saved their lives and helped their families throughout the First World War, has always resonated with me. She found her passion and vocation at a time when most ladies neither needed nor sought such things. Characterised by determination and courage, she illustrated what we each and all can do. Compared to what was possible in medicine in her time, and the appalling horrors of the trenches in the First World War, many of today's problems are much more easily solved. Almina had a passion for being the best, both as a leading nurse and a hospital administrator, and was a fine example of a strong and effective leader in her chosen field.

Thus my writing career began. Unexpectedly, *Lady Almina* did very well both here and in the USA. I think it might even be another example of geometric success. Further books followed about Highclere in the Second World War and a coffee-table book *At Home at Highclere* that gave a sense of what it is like to entertain here. Everyone who comes here, eats here; cooking is at the heart of life and rarely do I go by the kitchens without popping in to pass the time of day and find out what's going on, so *Christmas at Highclere* and *Seasons at Highclere* followed, with recipes and photographs that conveyed the beauty of the seasons. I then embarked on *The Earl and the Pharaoh*, thereby returning to the most famous of Highclere's Earls.

From panicked first-time writer to established author has been an unexpected journey for me, and the work is very different from my original training as a chartered accountant. Writing a book is a process, the publication of each marking the culmination of capturing different places and times and distilling them into a readable 'story', without ever losing touch with the truth. Nevertheless, it is very hard to make a living as an author so it remains only a part-time occupation for me, though one I love.

I think of *Lady Almina* and my succeeding volumes as evergreen books, offering me and those who choose to buy them an insight into inspirational real-life stories. Their themes of history, teamwork, leadership and change have led me on another career path: as a speaker for various organisations, both in the UK and globally.

Every week I write a blog, musing on a subject, comical or thoughtful, and every day is another opportunity for an Instagram post, an immediate way of sharing. This is a frequent cause of hilarity for Geordie and my sisters as my photography used to be so hopeless and I still like an ink pen, but at least it is all authentic. We also share a story on Facebook every day. Whenever we're asked, we reply to press and media queries, whilst a large charity event or the publication of a new book means there will be a flurry of press releases to approve. As an ongoing process we are continually seeking out new collaborations with like-minded partners who share similar values to ours because they make both parties stronger.

The founder and chairman of Viking Cruises, Torstein Hagen is a wise and valued friend who advocates expeditious decision-making – delays should be considered a waste of time and opportunity. In his business as in ours the implicit offer is of time out in a different world.

Geordie and I begin our office work every morning by reviewing data as Torstein has advised us, working out what it is telling us and what can we do better. We divide the estate up into two spheres of influence – he concentrates more on the finances, farm and higher-level challenges, whilst I deal with day-to-day life at the Castle, the forthcoming events and the marketing. Mostly it works, maybe because fundamentally we are a team. After several decades together, Highclere is not only surviving but has won its place in a global arena – in itself a real achievement.

CHAPTER TEN

October: Entertaining Royally

'But let us not take ourselves too seriously. None of us has a monopoly of wisdom and we must always be ready to listen and respect other points of view'

— Christmas broadcast 1991, Queen Elizabeth II

'Darling, she's accepted!' Geordie said, walking hastily towards me.

'Who?' I replied.

'The Queen!'

'Golly, crikey – what an honour!' My head immediately started spinning, mainly in panic.

My father-in-law, who sadly and very suddenly died in September 2001, had been a longstanding friend of Her Majesty. Since the 1970s the spring weekend visits to Porchey, as the 7th Earl was known, at his house on Milford Lake at the north end of the estate, were a world and time apart for the late Queen, who took the opportunity to see his thoroughbreds as well as her own horses at her stud by Kingsclere. Porchey and the late Queen shared a deep knowledge and love of thoroughbred horses and racing. From studying bloodlines to carefully looking over the strength and power of a stallion in his paddock, or watching a favourite broodmare, foal at foot, swinging through a grassy enclosure, head down to graze, or observing the promising adolescent yearlings – every detail was fascinating to them both. The late Queen simply admired and knew all horses. She rode out for over ninety years, from her first forays on a small Shetland pony to riding the superlative Burmese at Trooping the Colour, and later in life enjoyed her fell pony Emma. There is something about the rhythm and connections with a horse, looking over its ears, feeling its stride, which provides a calm, contemplative time out for both human and animal.

As my parents-in-law never actually lived in the Castle, by the time the 7th Earl died in 2001 it had not welcomed guests to stay for at least twenty years. In the meantime, the bedrooms, bathrooms, gallery and corridors had slipped into a state of rather faded grandeur. Geordie and his siblings grew up at Milford Lake House and it was here that their guests were entertained. During a house party with friends or hosting a game shoot in the autumn or winter, they would often have lunch at the Castle but would otherwise return to Milford for the remainder of the weekend.

Geordie's grandfather, the 6th Earl of Carnarvon, did live in the Castle, remaining there until his death at nearly ninety years old in 1987. However, he had been living more frugally over time and, in his later years, used confined and somewhat darkened rooms, with only a housekeeper and cook for company. There had been no significant investment in the material of the building for decades and repairs and maintenance were largely a matter of make do and mend. Friends who had been guests during that time would relate stories of cold, dimly lit state rooms counterbalanced by good food and wine, then having to set off after dinner to find dark, slightly spooky bedrooms with the aid of torches.

A year or so after Geordie's grandfather's death, the Castle was opened to the public for the first time and began a new life as part of Britain's heritage and tourist industry.

But even with their new role of welcoming visitors, my parents-in-law remained at Milford and running Highclere Stud, with great success. The sale money from winning fillies such as Lyric Fantasy could then be invested into re-facing the stonework of the eastern aspect of the Castle, for example.

Since no one was living there, the top floors of the Castle were closed off and the electricity supply cut for safety. The rooms in the tower were rarely entered and the main interest was naturally focused on the state rooms on the ground floor, whilst a few displays about past visitors or historic heritage were created in what were once bedrooms leading off the gallery. Many others were left shut up with dusty uncovered furniture piled randomly inside.

As ever, visitors enjoyed Highclere's architectural splendour, but the Castle's business began to concentrate more on weddings and corporate events, especially in the grounds. No one ever stayed in the building as the heating, hot water and fundamental comforts we've all become accustomed to barely existed there.

Geordie and I, however, felt Highclere was not a museum but a home. In 2003, we decided to open the Castle at Christmas to host a family party. My sisters and I had enjoyed many draughty Cornish winter holidays so I knew they would be happy to layer up, muck in and fill the place with laughter, despite the quirks and complications of staying in what was essentially a deserted building at this point.

Upside-down sofas were removed from bedrooms, mattresses — such as they were — turned and aired, and sheets and blankets found or ordered. Rooms were furnished with chests of drawers, armchairs and 'gentlemen's presses' – enormous wardrobes with hanging space and drawers. We hunted out mirrors, dressing tables and bedside lamps, most of which subsequently needed rewiring. The china cupboards provided decorative pieces to place on mantelshelves and I liberally piled books in every room. I also bought radios so people could at least hear the news as there certainly wasn't a television. Gradually, the clutter which should not have been present was replaced with the usual clutter of an English country home, albeit on a slightly larger scale than most.

There was no heating upstairs so we bought a number of white panel radiators for the bedrooms – far from chic but practical as they could sit in the fireplaces.

During their stay and over consecutive breakfasts, the 'complaints department' (myself and a rather long-suffering Geordie) opened up to listen to our free-speaking guests and family, and a rather long snagging list of items that needed replacement was created. This ranged from relatively easily resolved problems, such as saggy bumpy mattresses and disintegrating sheets, to rather larger and more expensive-to-solve issues, such as not enough hot water or light. Everyone was most informative and helpful with their comments and suggestions.

In a house the size of Highclere there is a strong visual relationship between architecture and landscape on the one hand and internal layout and decoration on the other. English country houses have a reputation for being a little fusty and faded, with their wealth of paintings and furniture positioned for life rather than the current aesthetic or fashion. They can be surprisingly eccentric, though today this approach would probably be classed as 'bohemian' or maybe 'heirloom chic' if it feels particularly battered, although they probably do not consciously try to be either. The photographer Cecil Beaton observed that the English country-house style had a 'healthy disregard for the sanctity of important pieces', in contrast for example to the French style, which tends to be more formal and symmetrically arranged. English informality and its apparent lack of order creates a more relaxed, lived-in feel where rooms show the patina of life and that their inhabitants enjoy living in them.

Highclere's state rooms lacked the usual clutter – photographs, cushions, throws and suchlike that create comfy corners to curl into with a book or shared crossword. There were few rugs, no lampshades, just plenty of bare bulbs supported by beautiful ceramics and pieces of sculpture. There were exceptional paintings downstairs but none to speak of upstairs. Rare antiques and mis-chiming clocks in the state rooms left it feeling empty and austere, with few personal flourishes. There was also a noticeable lack of the noise associated with everyday family life.

Nancy Mitford expressed her famous dictum that 'all nice rooms are a bit shabby', but there was not enough content for it even to be that. I remember an art expert sitting down with me and explaining that in a 'proper' stately home the paintings would be stacked on the walls two or three high to the ceiling whilst at Highclere our collection was 'a little sparse'. He was right. Rather too much had been sold after each war, more out of necessity than desire. Nevertheless, his words hit home and made me feel a little disconsolate and somewhat overwhelmed by the challenges of bringing back to life such a large house.

Given the pending Royal visit and my lacklustre post-Christmas family feedback, I did feel somewhat daunted. We only had nine months to prepare for the Royal weekend in early October, which sounds like a long time but was very short in terms of the sheer quantity of work that needed doing.

Luckily, I also knew just the person to call. Sarah Morris is a longstanding and unflappable friend who, fortunately for me, is also an experienced and much-sought-after interior decorator. She had established her business McWhirter Morris after working at Colefax and Fowler for twenty years. When I explained my predicament, she informed me there was no time to waste. She would be driving straight down as I needed help urgently – and she was absolutely right.

Geordie was more relaxed. The Queen was his godmother, and he'd had the honour of spending high days and holidays at various Royal estates with his parents and siblings. The sense of make do and mend and 'never complain, never explain' was inherent there. Why should we be worried?

Nevertheless, the Queen's acceptance was a huge honour, and I felt I must do what I could to make everything seem more practically habitable and a little less faded.

Sarah duly arrived with her assistant to begin making plans. The starting point was to refurbish the bedrooms and bathrooms that would be used by the Queen and the Duke of Edinburgh. We thought that Herbert and Arundel bedrooms would create an appropriate suite of rooms for the Royal party, but that their existing colour scheme of shiny avocado green and cream left something to be desired.

In fact, there was nothing in Herbert bedroom that was not painted a sludgy green; it covered the walls, fireplace, ceiling, skirting boards, coving and doors. Meanwhile in Arundel, the shiny cream paint was peeling, and a large watercolour map was propped up behind cracked glass on the far side of the bed.

The 6th Earl had separated from his second wife Tilly Losch after the end of the Second World War and since then the task of redecorating had been left to his land agent. Castle bedrooms and corridors were painted in rotation every few years post-war, and the least expensive paints available in any quantity tended to be either shiny cream or avocado green. The land agent simply looked at the cost, went for the cheapest option and bought in bulk. Unfortunately, this method of 'decorating', and I use that word lightly, continued for the next forty years.

The Highclere decorating team comprised Pat and Mike Withers with their sprightly assistant 'Young Richard'. They had dutifully repainted the gallery and bedrooms and had an encyclopaedic knowledge of previous decorating iterations, as well as numerous stories of life in the Castle with the 6th Earl. I immediately called them to see if they would be willing to return and help us renew and renovate a series of rooms and corridors in very short order, the incentive being that at least the colour palette would be rather more imaginative this time.

They rapidly got the measure of Sarah, forming a determined and strong partnership with her to get the job done. Technical knowledge and knowhow matched with Sarah's experienced eye began to breathe new life into beautiful but long-neglected rooms. Sarah has such an infectious laugh and soon the whole Highclere team was working together willingly to get the place ready.

With her oversight, planning, experience and inherent good taste, she sent detailed colour boards and fabric treatments for me to consider. For any decorating scheme in a building like the Castle, there is always a balance that needs to be struck between paying homage to the architectural intent, noting my predecessors' preferences garnered from stripping back the subsequent layers of paint to the original scheme, considering what visitors might think, and last, but hopefully sometimes not least, my own preferences. I spent many quiet moments wandering around the main rooms to gain a sense of the hierarchy of the spaces, of how the rooms might originally have looked and been historically arranged. Old photographs were eagerly examined but we were not trying to reconstruct the past.

Ceilings were painted a flat white, the rolls an alternate off-white, and the mouldings and covings further different shades of off-white. The flat face of the skirtings was to be mousy brown, the profile or moulded part would match the other woodwork, whilst that may well be painted in yet another off-white. In Stanhope dressing room alone, we counted no fewer than seven off-whites. I had read that John Fowler, doyen of English interior decorating for whom Sarah originally worked, had a three-off-white system, but in some rooms Sarah was surpassing herself. The variation added depth and texture, light and warmth, to otherwise large and rather austere spaces.

Throughout the Castle, the Charles Barry linenfold doors and the architraves would have their own signature scheme: Sanderson Spectrum Neutral and Neutral Light. Twenty years later, Pat and I can still never remember which way round they are applied.

For Herbert bedroom, Sarah suggested stippled and dragged marmalade-coloured walls, deep-cream textured curtains generously edged in a wide old-fashioned moss-coloured velvet with deeply fringed pelmets above, and a half-tester for above the bed. I cannot quite remember whether I ran it past Geordie but, in any case, he loves marmalade – albeit on toast. Team Withers cross-lined the room and applied the base paint, after which a specialist arrived to marble the mixed shades of marmalade, all of which took several days to apply. I love it.

Herbert is one of only three bedrooms on this floor with an en suite bathroom. The bathrooms each occupy corner towers of the Castle and have views across the park from their three windows. We therefore chose a gentle green for the walls with golden honey-coloured curtains to create a peaceful sanctuary in which to enjoy a luxurious bath. All the bathrooms have large Victorian baths with old-fashioned plungers that turn to release the water. They are amazingly deep and can take quite a while to fill, but fortunately there was now no shortage of hot water. However, there are no showers in the Castle. I had mistakenly bought rubber-hosed shower attachments (a legacy of childhood holidays) to have a means of washing my hair in the bath, but had not checked into the technicalities of Victorian plumbing. I soon realised that an honest plastic jug would be the ultimate solution to this dilemma.

Carpet in bathrooms is not a fashionable choice nowadays. However, I find the comfort of emerging from a deep scented bubble bath onto a thick towelling bathmat with a soft carpet underfoot works well in the Castle. The Victorian heated towel rails, innovative at the time, still work admirably well and can hold large warm fluffy bath towels.

Arundel bedroom had a charming portrait of a girl in a white corseted dress with pink ribbons, and this soft, pretty portrait of Rebecca, Lady Abergavenny, led us to use warm pink colours in this more north-facing room. However, finding the right pink was a little challenging. As is the tried and tested way, multiple tester pots from many paint suppliers were painted in splodges around the walls to view in different lights at various times of the day. The dressing room, by contrast, was wallpapered in a stripe. All the curtains were in reasonable condition and the beautiful, handstitched quilted bedspread was still, after a clean, in remarkably good order considering its age.

At that time I started reading archive records about Almina Carnarvon. She too had welcomed a Royal visit to Highclere in 1895 and at the time had been just nineteen years old. To my surprise, it seemed she had concentrated much of her energies on the practical side of life in the Castle: putting in electricity and updating the plumbing. I had always thought choosing fabrics and colours would be the more appealing side of renovating a property, but of course now I realised that I too had to grasp the underlying needs of the building before concentrating wholly on the look of things. Everything Almina did really stood the test of time, but by now every bedroom and bathroom needed to be rewired and David and Andy the electricians became an indispensable part of the Highclere team. I was soon quite au fait with 3-phase 16-way electric boards, cable runs and final distribution circuits and conduits. David and Andy soon realised plastic light switches were anathema, brass-mounted light switches a must, and we have had many debates over the years about finding good-looking bathroom lights that comply with regulations.

The hot-water boilers in the basement are looked after by Geoff and Mark the plumbers. These substantial pieces of engineering have their own room. Their sheer size and unreliable character fill me with trepidation.

The central bedroom over the front entrance had also joined the to-do list. It had a leaky hand basin, which definitely needed replacing, but I had also gathered that it had been my father-in-law's room in his youth and for that reason alone I felt it needed to be refurbished. It lies centrally off the gallery and Sarah Morris had found a Cole & Son wallpaper, which was subtle but very parliamentarian as befitted a house designed by Charles Barry. I really like wallpapers with original designs, and they are also useful for disguising any lack of paintings. Sarah had cleverly recognised that the curtains in Portico bedroom were a pattern that dated to 1911 and were designed and made by the fabric designers Watts of Westminster. They were so pretty and if re-lined would still be perfectly fine.

After I had bought two large single beds (as they are always useful to have), I discovered that Watts were miraculously able to print ten more metres of matching fabric and thus I had headboards and valances to match. Luckily, my number-three sister, Lucy, makes curtains so she and Sarah began busily ordering the fabric to dress other windows.

There were really no paintings at all left in the bedrooms so Geordie had the task of buying framed landscapes in different shapes and sizes. He also had to buy carpet runners as there were no rugs anywhere. He would happily peruse catalogues from auction houses at the more affordable end. Lacking much experience at that point in the art of bidding at auction, it was a little chaotic when he bid for one rug but had in fact bought another, or bought one painting not realising it was from a group of ten. Attention to the small print and catalogue details can nevertheless have surprisingly productive consequences.

Not to be left out, I started framing prints and drawings from the archives. It is a wonderful way of sharing what I find so fascinating as well as providing points of interest for visitors. Fortunately, a girlfriend of mine, Anna, who lived nearby, was importing rugs that were not too expensive, so I kept buying a few that I liked each month in different sizes. I thought I could just keep switching them around as necessary until they found a permanent home in one of the bedrooms.

Some of the paintings Geordie bought had moonlit or night-time themes, where I might have hoped for more pastoral light-filled landscapes – some are still propped up in cupboards waiting to find a home. However, undeterred by early teething hiccups over his auction efforts, the search continues and Geordie's acquisitions have improved in variety and with the benefit of his by now more informed and discerning eye. In the meantime, Sarah was also on the lookout for paintings, antique rugs, bookcases, luggage racks and old vases we could use for lamp bases, but she had a more organised approach which involved measuring the space first and buying second.

The tall cedar cupboards in the robing room proved to hold quantities of wire lampshade frames that just needed re-covering in a slubbed silk with some fringing. Each of the candelabra lights in the saloon, dining room and library have between seven and nine arms, all of which needed new candle shades. Another local girlfriend began to make four new shades a week for us. There were about a hundred needed in the first instance, and she felt this was a more manageable way of breaking down the order as well as making the billing slightly more palatable!

Whilst the upstairs bedrooms were proceeding apace, the main state rooms were also in dire need of attention. The central saloon of the Castle has a fifty-foot-high ceiling and is an inspiring and uplifting space. The walls are clothed in exceptional gilded and painted leather hangings which date from 1661, whilst the alcoves above are hung with eighteenth-century tapestries. The rooflights mean that daylight filters into the space throughout the year and the upper gallery from which the main bedrooms lead is framed by pale sandstone Gothic arches that also let in the light.

Despite this, it proved hugely challenging to find a paint colour for the gallery that was both elegant and appropriate to this inspiring space with its frequent changes of light levels. Small areas of paint were applied to various walls but still I could not choose. Each day they looked different. Eventually, I made a decision and ordered fifty litres of paint to begin with. As an afterthought, I showed Geordie the colours and he said he liked most of them but not that one, pointing to a testing patch. That was of course the one I had ordered. I just said, 'Noted – absolutely, darling.' Layers of old paint were removed, walls cross-lined and relined, and woodwork and cornices mended.

The wooden floors of the saloon, polished and back to their best, needed a carpet to complete and complement the grandeur of the space. It had to be very hardwearing and a 'statement piece' as every visitor and guest would enter through the saloon. It also needed to be huge but with no central pattern, and, Sarah advised, have a substantial border, which would make viewing it from the gallery above as much of a pleasure as it was within the room. Geordie's principal requirement for this enormous carpet was that it should please not cost too much.

Through a friend of Lucy's, an Iranian carpet dealer arrived, and with measurements taken and colour palettes discussed, our carpet commission was ordered from India. With exuberant ivory flowerheads, trailing and alternating red and green flowers and leaves, this vegetable-dyed rug exceeded our expectations – it is stunning.

The armchairs in the saloon were a faded pretty peach colour that was not quite strong enough for such an imposing room. They were re-covered and upholstered in ribbed green velvet. Cushions were another challenge as I did not know where to go to find strong fun patterns. I arrived at Sarah's studio with a paltry collection of unsuitable swatches, explaining my unhappiness. She cast an eye over my offerings and said to leave it with her. Curiously, cushions can be remarkably complicated to get right. Never requiring significant volumes of fabric, the trimmings – often more expensive than the fabric – can elevate something so simple into the complete finishing touch.

I have discovered over the years that the house lives and breathes through the seasons with us. Listening to its creaks and sighs, the minute adjustments of floorboards as the house cools in the night hours, the way the catches on some doors take a while to click home, brings the comfort of familiarity. On a quiet evening after the shutters are closed, lights dimmed or turned off, the Castle settles peacefully as do we, respecting the age and enduring timelessness of this ever-evolving house and home. It feels like a living entity and a touchstone of values, and it is this atmosphere more than any decorating style that matters to me most.

Before the Royal visit, however, every day counted if we were to renew the old colossus in time for the Queen's arrival. Taking too long to make decisions would not help. We needed to keep going.

In the dining room, looking at the portraits of family and guests who had lived and dined here over the last two or three centuries, it was clear that the frighteningly frail picture wire suspending them from picture rails was damaging the corners of the frames – to say nothing of the notorious instability of this system, which clearly needed our urgent attention. Consulting Les Taylor, our unflappable head of security, who knew everything but was discreet and diplomatic in his advice, I decided to order 100 metres of gold chain and 100 hooks. Les, like everyone else at Highclere, wore many hats and knew an amazing amount of practical detail about the objects in the state rooms. I had learned that he liked to be involved in picture hanging. Pat Withers found a local blacksmith to make the rail hooks, and although I was not going to be able to sort them all out in a day, we made a good start, and the 100 metres of chain was soon diminished.

The same blacksmith was then commissioned to make a triangular hinged frame in order both to hang a lantern to light the red stairs and to be able to swing it sideways when changing the lightbulbs. There were few proper lanterns in our many corridors and being able to see the way is always useful!

In the meantime, there were a few other pressing matters to consider. Who do you ask to stay in a house party with the Queen and Prince Philip? Who do you ask to shoot or to dine during their visit? My mother-in-law must be invited, of course, but thereafter I turned to the one person I knew who could help me decide on the rest, the oracle: Mrs Sutcliffe – Nora.

Mrs Sutcliffe had worked for my father-in-law as his secretary for three decades. Devastated when he died, she kindly agreed to come and work for Geordie and me, helping with cricket, shooting and diaries albeit just part-time. As is often the case at Highclere, I wasn't entirely sure what we might be doing together, but I was sure she should come and be with us, given her long experience of working with Geordie's father.

It seemed she had always typed letters on a typewriter whereas we had moved on to screens, computers and printers. Neatly dressed in skirts, cardigans and sensible shoes, she said she was not sure she could navigate these new-fangled machines and wondered if it might not be better to bring her own typewriter. Following a brief and very courteous debate, Nora finally agreed to try a computer. With huge enthusiasm, I showed her the electronic diary and set up a folder with sub-folders called 'Nora' – a positive starter for ten.

OCTOBER: ENTERTAINING ROYALLY

We already had a printed list of friends and neighbours who could potentially be added to the guest list for the Royal visit and the old methods of leafing through address books and correspondence was briefly reintroduced, to see if anyone should be added. Nora was integral to this. I can still hear her voice or momentary telling silence when I came up with a bright idea, and then the gentle deterrent: 'I think not.'

I had been fortunate enough to meet the Queen before Geordie and I were married. One Friday afternoon he said to me, 'Don't forget, we're going to my parents' for supper. By the way, the Queen is going to be there.' I enquired about the dress code, which was apparently just 'neat and tidy'. Recollections of my schooldays and severe headmistresses scolding us to pull up our socks or tie back our hair filled my mind. Geordie reminded me that the Queen would speak first, and one would then acknowledge her with 'Your Majesty' before curtseying. Thereafter, she should be addressed as 'ma'am' – rhymes with 'spam'. As so often, I had no further time to think or worry. It was both extraordinary and simple, just the five of us there and everything very cosy and relaxed. The Queen was wearing a cardigan over a pleated skirt and her voice sounded so oddly familiar. Of course, the main topic of conversation was horses. Luckily, I had ridden all my life and had in fact ridden out a few times in the early morning for Nick Gaselee in Lambourn, so had some experience of the world of racing, but I followed jump racing rather than flat. Nevertheless, I listened and enjoyed being part of this rather special gathering and the evening was certainly convivial.

I had not really expected the tables to be turned so quickly – my father-in-law having died so suddenly and relatively young – and if I thought too much it all seemed rather surreal to be welcoming the Queen and the Duke of Edinburgh myself.

The next element of the weekend planning was to finalise the invitations. Following suggestions from my husband, Nora and I wrote to ask friends to stay, or to join us for dinner, for the game shooting or for Sunday lunch. There would also be a policeman staying inside the Castle, another in the flat at the rear, whilst presumably others would be discreetly secreted in the general environs, although the details would thankfully not be for us to worry about. The Queen's dresser, Angela Kelly, would stay in a room on the same floor as her, and my brother and sister-in-law were asked to join the party, along with local friends of the Queen and Prince Philip. The Duke and Duchess of Wellington were asked for Friday night and Colonel and Mrs (Jean) Gerard Leigh for Saturday night. As a note of interest, it was Jean who was photographed as 'Pam', the fictional girlfriend of the 'Man Who Never Was', as part of the deception in Operation Mincemeat during the Second World War. There were also Lord and Lady Ashburton plus other friends I had met either whilst staying with the Queen and Prince Philip or who had been invited in the past by my parents-in-law. I asked my sister Lucy to come and be my right hand and invited a friend of my son Edward's to keep him company as I would not be able to entertain him so readily – Vivi was of a similar age, in his form at school, and the daughter of one of my girlfriends.

Nora's perfect letters were dispatched, phone calls made, and times and dress code for dinner confirmed: long for the ladies and black tie for gentlemen. Strictly speaking, only the host could wear a smoking jacket as he was in his own home. Every detail, including all the guest lists, was relayed to Buckingham Palace.

I had often studied the photos and accounts book from the 1895 Royal visit. Coincidentally, the Lord Ashburton of that era had been included in the visit and official photograph, and now I was asking the current Lord Ashburton. When my predecessor Almina needed to plan a similar weekend's entertainment in 1895, her father Alfred de Rothschild helped her employ the best chefs from the Savoy Hotel in London to create the finest possible dishes. He also produced an orchestra for one evening and magicians and entertainments for another. Flowers from the fashionable florist Veitch filled the house and supplementary furniture and rugs arrived in quantity. The drawing room had been specially refurbished: the walls were lined in turquoise-green silk from France, emulating the Dauphin's room in Versailles, and the bedroom designated for the Prince of Wales (later Edward VII) was lined with deep red silk.

In 1895, the Castle had some basic heating: fourteen radiators had been installed in some of the major rooms by the 4th Earl, Almina's father-in-law, whom she never met. Following the desire for modernity embraced by her own father, she undertook to update all the plumbing and to wire the Castle, bringing electricity in for the first time from a new battery house just off to the west of the building. The nineteenth century was a period of rapid technological change and there were many practical advantages to electric lighting, not least of which that it did not produce the unpleasant and damaging fumes oil lamps did and was far safer than a naked flame in regard to fire hazards.

Alfred de Rothschild had been one of the first owners to instal a proper heating system and electric lighting at Halton House, but it was a 'new build' and thus could be well planned from the start rather than having to adapt an ancient house to accept new technology. Highclere was a far larger undertaking, but again thanks to her father, Almina had experienced engineers and workers to hand. She also introduced a state-of-the-art electric bell system to help make the running of the household as efficient as possible, and there was even a version of a speaking tube so that instructions could be relayed directly from the upper floors to the depths below stairs.

It was strange the way my first foray into entertaining Royalty echoed hers, though Almina's efforts between June and December 1895 were on a far grander scale than my own.

—

It was not the first time the Queen had stayed at Highclere. Geordie's aunt Patricia Leatham remembered when the then Princess Elizabeth and her sister Princess Margaret, together with Prince Philip, came to stay at Highclere in the autumn for a weekend shooting party. As her cousin Penelope was ill, Patricia was designated hostess for her uncle the 6th Earl. She was very nervous but the Royals were so nice and appreciative that it all turned out to be great fun. Unfortunately, Saturday was so wet that the shooting was cancelled and they all had to play indoor games instead. There was a lot of Racing Demon at which the princesses were brilliant and so quick – it was impossible to win against them. They also played The Game which is a form of charades. Patricia was a hopeless actress so she found the whole thing complete agony. In the evening, the princesses played the piano and sang; they were so good that Patricia said had circumstances been different, they would easily have made a name for themselves in the world of entertainment. Geordie and I were hoping for better weather this time . . .

Just as in Almina's day, the entire household was thrown into turmoil by the renovations, but here in the twenty-first century we were also trying to cope with our weddings and corporate events bookings as well as summer visitors.

So many hostesses went to so much trouble to make everything just perfect for the Prince of Wales (the future King Edward VII). I remember reading somewhere that Lady Warwick had remarked as he was leaving that she hoped he had found everything to his satisfaction, and that the Prince of Wales had replied that it was all perfectly satisfactory, but there had been no hooks on the doors for his dressing gown. I think she was mortified, and as a nascent hostess I have, since reading this, religiously checked doors for hooks, hangers in cupboards, whether radios work and if lamps have working bulbs.

Any Royal visit is preceded by the arrival of Royal Protection. On this occasion they conferred with Les Taylor. They walked and talked their way around the Castle, making plans. Les was integral to the seamless and discreet security operation, keeping tabs on the officers' numbers and locations so that we could ensure that they were all well fed and watered.

Thanks to this cooperation, we were aware of exactly when the Royal party would be arriving at Highclere, and I followed Geordie out to wait on the drive as they drove through the gates. I clearly remember my nervousness as the large car swept to a standstill on the gravel. The banqueting team were ready to open the car doors and Geordie was soon walking forward to bow and shake hands. I followed, to be greeted warmly and then to curtsey. Having welcomed them, the first order of the day was tea and sandwiches in the library, sitting on the same red sofas that later would become so famous thanks to *Downton Abbey*.

All the room lists were printed out, the outline for the weekend set out and printed for each bedroom, heaters were turned on and shutters closed to keep the warmth in. Plants from Highclere's greenhouses featured in profusion in all the state rooms and on the landings. I had picked flowers to arrange in all the bedrooms and for the dining-room table. All was nearly done, but in checking that everything was perfect, mindful of Lady Warwick, I ran up and down more steps and staircases than ever, never quite allowing for the time it takes to cover all the rooms.

Menu-planning for any dinner party is fundamental but providing a weekend of food and drink for a Royal visit can be more than a little daunting. Sitting down with Chef weeks before the event, we had proposed a series of menus with three rather than five courses, which provided delicious straightforward food (no garlic) that wasn't overly fussy. There needed to be a balance between meat and fish. Dinners tended to be served with few or no potatoes as that made it easier for the butlers of the time, Jose and Colin, to plan how each course was to be served.

Most importantly, we needed to make sure there were good stocks of Dubonnet and gin, which when combined create a beautiful rose-coloured cocktail. Less fashionable today, it is a lightly aromatic drink, made with two parts Dubonnet to one part gin, large chunks of ice and a slice of lemon, and something of a favourite of the late Queen. In the summer of 2022, Highclere sponsored a race at Salisbury Racecourse, which coincidentally was won by an exciting filly owned by Queen Elizabeth. Geordie was delighted to send her the prize of a bottle of the new Highclere Castle Gin and to receive a lovely letter in reply.

Prince Philip always liked a beer so it was essential to have some to hand – his preference was for a pale ale. A drinks table was set up in the saloon before lunch and a second left ready and prepared behind the red sofas in the library for after dinner. Drinks before dinner would be tray-served and included a Highclere cocktail of the evening, as well as the Dubonnet and gin.

Completing the placement for lunches and dinners was like doing a crossword puzzle, and it took many scribbled sheets of A4 paper to ensure that everyone was sitting next to someone different each time. I had found the proper old green-leather table planner for the dining room and carefully cut out some rectangles in white card to slip into it, writing out the names as neatly as possible.

As this was our home, we remained in our usual places. The Queen, as guest of honour, was seated to Geordie's right and Prince Philip to mine. As always, Geordie would turn to speak to the guest on his right and then everyone would follow suit around the table. After the main course he would turn the other way.

After dinner each evening, I would follow the convention of asking the ladies to leave the table and retire, whilst the men remained in the dining room. We then needed two teams to offer coffee, teas and petits fours to each group before all found themselves together once more in the library. The original idea was for the men to be able to chat amongst themselves and smoke cigars but as times have moved on, and smoking no longer takes place in the house, Geordie and I have now moved away from this tradition of separating the sexes immediately after dinner.

The extraordinary long reign of the late Queen is now history but her poise and calm, her quiet authoritative voice and the way she effortlessly commanded global attention, is a legacy that will long be remembered. Looking back, especially now, I recall the extraordinary weekends I spent with the Royal Family in an entirely random, light-filled sequence.

The Friday morning of the first Royal weekend I arranged, for example, I had been in good time to strap Eddie into his car seat and drop him off punctually at primary school. I returned to check and feed his pet rabbits, Cottontail and Daisy, only to find to my horror that both had disappeared, having dug under one corner of their pen. Knowing he'd be absolutely heartbroken and that I would not have time to deal with the subsequent fallout, I thought that the quickest solution would be to set off to our local pet store to see if they had any more-or-less identical-looking rabbits as the ones now missing – the same sex obviously.

Just as I got into the car, I looked out of the window to see one of the rabbits, Cottontail, hopping across the lawn. I rapidly called Geordie to come and help and we gingerly worked our way across the garden to try and corner the rabbit against the wall in the vegetable patch. At the first opportunity, Geordie launched himself into a flying rugby tackle, hands outstretched to grab the rabbit just as it made another dash for freedom. He landed horizontally on the lawn, the rabbit clutched to his chest, whilst I cheered him on. One rabbit was better than none. The pet store could wait until the following week.

Swiftly replacing the rabbit in his pen, we covered over the holes with wide slates and stones, temporarily blocking the escape route, and I then rushed off to do a detailed check on the home team. I had a lovely lady helping me with Edward and his friend over the weekend so that I could concentrate on looking after our guests and my husband.

For all my efforts in advance, of course nothing ever does go quite to plan. Having written and confirmed the Duke and Duchess of Wellington for 7.45 p.m. on the Friday evening, there was no sign of them when the time came. The Queen

OCTOBER: ENTERTAINING ROYALLY

and Prince Philip walked into the drawing room and everyone turned towards them to curtsey or bow. Ten minutes later, still no Duke and Duchess.

Noticing their absence, the Queen turned to me and asked if I had phoned them. I said I had but would try again. There was no answer and everyone was a little anxious. To add to this worry, Lord Huntingdon, who had trained horses for Her Majesty, had not arrived either. Again, I phoned to be met with no answer. Unable to wait any longer, I slipped into the dining room for emergency action with the Highclere team. We took a leaf out of the table, removed three chairs and all the placemats, glasses, napkins and cutlery with some speed and reset the remaining table. Panicking more than a little, I had to change the placement which was now muddled and with uneven numbers. Returning quickly to the drawing room, I then invited the Queen, Prince Philip and the rest of the party through to dine.

After dinner, the gentlemen came into the library promptly. My sister Lucy, standing with me, exclaimed that dinner having been quite so delicious and her stomach being more than full, she was going to 'quietly explode' – an utterance as comical as it was ridiculous, and regretted as soon as it was spoken. Prince Philip promptly seized upon the nonsensical contradiction, taking her to task that nobody ever quietly explodes since explosions are renowned for making noise. Henceforth, she loudly explodes.

The next morning, William (Lord Huntingdon) arrived for the shoot and wandered into the Castle to be met by a volley of questions. It turned out he had quite forgotten dinner and instead eaten fish and chips in the local pub in Kingsclere. The following week he sent me a magnolia tree 'Royal Crown' as an apology, which is planted and doing well on the east lawns.

Edward and his schoolfriend Vivi came out for part of the morning shoot with me. We all stood behind the line of guns in a corner of the dappled brown fields, 'landscape plotted and pieced' in Manley Hopkins's words, in the beautiful clear October sunlight. The Queen was standing with her spaniels a few yards away. Vivi pulled at my sleeve, saying, 'Mummy said the Queen was going to be here today.' Leaning down, I replied, 'She *is* here today – the Queen is just over there,' nodding in her direction. Vivi replied somewhat indignantly, 'That's not the Queen – she's not wearing a crown.' Overhearing, the Queen kindly explained that she didn't wear a crown every day as it got in the way. Vivi was still rather unsure and for a long time was not convinced that Her Majesty had been the real deal. As the drive ended, the Queen's dogs swung into action picking up, before we all stopped for elevenses with plenty of soup and hot sausage rolls.

Saturday evening found me in a quandary – I had chosen not to keep ringing the Wellingtons, thinking that perhaps they might arrive for dinner on the Saturday evening instead. I had arranged two new placements, one including them and one without them (just in case) and had laid the table to include them. They duly arrived promptly at 7.45 p.m. Prince Philip walked into the drawing room, spotted them and said to the room in general how nice it was to see them after all, albeit twenty-four hours later than expected.

By the end of the weekend, everyone involved was rightly immensely proud of their efforts to turn the Castle back into a home and, furthermore, one which had welcomed a Royal party. It didn't quite end there, though. Both the Queen and Prince Philip were kind enough to sign our visitors book, with fairly large and conspicuous signatures. Unfortunately, one of the other, perhaps a little more myopic, guests failed to realise the honour and promptly scrawled his own name in between theirs. As the French would say, '*C'est la vie!*'

—

The Castle has its own personality and, over the years I have lived here, my relationship with it has undoubtedly changed and developed. From time to time, it still seems overwhelming, but I am now more used to the inherent chaos of living in such a large and old building. Highclere is, of course, not wholly Charles Barry nor Victorian. The back is Elizabethan, parts are Georgian, and there are still traces of the original medieval building incorporated into it. Its shape is rather square and masculine, a strong statement, with large rooms that can take bold patterns. It does not suit pretty or fluffy. Whilst the Castle itself needs to feel as if it has a central theme, the many rooms are very varied and speak different 'languages'. The house has different styles of furniture and paintings, which reflect previous generations' tastes and obsessions, from Chinese lacquer furniture, French clocks, Dutch paintings or Italian embroideries. Highclere is first and foremost our home, and we strive to preserve and conserve it so as to share its glories, however imperfect. Slightly shabby can still be chic and most certainly tends to be comfortable, and a little bit of silliness here and there proves it is a home rather than a showcase.

In between entertaining visitors from all over the world and, for the last few years, welcoming television and film crews, Geordie and I continue to host house parties, though most are not nearly so stressful as a Royal visit. Some go smoothly, some less so. Highclere continues to throw out challenges in the form of leaky plumbing or occasional pieces of masonry falling off the roof, but we have come a long way from the early days when a bucket left in the north-east corner of the saloon related to a leak high up in the south-west roof where the lead or slates had worn thin over time.

Animals are unpredictable and many a useful house-party guest has had to don their macs and wellingtons over evening gowns or black tie to help a colicky horse or round up sheep who have got out of the fields. Gates have been inadvertently left locked, forcing guests to climb over them and walk the last mile to the house, a somewhat extreme sport – working for one's supper!

Mobile-phone signals can be patchy at Highclere and there is only one telephone in the central part of the Castle, so alerting us to any delays or complications can be a challenge in itself, but is all part of the fun of living and entertaining here.

As the years go by, we continue to renovate and renew, room by room, corridor by corridor, slowly and incrementally breathing new life into the bones of this old and much-loved house, bringing a little magic and excitement instead of museum-like austerity. In real life, houses like Highclere are never really finished. They are ongoing projects as each generation remodels, rebuilds and repairs; a constant evolution that will hopefully allow them to stand long into the future.

CHAPTER ELEVEN

November: Curses and Ghosts

*'A sad tale's best for winter: I have one
Of sprites and goblins'*
— *The Winter's Tale*, William Shakespeare

Safely tucked away in the bottom of a desk drawer is a battered, thick, typed manuscript. It is the unedited autobiography of the 6th Earl of Carnarvon, written in a different time and with much vivacity and colour. The opening scene, told very much in his own voice, is set in Cairo on 5 April 1923. In it, he describes being woken in his hotel room in the early hours of the night by one of the nurses who was helping his mother tend his desperately ill father. 'Hurry, hurry! I am afraid your father has just passed away. Your mother has just shut his eyes and she would like you to go and say a prayer while his hands are still warm.' He continues: 'Snatching my dressing gown and running a comb through my hair, I picked up my pocket torch and went out into the corridor. Even as I began to walk toward my father's suite, the lights in the passage suddenly went out and the whole hotel was plunged into darkness.' He then had to feel his way along the corridors to his father's room where he found his mother on her knees, crying quietly. It was 2 a.m.

No fewer than three Cairo newspapers recognised the death of the 5th Earl of Carnarvon by publishing a black mourning border all around the front page.

General Allenby, High Commissioner of Egypt at the time, asked the new Lord Carnarvon to call upon him at the Residence at 10 a.m. He said, 'I don't know if you read this morning's papers but they give some prominence to the failure of the electricity supplies during the night. Naturally I made some enquiries which is why I asked the Head of the Cairo Electricity Board to come along to see me.' The story unfolded that the senior duty manager of the board had rung the Head in the middle of the night to report a major power failure throughout the city. He had been unable to locate the cause and noted that the time was 2 a.m. However, five minutes later, to the surprise of all, the street lights went on again. Cairo was divided into four separate power jurisdictions and in each quadrant the story was the same. For just over five minutes, the lights went out before coming on again. The Head of the Electricity Board reported, 'I'm afraid there's no technical explanation whatsoever.' Later, on his return to Highclere, the new Earl found that his father's beloved dog Susie had died at the same time as his father in Cairo.

Another strange coincidence, which added to the general air of mystery, concerned the famous golden mask of the young Pharaoh Tutankhamun. When it was carefully examined some years later, it was found to be of equal density of gold, except at one slightly weaker point on the left cheek, exactly where a mosquito had bitten Lord Carnarvon. The precise cause of death of both Tutankhamun and Lord Carnarvon is not clear. Carnarvon probably died of sepsis brought on by the infected mosquito bite, but both men died suddenly and relatively young.

NOVEMBER: CURSES AND GHOSTS

It did not take long for newspapers around the world to latch on to the idea of a curse. Although Howard Carter tried to refute the claim, even he was not immune from mysterious occurrences. He owned a canary that lived in a cage in his bungalow, built amidst the desolation of the dusty landscape near the Valley of the Kings. This comparatively luxurious accommodation brought much pleasure and enjoyment to the archaeologist and his friends. He used to place the cage outside in order that the little bird might enjoy an airing, but on one occasion, after it had been trilling to its heart's content, it suddenly fell silent. Carter's manservant rushed outside to see what had happened and saw a swaying jet-black cobra in the very act of swallowing its prey. Somehow, it had managed to infiltrate the bars.

The sacred cobra was of course the guardian of the ancient Pharaohs and the news spread like wildfire. A week or two later, the new Lord Carnarvon received a phone call at Highclere. The voice on the line said, 'You won't know me at all, but I'm a spiritualist and worked very closely with your father. In fact, at our séances I acted as his medium.' The lady continued, 'I have to tell you, I had a message from your father two days ago. We had a very long conversation and he asked me to pass on an instruction. It is that on no account whatsoever should you step inside the tomb of Tutankhamun.' She repeated this again and said, 'Your late father asked me to tell you that if you disobey this you will surely die and you will have no children.'

Despite his scepticism, the 6th Earl could not dismiss the matter out of hand. Some weeks later, the same lady called again: 'I hate to disturb you but your father came through again last night. He asked me if I passed on his message and whether you had agreed and whether you had answered both questions in the affirmative. He said that he sent you his love and was glad that everything was going so well for you.' Whilst claiming that he did not believe in superstition, the 6th Earl also stated that he would not enter the tomb for £1 million, remaining true to that promise to the end of his life.

Much of Victorian and Edwardian society had been deeply preoccupied with spiritualism and the study of the occult and this lingered on well into the twentieth century. Séances, mesmerism and clairvoyance were all highly fashionable and frequently practised. Lord Tennyson's poetry reached across the bar and Arthur Conan Doyle and other novelists frightened their audiences with stories that were not easily explainable. Even devoted Anglican Arthur Balfour, who later became prime minister under Edward VII and was a mainstay in British politics for nearly fifty years, was involved in the Society for Psychical Research and served as its president for a time.

One famous society psychic was Cheiro, otherwise known as Count de Hamon. He was consulted by many well-known figures seeking his advice: Dame Nellie Melba, Mark Twain, Oscar Wilde, Lord Kitchener and Joseph Chamberlain, to name but a few. He claimed he had written to Lord Carnarvon asking him to abandon any future involvement in Egypt, but that the 5th Earl had replied that not only would he return there, but there could be no question of his failing to finish what he had begun.

Notwithstanding his alleged refusal to follow Cheiro's advice, the 5th Earl was known to have consulted a clairvoyant called Velma from time to time and apparently saw her shortly before he left England in January 1923. Velma reportedly said she considered he had a fairly long lifeline but that it was thin in the centre and there was an ominous spot, which, given a combination of other circumstances, might indicate death. In addition, there was a spot at the junction of the lines of the heart and Apollo that indicated great peril, although the line of Apollo also predicted glory and success.

The 6th Earl's memoirs also relate a story about Velma and the Duchess of York, later Queen Elizabeth and later still the Queen Mother. Apparently, they met at a charity pageant held at Hatfield House in Hertfordshire. Velma had been provided with a booth in the 'Gypsy encampment' at which the young Duchess arrived, laughing, and agreed to a reading. Velma read her hand commenting on the indications of great capacity for loyalty, affection and clear sense. She continued that there were good omens, and several other features in her hand promising a happy and successful marriage. Furthermore, there would be the arrival of a child who would be worshipped from one end of the Empire to the other; that she would be of great importance to the history of the country and an influence for good – 'the crown of happiness'. Perhaps an unexpected outcome to mull over for a group of young people at a party.

There are additional claims that the 5th Earl's half-brother, Aubrey Herbert, also suffered from King Tut's curse simply by dint of being related to the Egyptologist. Aubrey was a polymath who spoke ten languages, a remarkable man and a hero to many of his generation. However, he was born with a degenerative eye condition and became totally blind later in life. A doctor suggested his rotten, infected teeth were somehow interfering with his vision, so he had every single tooth pulled from his head in an effort to regain his sight. It didn't work. Instead, he died tragically of sepsis as a result of the dental surgery just five months after the death of his supposedly cursed brother. In 1929, Aubrey's younger brother

Mervyn died at the British Embassy in Rome of 'malarial pneumonia' at just forty-six years old. Like his brothers, Mervyn was much admired for his intellect and was also a first-class cricketer.

Today, over a hundred years later, tales of 'King Tut's curse' are still going strong, still widely discussed and generating column inches.

Technically, All Hallows' Eve is supposed to be the day when we reflect on those we knew who have died and take the time to remember and honour them. It was also, in pagan times, the night the dead walked again and these days, certainly in the West, that side of the old belief is the one that takes precedence. Hallowe'en now is more about visions of poltergeists, shrouded figures and spectral skeletons rising up from long-closed graves than an evening of quiet mourning for those we have lost.

Hallowe'en activities abound, ranging from trick-or-treating and carving pumpkins into jack-o'-lanterns to the telling of ghost stories in myriad forms, from books to films and everything in between. The long, dark winter nights in the northern hemisphere lend themselves particularly well to ghost stories and things that go bump in the night. By reputation there are a number of ghosts or presences at Highclere. A few appear in the park, there may be some restless souls by the Bronze Age tumuli or the Iron Age fort (I have to admit, I have not looked), and there were sightings of one in a yew tree. Inside the Castle, there are many and varied presences, of which more later. Everyone here has their own story of strange events and parts of the Castle that they don't like to visit on a gloomy evening.

The ruins of Highclere's ancient church of St Michael and All Angels lie just outside the back of the Castle and are embraced by banks of yew trees, one of which is apparently 1,000 years old. The church was named for St Michael who performed many miracles and went into battle with Satan to cast him out of heaven, which is why he became the guardian of the Church. In some legends three further angels, Raphael, Gabriel and Uriel, are involved in this battle, and in others up to seven. As a result, St Michael was revered by most military orders of knights. The original Anglo-Saxon church was likely of a simple design, having just a nave and a chancel, but after 600 years was in need of restoration. At this point, Highclere was owned by Geordie's ancestor Sir Robert Sawyer, who rebuilt a larger version in brick with a new tower at the western end, leaving the cemetery to the northern side. His grandson then removed the cemetery to its current position in a new area of hallowed ground a mile away. Not all the local communities were happy with this decision as there had been no consultation and in those days a mile was a long way to carry a coffin.

By 1870, the church was once again in dire need of restoration. The 4th Earl decided to dismantle it and commissioned Sir Gilbert Scott to design and build a new church in the village of Highclere rather than by the Castle. It would be far easier for the parishioners to reach and much nearer the burial ground. An alley was named to connect the new church to the revised cemetery, and the new church was consecrated in November 1870. It is still there and remains a beautiful place of worship today. Some of the effigies and monuments were removed from the old church to the new one, but there are vaults under the grassed-over nave of the original church by the Castle and various monuments remain in the crypt.

Perhaps due to these upheavals, a rather challenging ghost disturbed everyone living in and around the old cemetery. He became known in local legend as Grampas, which, rather than being a misspelling of Grandpa, is actually derived from the Anglo-Saxon word *'grama'* meaning 'a fiend'. History does not relate who Grampas originally might have been or exactly when he began to materialise: perhaps he was just a local bad spirit. In any event, he made himself very troublesome to the neighbourhood, to the extent that, in medieval times, an assembly of priests sought to lay him to rest in an old well on the north side of Highclere. For some time afterwards, Grampas remained quietly in limbo but after a while he broke out again and assumed his nightly wanderings over the countryside. Once again, another congregation of priests met to exorcise him, but their number – eleven – was clearly not sufficient as Grampas appeared in the middle of their meeting and drove them apart. Another priest was found and they met again. Apparently, twelve was a more appropriate number and Grampas was banished into the oldest yew tree near the church, where he remained in safekeeping.

However, some years later during a storm, the yew tree was split in two by a bolt of lightning and Grampas resumed his career of mischief for a considerable time, by all accounts. Mr Gowen, who was secretary to the 1st, 2nd and 3rd Earls, remembered that an old clerk used to recall how on a dark winter's night he was walking home past the beginning of Gines' Copse when he heard a strange rumbling of wheels. Turning, he saw a coach and six, complete with headless coachman and horses snorting fire from their nostrils, driving straight towards him with Grampas sitting inside. As he leaped aside, the coach continued on towards Siddown Hill. The next morning, the clerk traced three distinct horse's hoof-marks leading up to the brow of the hill.

This time, six bishops were brought in, resolved to make

quite sure their enemy was subdued: allegedly they laid him down for a hundred years in the Red Sea, where hopefully he still remains. The bottom of the yew tree is now carefully bricked up, both to support it and to prevent any possible ghostly re-emergence. The 4th Earl wrote that, in the winter of 1864–5, he filled up the hollow with cement and brickwork and cut back some of the boughs, and that later on, when a new limb was torn away, the tree was trimmed and the brickwork checked. Similarly, I too have carefully removed all the ivy and any dead wood from the tree and, like the 4th Earl, am watchful that the old yew continues to thrive and no one tries to interfere with the brick structure around it. Nevertheless, on a wintry evening walk around the far side of the church remains, in the lee of all the yews planted by the 4th Earl, it does still feel rather unsettled, full of deep troubling memories, and the sounds of the owls and bats are unnerving rather than reassuring.

There are other walks at Highclere that also carry echoes of memories and Lime Avenue is one such. A beautiful eighteenth-century avenue, with wonderful scents in the summer and colour in the autumn, it is part of the remains of the original pleasure gardens, built for frivolity and assignations. These days, the avenue has a nice even tarmac surface and *Downton Abbey* filmed a number of scenes along it, with characters on horseback or on foot. It is a regular walk with my sisters and was a lovely route on which to push Edward in a pram or help him balance on a bicycle. Walked on your own, however, it reeks of history.

On one of his last days at Highclere, in early January 1923, the 5th Earl was walking back along it with one of his keepers, Tommy Richardson. 'Oil the guns well, please, Tommy, and put them away – I am off to Egypt and will not need them again this season,' he allegedly said. I can almost visualise them, the two straight-backed figures, silhouetted under the spare high grey branches of the avenue, which seem to lean in as if listening.

One of the past keepers, Keith Radwell, reported that he was just passing through to check some pheasant pens and water the far end when he noticed an old-fashioned pram being pushed by a well-dressed woman in a long black skirt. Keith stopped because he did not expect to see anyone there and wondered why they had turned off as if they were going towards the gardens. He reversed his Land Rover and went back to enquire, but there was no sign of anybody except for the woodman George Hillier. When George was asked where the lady had gone, he simply replied, 'What lady?' Keith said that he had not felt either fearful or threatened. He was just bemused to find there was no explanation for what he had seen.

The glasshouses and cold frames lie not far from Lime Avenue, and at one point Pat the decorator was up a ladder in order to paint across the top of the carnation house. It is an old part of Highclere's world in that the wall on one side originally formed part of the Monks' Garden during the Middle Ages. She heard footsteps come around the corner but despite her calling out to see who it was, no one answered. Instead the footsteps carried on. Pat could not see anyone so came down the ladder to investigate, leaving the paint pot balanced on top of it. No one was to be found and, thoroughly unsettled, she said there was no way she was working there on her own any more.

Pat has worked at the Castle for some sixty-five years, first with her father and then with her husband Mike, and has had numerous strange sightings over the years including a couple courting by 'Charlie's mine'. I was always a little puzzled by this until I realised she meant Charlemagne's statue. Personally, I have never come across them but then I have so many dogs that such a couple would undoubtedly take refuge elsewhere for privacy.

It is a different story inside the Castle. In the early months of getting to know my way round, there was always one hallway I preferred to avoid. There is a large portrait of a lady there who for some reason I always felt used to follow me, especially when I went upstairs and around the gallery. I did not really like to mention it to Geordie, until one day a visitor touring the house went into the Castle office and reported to Jackie (Lessware), who was working there, that a lady from a painting had followed her around the gallery.

I asked the archivist what was known about that portrait and was told that it had been started in 1875 but that whilst the lady's face had been painted from life, she had then sadly died and her maid had sat in her clothes so that the work could be finished posthumously. If you look closely, there is a cut-out circle around her face that is carefully disguised and smoothed into the portrait. It may well have been the dead woman's dress that the substitute wore, but what has always worried me is that the arms and hands in the picture look wrong, as if they do not belong. A marble cast of one of the subject's hands had been made; it was very elegant with beautifully shaped fingers, whereas the arms and hands in the portrait are much plumper.

The portrait is of Evelyn, the 4th Countess of Carnarvon, who sadly died in childbirth, leaving behind four small children ranging from two weeks to eight years old. I began my book *The Earl and the Pharaoh* with her story and have rearranged the family portraits by the red stairs so that a young

5th Earl now hangs to one side of his mother, her brother opposite, her mother-in-law high up nearby, and the portraits of Geordie and myself on another wall. The staircase itself has been painted for perhaps the first time in a century, a new rug grounds the hallway, the chandelier once more hangs straight and her story has been told. We are all friends and if she chooses to have a meander around, it is fine by me.

The painting over the fireplace in the drawing room shows the children of the 1st Earl, four brothers and their sister. One of those young men, Charles, joined the Navy but, to the distress of his family, died at sea. Some thirty years later his beloved nurse died at Highclere. Her last words were: 'The Captain is in the drawing room waiting for you, my lady.' They missed him so much but she could still see him.

When she began her tenure at Highclere, my mother-in-law Jeanie had been concerned to 'set the house at rest' and, after inviting some alternative therapists to help her, felt that the main rooms were fine but she still had not tackled certain uncomfortable sightings, both upstairs and downstairs. She told me she had once felt a cold presence in a lower corridor in one area, as if someone or something had walked past her. One wintry Sunday afternoon, when my son was only about three years old, Geordie, a photographer and I were alone in the Castle taking photographs of the paintings in the smoking room for a new guidebook I was writing. Around 4 p.m. I thought I would bear Edward off for tea, so he and I left through the green baize door into the servery that sits behind the dining room and then went down the old servants' stairs into the basement. I had parked Eddie's little red battery-powered ride-on car there and it was also time to retrieve and feed Percy the puppy.

With Edward in his car, we went through a set of doors

and made an awkward right-hand turn along a rather poorly lit corridor, then through another set of doors, followed by a second right-hand turn. The little car was buzzing noisily and, sensing someone was there, I glanced to my left to see a man coming towards us, dressed in dark clothes, with some sort of pale necktie or cravat. He was slim and about my husband's height but seemed slightly indistinct. I could hear Percy barking madly, trapped a way off behind a further set of doors. With Edward in front of me, as usual keeping a steady speed, I urged him to go faster. Glancing behind, I saw the figure appeared to be following us. I began to push the back of the car – 'Faster, darling, put your foot down' – and eventually we burst through the heavy swing doors and found Percy, who was very loud and very anxious. The figure paused at the doors. As we hurried along the last stretch of corridor, I did not look back.

I remembered my mother-in-law saying it was a particularly old part of the Castle, and thereafter I always preferred to avoid this corridor conjunction when I was on my own, which made my progress around the building somewhat convoluted. After telling a friend about it, they suggested I seek help and I was given the number of Father Peter, an Anglican monk from Westminster Abbey. He would come down and bless the Castle for Geordie and me, suggest that this spirit could find peace elsewhere and, in addition, try to calm down the atmosphere in the bedroom where séances used to be held.

House blessings often take place on 6 January, which is the twelfth day of Christmas, the Feast of the Epiphany. I was unwilling to wait that long, and Father Peter undoubtedly had other duties to perform on that day, so he arrived one Saturday morning soon after we had spoken, with prayer book and holy water. Prior to his arrival, he had asked me if I could try to find out who the man in the corridor might have been and what had happened to him. The most likely candidate was a footman called John from the nineteenth century who had been having a romance with a nursery nurse. Whilst she was absent from the nursery, the Countess's baby had died. It may have been cot death or something similar, and most likely not at all the fault of the couple, but in the pain, grief and misery thereafter, the footman committed suicide not far from where I had seen him. I was a new Countess with a young child and perhaps he had hurried behind us anxious to ensure all was well.

Father Peter arrived and we spent a peaceful and thoughtful morning, beginning at the front door to bless the spot where we welcome guests – 'Peace be to this house and all who live here.' The dining room was next on the list as at every big social event we sit there and eat together.

After that, the focus was the bedroom in which the 5th Earl of Carnarvon was rumoured to have held séances a hundred years previously. Father Peter thought the blessing 'of this room with God's overshadowing love would help ensure anyone sleeping here might be bathed in light and tranquillity', and therefore awake refreshed.

From there, we went back downstairs and I took Father Peter to where I'd had my unfortunate experience with John the footman. I nervously hoped this would work and that Father Peter's prayers would encourage the spirit to forgive and move on. It was a prayer and not an exorcism and, on the whole, I am now comfortable here, but other members of the team at Highclere still occasionally see a figure at the end of this corridor. John G has felt someone there sometimes and always whistles a little or talks loudly as he exits without wasting any time. Occasionally the dogs lose all confidence and, with hackles raised, back off. If possible, we all follow their example.

Over the last few years, we have rearranged various rooms in the cellars in which the Egyptian exhibition resides and the alarms were always going off there for unexplained reasons. A number of times I went there with Les Taylor to help him check out the area and reset the alarms. There was never anything there, but they had been triggered and we always used to look at each other knowingly. Les himself always advised anyone visiting the Castle to knock loudly before going up into the main tower.

Father Peter said he could return with more reinforcements if needed, but we have muddled on through the years without seeking further help.

Pat Withers has many stories to relate about strange events inside the house as well as in the grounds. One day her father was painting the staff-room door and as she walked towards him, she heard him say 'Good evening' to someone out of her sight. When she arrived a minute or two later, he reproached her for her poor manners in not greeting the lady, telling her he hadn't brought her up to be so disrespectful. Pat replied that nobody had come back down past her, but her father insisted that the lady had come down the private stairs from His Lordship's room, passed him and then must have passed Pat as she went down the corridor. Pat was rather indignant, but her father was not the only person who saw this lady walking along purposefully in a floor-length, bustled black dress whilst rounding the corner from the Gothic stairs.

On another occasion, Pat and her team had been working up in the base of the great Barry Tower. It is such a beautiful staircase and hall, and I had decided to wallpaper it to bring it back to life. The project was almost finished although, unfortunately, I still had not quite found the moment to mention it to my husband. One lunchtime, however, he decided to make his way up there, having got wind that something was going on. Pat, fully aware of the situation and wishing to steer clear, disappeared at some speed down the red stairs, whilst I tried to waylay Geordie, muttering something about 'a little restoration work'. He was surprised perhaps but also very pleased with the effect, saying he thought it looked amazing. I explained it was a specially commissioned wallpaper . . . another fantastic idea of Sarah Morris's, and he groaned, thinking of the expense, but I reassured him it had all been paid for under the contingency line in the budget. I find it an extraordinarily useful miscellaneous line.

This was not the only time Pat had descended this staircase at speed. Years earlier, some lads working for her were rubbing down the window frames in some of the more distant rooms on the top floor when, all of a sudden, the two boys took off, running along the corridor towards the stairs. She wasn't sure what had happened but followed them down to find they had not stopped running until they were outside. They would never tell her what had happened but adamantly refused ever to work up there again. It remains a mystery. However once, when I was in a bedroom on the floor below, I heard a huge commotion in the rooms on that upper floor. I couldn't make out whether it was a party or a fight but decided that tea called and beat a hasty retreat.

The 6th Earl had just one sister, Evelyn, who in turn had one daughter, Patricia. She was born in 1924 and lived at Highclere with her cousins during school holidays and throughout the Second World War, when she was often on her own in one of the gallery bedrooms. She was normally allocated the same dressing room and would sleep there with her beloved little Norwich Terrier dog Tom Thumb. Her diaries tell that she would often wake up in the middle of the night convinced that someone was sitting on her feet, but that she didn't think it could be anything too sinister as it didn't seem to have any effect on Tom Thumb. Many years later, an American relative was staying at the Castle in this same room. I asked him how he'd enjoyed his stay and he replied very much but he had been unable to sleep as someone kept sitting on his feet. Still today, the end of that bed sometimes has a depression in the morning when absolutely no one has been in the room. I am not sure it is a worrying ghost, but it might possibly be the 3rd Countess who reportedly returned to Highclere to nurse her son when he became very ill during his forties.

Sometimes, however, Patricia was given a bedroom on the top floor and found that one very uncomfortable to stay in, and it is still not a favourite room for any of the team today.

These rooms high up in the Castle are a fascinating place to explore. We have slowly been finding new purposes for them, focusing on fresh stories to tell in our visitor displays and renovating the worst ones. It means we often need to go up there and check them out . . .

One of our favourite Highclere entertainments is to make people jump. This may involve hiding in cupboards or behind half-open doors and there have been some spectacular successes. A young intern, James (Hunter), who is by no means small, worked here for some years in the estate office with me. He was studying property and estate management at university and this was his holiday job. As a ruse I had asked him to help find something on the top floor of the Castle – we are always looking for things so this would ring entirely true.

In the half-light of a long corridor, he was asked to look

behind a door to his left . . . he opened it, screamed, collapsed in a heap on the floor and burst into tears. It was quite spectacular, and his 'friends' collapsed in laughter, unable to speak. Inside the cupboard was 'Gladys the nurse', a dummy with a pretty face and slightly lopsided wig, dressed in Almina Carnarvon's raspberry-red-and-white nursing uniform. Quite realistic. She comes out for various themed events. The search party did not continue and something restorative was needed.

Another member of our team, Hannah G, thinks she is quite on the ball and would certainly not fall for any sort of practical joke. At the back of the cellars in the Egyptian exhibition is a long narrow chamber accessed down a few steps. It was once a Champagne cellar but now the alcoves either side are empty, whilst three Egyptian statues within the cellar light up to catch the visitor's eye and look rather wonderful. It is rarely open but we were doing some filming and therefore had unlocked the traditional door with its barred grille. We were having a meeting in the tearooms and I burbled away, telling Hannah she must come and look as the room was not usually accessible. I wondered whether she thought we might improve the lighting? Completely relaxed, we walked along the corridor, round the corner and into the back of the cellars. Whilst she was exclaiming with delight that she had never been down there before, I guided her to the chamber, staying back as she stepped down into it. Caitlin was hiding behind a wall in the alcove to the right, whilst Guy was on the other side with a mobile phone ready to record a video. Caitlin said 'Boo', Hannah screamed, called me naughty names and screamed again. She could not believe it – we were bent double with hysterical laughter. Caught – hook, line and sinker.

I knew Hannah would want to get me back and she'd probably bide her time until I had completely forgotten to be

NOVEMBER: CURSES AND GHOSTS

careful, and I was quite right. She persuaded Ted, a TV presenter and craftsman who was restoring candelabra here, to record a deep and breathy utterance of 'Fiona' on her phone. I was on my way up to Orient, a room on the top floor that I use when I'm writing, and Hannah and Caitlin rushed up another flight of stairs ahead of me and hid under my desk. It was not a big space and I had taken my time to get there with various impromptu meetings en route. Entirely oblivious, I walked across the room to open the shutters when suddenly this voice came out from under the desk – I did not jump quite as much as Hannah had but it was nevertheless a successful ambush.

Curiously, footsteps do walk past this room quite often in the evening – usually around 5 p.m. Once I thought it was John letting me know he was off home or bringing me a mug of tea or something stronger. I leaped up from my desk to let him in but there was nobody there. I radioed John to find out where he was and he was on the gravel outside the Castle. Two Labradors often work with me in there – they have a lovely big cushion to sprawl on and a tin of treats, as well as the chance to steal my apples. On hearing the footsteps, they always bark madly and run to the door. I have been a bit worried that this chap (the footsteps have the measure and sound of a man's tread) might be annoyed that someone was pretending to be a ghost and, in fact, after Hannah's triumph, he walked up and down twice, which I found more disconcerting than the ambush.

Another time, I was once more trying to finish a book and had borrowed another desk as every surface in my writing room was already covered with my notes and jottings. As usual the deadline was fast approaching and I was running late, so I'd got up quite early to start writing when I heard the fabulous sound of china cups tinkling on a tray coming along the parquet floor of the corridor. I jumped up, thinking it might be Diana, the housekeeper, coming to my rescue with a cup of tea. However, opening the door and looking out, I was sad to see there was no one there. Strangely, the same thing happened to Sally from the gift shop when she was working in the Castle office during Covid – she told me someone had walked along the corridor and that she had thought it was me coming with a much-needed cup of tea. There were only the two of us in the Castle at that point. Finding out that I hadn't moved from my office across the courtyard that morning, and having heard my similar story, she decided to work remotely after that. It is a big building to sit in entirely on your own, even during the daytime.

People – families – have lived at Highclere for millennia and survived and enjoyed the trials, tribulations and joyous moments of life. Conscious of the way the threads of time link us together, I had an idea for giving new purpose to a fallen cedar. The park at Highclere is lucky to have quite a few of these iconic trees but they are vulnerable in stormy weather and high winds. They are almost too greenly magnificent and sometimes we lose boughs and occasionally an entire tree.

This particular tree, situated halfway up the main drive to the Castle, split and fell one winter, leaving only part of the trunk standing, perhaps now eighteen feet high. I decided to call in an extraordinary wood carver I had heard of who creates amazing sculptures using a chainsaw rather than more conventional tools, and asked him to turn the trunk into Highclere's own version of the Green Man.

Partly, I got the idea from Dickens's *A Christmas Carol*, which is performed in the Castle each year at Christmas. Essentially, it's a book of ghost stories, but the purpose of the visitations is to bring about change for the better rather than fear for fear's sake. Scrooge becomes a better man as a result. One of the characters, Christmas Present, is described as wearing a 'deep green robe, or mantle', 'a holly wreath, set here and there with shining icicles. Its dark brown curls were long and free.' He does seem quite a jolly figure but quite scary and is an almost quintessential description of folklore's Green Man.

Whilst often incorporated in ecclesiastical buildings, the Green Man has a far older pagan heritage embodying our ancestors' connection to the earth and woods. Green Men were often part of Roman mosaics, and of course the Egyptian God Osiris is regarded as a 'grain' deity, depicted with a green face to represent the annual rebirth and resurrection of the fields around the Nile as they return to fertility every year. Look around an ancient stone church and inspect its carved architectural detail. On the inside or outside stonework, or in the detail on the decorative wooden carvings ornamenting pews, stalls or beamed roofs, you might see the representation of a man's face surrounded by leaves. Vines, flowers, fruit or branches sprout from his mouth; sometimes this motif is partly disguised, sometimes it's more obvious. Notably, over a hundred Green Men are carved into fifteenth-century Rosslyn Chapel in Scotland.

The Green Man is often viewed as earth's spiritual protector and is part of our common folklore, so I thought an image of him here would not be out of place. I hope later to grow roses and honeysuckle up and over him.

The very word 'spirit' has a benign etymology, in that it is all about breath and breathing, which is a much more reassuring concept than an otherworldly being, whilst 'ghost' likely links to the Germanic *'gast'* and thence to our word 'guest'. So, they are not all bad and, despite the stories, Highclere has a warm and homely atmosphere that welcomes guests and will continue to do so. Of course, in a building like this it is all too easy to imagine guttering candles and dark shadowy corners, shutters and doors creaking in unexplained draughts. For all our modern technology and means of controlling our environment, the fear of curses and ghosts, of spirits wishing us evil, does not fade but is deeply embedded in our subconscious.

Personally, I prefer to believe that any ghosts are just people who have slightly lost their way; missed the right turning, if you like. Living in and around the Castle, I don't really think it is haunted – mostly – so much as that there are other spirits and times that sometimes occupy the same space as we do. Having said that, when I finished writing this chapter, I did require the reassuring companionship of two dogs when returning books to the archive room on the top floor.

CHAPTER TWELVE

December: Christmas at Highclere

'I will honour Christmas in my heart and try to keep it all the year'
— *A Christmas Carol*, Charles Dickens

At Highclere, Christmas begins in January. The month is named for the Roman god Janus, the god of beginnings and endings, who is always portrayed looking both ways, facing the past and the future. He holds a key as he was conceived as the doorkeeper and therefore symbolises transition in time and space. In some ways our month of January perfectly reflects this duality.

In past times, the eve of Twelfth Night was one of celebration and as large a party as Christmas Day itself. In the West, it may still be celebrated as the day the Three Kings or Magi arrived at the stable with their gifts for baby Jesus. Epiphany remains a national holiday in many parts of Europe, though sadly not in England and definitely not at Highclere.

At this time, Sally and her team of elves are far from at leisure as 6 January marks the date by which we need to remove all the Christmas decorations from the Castle. From the gardeners and the banqueting team to those in the office and the gift shop, everyone kindly appears to help dismantle the garlands and trees. The different-coloured baubles are sorted, wrapped in old newspaper and put in labelled boxes.

That may sort out the past but the next endeavour is to pre-prepare for Christmas to come in eleven months' time – the future.

As ever, much coffee and hot chocolate is consumed and Sally tempts anyone who offers to help with yummy spicy biscuits, perhaps inspired by the spices brought by the Magi. Traditionally, this time of year is celebrated with heavily fruited Twelfth Night cakes and Epiphany tarts. In any case, it encourages everyone to find half an hour here or there to join Sally's gift-shop elves who are now beginning to rework garlands, trees and floristry into the theme for the following year.

Christmas themes evolve from eureka moments, fuelled by coffee, in which Sally and I try to plan at least two years ahead. Sometimes we share the magic idea that just pops out and sometimes creative inspiration is harder to find, requiring more coffee. It is quite comforting to be able to look further into the future as it means there should be less firefighting and crisis management in at least one area of Castle life.

All of the remaining days of January are therefore taken up with looking forward. It is done at full throttle as the temporary marquee area in which we work is taken down at the end of the month, so we transition into the future in true Janus style. Of course, what we are really doing is anticipating February, a month traditionally associated with purging and cleansing, with the idea of getting rid of all of the things that no longer bring you joy and happiness and removing clutter, both physical and emotional, which is also rather positive.

To empty the marquee in the most efficient manner, we rent a little white van with a tailgate which, over several runs, takes all of Christmas down to Sally's sheds. These have rather grown in number over recent years and include shipping containers, which are an improvement as they are more resistant to mice and damp weather.

Sheds have always been a matter of contention at Highclere as everyone wants one. In the past, Sally used to borrow corners of rooms on the top floor of the Castle and parts of other people's sheds for Christmas storage. However, as Christmas at Highclere attained more ambitious levels of decoration and public expectation increased, her shed requirement became key.

In fact, she was visibly moved when I said I thought she should now have her own space – 'You mean I too can have my own sheds?' Not knowing whether to laugh or nod reassuringly, I confirmed she could indeed now have two sheds, which soon increased to three shipping containers. Even better, they have lights, low-level heating and doors that lock: what more could she possibly want?

All the Christmas decorations were moved down from their various hidey holes to Sally's new kingdom, so she could sort it out and see exactly what she had. It was something of a mammoth task, and we all had a good workout carrying everything down three flights of stairs, but at least it would all now be in one place. It was extraordinary to see how much had accumulated.

I said I was not sure if her herds of reindeer would fit as well – she had been collecting reindeer of the willow variety for the Christmas events we hold. Worried about not having enough, she'd ordered two herds of different sizes, plus a red sledge. Perhaps, however, they could occupy a shelter rather than a shed.

During the years *Downton Abbey* was being filmed, we enjoyed our first Christmas in July when the Christmas special was being made. With the sun blazing outside, the cast would stoically dress in warm clothes – coats and hats – whilst singing 'Silent Night' around the Christmas tree in the saloon, or Great Hall as they called it. The *Downton* tree was always put in the same place we have our own tree, which gives a real sense of nostalgia to visitors who come to see Christmas at Highclere and blurs the gap between reality and fiction.

The film crew would be in shorts and trainers, an ice-cream van parked around a corner, and in between takes everyone was outside under the trees with cold drinks: it's the magic of the movies. Those few days of Christmas in summer inevitably had a de-mob feel to them as they were usually also the last days of filming for that season.

Planning for Christmas on the scale we do today only really began in 2019. My parents-in-law never opened the Castle in the winter, but Geordie and I thought it was a lovely time of year to share Highclere, although our focus initially was on just a few charity events.

It then dawned on me that many other stately homes were very successful at Christmas which, in business terms, helped them through the leaner winter months. Lacking their large car-parking areas, however, we had to make sure that whatever we did was both practical and possible. Writing a book about Christmas gave me several ideas for various events suitable for smaller numbers of guests. We would have to box and cox in a slightly different way from other stately homes, which led to creating events around the various Christmas themes of eating, carols, storytelling, gifting, evening receptions amongst the twinkling lights, and a play about Christmas: *A Christmas Carol*.

After an enthusiastic beginning in 2019, we then had to think very carefully about the following two years during Covid. Instinctively, we felt we should do something despite

DECEMBER: CHRISTMAS AT HIGHCLERE

the pandemic and, with careful spacing and one-way tours, did manage to welcome visitors albeit in limited numbers. Inspired by the first global media event, the discovery of the tomb of Tutankhamun by the 5th Earl and Howard Carter, Christmas 2022 became Egyptian-themed. It was, in every way, a cheering and unexpectedly positive experience for those wishing to visit Highclere, a glint of gold amongst some rather dark years. Highclere then became medieval and purple, drawing on its early ancestry under the ownership of the Bishopric of Winchester and referencing the purple bottles of our new Highclere Castle Gin – both spiritual guidance and a spirit to cheer the spirits so to speak. Following that, we returned to the idea of journeys with the Three Kings, before reverting to a more traditional look once again.

September marks the end of summer opening and the time when Paul the gardener and Sally go in search of Christmas trees. Given the scale and number of trees required, it is important that they are right. Their first away day is to a local farm to choose *the* Christmas tree for the saloon. Sally tends to reappear looking as if she has been through a hedge backwards, her hair and attire all slightly askew but happy that they have once more found a good tree, marked it and decided which side will be the front and which the back – also marked.

At this point, John G tends to appear, to ask rather nervously how tall it is. He prefers a tree of eighteen feet or perhaps, at a push, twenty, whereas I hope for twenty to twenty-four feet. In practice, twenty-four may be too big if the tree is also very wide. We did put one tree up and have to take it down again to reduce it as I had not really appreciated that twenty-five feet was very much bigger than twenty. Paul has gained so much experience by now that he feels he can cut an otherwise suitable tree to the right length and is less worried.

Sally then leads the next foray to another Christmas tree farm to choose the fifty or so other trees that are needed. These range in size from twelve to fourteen feet down to the twenty-four waist-high trees that line the driveway. The gardeners, dressed in their usual waterproofs, look much the same on their return, whilst Sally once more looks as if she has been hiking through an unexplored wilderness.

None of this part of life was ever covered on *Downton Abbey* but we have made various TV documentaries that share the process – although, since we try to be at least slightly dignified and grown up for TV, they never quite reveal the full hilarity. The office team begin to put up a cheery board stating how many days to go to Christmas: 78 days . . . 65 days . . . and John expostulates in despair. He is the Christmas Grinch.

Dressing the Castle for Christmas is no ordinary project. The rooms are not merely large but numerous as well, and the central saloon is fifty feet high so there are quite a few challenges. More is more or else it looks rather inadequate. There are also various housekeeping rules: no water, no gaffer tape, no wire to hold garlands in place or mantelshelf decorations in situ. There are also health and safety rules: nothing that can fall over or detach. Geordie, of course, imposes a budget. We reuse as much as possible from previous years, attempting to be economical with resources, but inevitably there is fresh expenditure each year.

For all the planning and preparation, Christmas is always something of a test and, therefore, the main ingredient required is laughter amidst the teamwork. Some of us may be working at height – quite a few of us did a course in that, and then we had to do a manual-handling course about lifting things – though the ladders are never where they need to be.

By early November, Christmas – as far as the Castle is concerned – is nearly upon us. It does not matter if you normally work in an office, in the gardens, with the horses or in the tearooms, Sally will be looking for you. The time has come to retrieve the Highclere trees, floral displays and garlands from the sheds and unwrap them, wondering if they are still intact and will still work. There are long emails from her with lists of things to do for each day and calling out for elves.

It is always rather easy to tell who has responded to her call and who has not, as the helpers always sparkle and glitter when they reappear at their desks. Furthermore, if you then sit where any of them has been working, then you too glitter from behind as you walk away.

Amongst Sally's seasonal statistics, with which she likes to entertain her 'troops', are the facts that we use over 10,000 baubles and tree decorations, each one wired up, and two kilometres of garlands, all reflecting this year's Christmas theme. Some of the thirty-four floral displays are enormous and decidedly unwieldy, so two or even three people have to carry each one and they don't fit very well through the windows. The first day is spent simply trying to put the right trees and displays in the correct rooms.

Meanwhile, the farm has kindly collected the forty to fifty real trees and returned with them to the old garages behind the Castle (made rather famous by Lady Sibyl and Tom Branson), as well as collecting the main tree, which is then left to dry in a barn over the weekend.

The gardeners and farm workers begin all the Christmas tree work outside for the first three days. They bring up a small digger to fill the containers for trees lining the drive as well as the huge pots for the tall ones clustered outside by the front door, with a wooden frame fixed into place in each bucket, before proceeding around the back to the courtyard for the next six to eight really quite large trees. Whilst inside garlands begin to wind their way upstairs, two or three of us begin threading lights around the outside trees before carefully attaching baubles so they will withstand the wind.

Christmas trees are a relatively modern concept and, in a way, a Royal tradition that was introduced into England by the Hanoverians in the eighteenth century when they took the English throne. The idea was reinforced by all those charming engravings of Queen Victoria, Prince Albert and their children, gathered around their Christmas tree, after which trees rapidly became an essential part of Christmas. They bring the beauty of the woodland world into our homes, make us smile, and if they are real, they have a wonderful scent. Whatever your style of decorating, whether it be over-the-top abundance or a more minimalistic approach, they are a focal point round which to gather and centre the festivities.

The Friday of decorating week is always Operation Chief Christmas Tree, for which the dress code is your best Christmas jumper. The betting is on Paul Mac or Luis to find the most eccentric design but late entrants may surprise everyone. John G is not at all keen on Christmas so it is ironic that he plays a lead role in helping the team to fulfil Sally's every Christmas wish. He is always the first out in front on the gravel, wearing thick gloves in readiness and offering an endless commentary as the farm's tractor and trailer eases between the stone entrance pilasters and sweeps around parallel to the Castle door.

The straps securing the tree are undone and the farm team, as well as the rest of us, take up position either side of the long trunk as it is slowly levered off the flatbed and onto our shoulders. Wheeling round with much shouting and laughter, the tree heads bottom first into the saloon where the carpets are covered with plastic. Wooden props are hastily pulled into place under its length, before it is carefully lowered and tested for stability.

Stage two is now to release the branches and fit the large Highclere-made stand around the bottom of the tree. The base was specially made with reused floorboards from a cottage renovation and is a work of art; it is beautifully constructed and has clamps to ensure the tree is held straight.

Whilst this process is taking place, Sally and her team are attaching Christmas decorations to the top, given that it is temporarily accessible. This means lying on the ground to reach under some branches. Then ropes with slip knots are attached to the top third of the tree, whilst John repeatedly reminds everyone of the joy of Christmas and Paul Mac lights up his sweater and heads for the sausage rolls.

Caitlin and I will be filming the scene for Instagram and much of the proceedings will have to be drowned out by the backing track, to disguise the frank exclamations from the team. Geordie appears in the saloon as he likes hauling on the rope that pulls the tree upright, with the gardeners' and often the grooms' help. They head up to the gallery ready to brace themselves, Luis balances on the highest wooden spoke of the tree stand, and when we are ready, most of the team heaves, a few pull, and it starts to lift off the floor. It mustn't, of course, crash into the leather wall hangings or the painting behind it, and a huge cheer goes up when the tree is successfully upright. Whilst this is a tremendous achievement, it is just the start of a long day.

All the ladders come out and the first job is to get the lights on. Long wooden broom handles with hooks on the end are the key tool for reaching into the tree to hang the rest of the decorations, and three of us head up ladders whilst other people hold the bottom steady. Slowly, the deep green tree is transformed into a golden or frosted or Victorian or medieval-themed wonder.

As the day develops, many of the team fade and exit stage left, their initial enthusiasm waning. Sally has by now pulled up a chair and is sitting in state in the middle of the room nearest the front hall, issuing instructions as to what is missing from where. It is a good viewing point and she has now become known as Queen Elf.

At the end of the afternoon, we all stand back for a final check that all is as it should be, before slowly working through each room clearing up. By this time, we will have attached 10,000 baubles, installed fifty-seven outdoor trees, twenty-two indoor trees, the twenty-three-foot principal tree, over thirty large and opulent floral arrangements, mantelshelf decorations, fireplace decorations, table decorations, 600 metres of garlands – and all of it handmade. There are often hundreds of battery-operated floating candles and consequently we have unwrapped and used hundreds of batteries.

We then have the weekend, as well as the two succeeding days, in which to make any final preparations needed for the Christmas opening. It is the prudent accountant within me that leaves this interlude before we officially open – something always goes wrong.

In the meantime, the kitchen is busy preparing for the upcoming events. All the cakes, scones and sandwiches are made in-house. Over the next month they will, for example, use four and a half tonnes of flour, 4,500 eggs, four gallons of brandy, 100 kilos of turkey, forty-five gallons of milk, twenty kilos of sultanas . . .

Christmas at Highclere is really the story of innumerable journeys, from the countless deliveries that make the holiday what it is today, to the nostalgic heritage of a family that has lived here for 350 years with all the accordant traditions that have developed over the centuries, as well as the various gatherings of visitors, family and friends. Thus every year Christmas re-establishes the relationship between the past, present and future.

—

One of the events central to Highclere's Christmas each year is the one-man show acted out in the saloon by Charles Dickens's great-great-grandson Gerald Dickens.

Charles Dickens made an extraordinary contribution to our view of Christmas today. In a way, he is responsible for introducing us to the kindlier aspects of the season – thinking of others, looking after those who are less fortunate, the idea of sharing and goodwill. To quote: 'Every traveller has a home of his own, and he learns to appreciate it the more from his wandering.'

When *A Christmas Carol* was published on 19 December 1843, Charles Dickens was only thirty-one years old and his previous novel was not selling at all well. However, the first impression of the new book sold out before Christmas and it has never been out of print since. In some ways, it is best read aloud. Dickens was himself an actor and his stories are a performance. The colour and immediacy of his language brings characters and situations alive in a way no other author seems able to match. He was also, by our standards, a campaigner, using words and stories to ask us to think about and change some of our behaviours and prejudices.

A Christmas Carol is written in three parts – or should I say in three ghosts? The first spirit to visit the central character, Scrooge, is the Ghost of Christmas Past. This ghost is described in great detail and spends a fair amount of time with Scrooge, who to begin with is not at all keen on the idea of a spectral visitor. In fact, he does his best to ignore the memories that the ghost insists on evoking for him, and the form the visitor takes constantly changes as these memories fade and change shape.

The second ghost is the Ghost of Christmas Present. Huge, vibrant and generous, this spirit represents our current everyday lives. He brings a feast with him, which does manage to hold Scrooge's attention, but his visit is much briefer and at the end of it he shows Scrooge Ignorance and Want. In the final part of the story, the menacing Ghost of Christmas Yet to Come reveals a terrible Christmas Day in the future. This ghost remains silent and Scrooge sees a vision involving the death of a much-disliked man, whose funeral is only attended by local businessmen if they can be assured that lunch is provided. Scrooge asks the spirit to show him a single person who feels any sentiment over his death and the final scene is of an unloved, neglected tombstone bearing Scrooge's own name. Utterly terrified, he pledges to change his ways.

Many of the themes of *A Christmas Carol* are implicit in everything we plan at Highclere and so it is perhaps appropriate that our Christmas events culminate with a performance of the play. It takes place in the shadowy, dimly lit saloon with only the huge Christmas tree offering light, which makes it hugely atmospheric.

Given food is such an important part of Christmas,

however, our events start with Christmas tours and afternoon tea, organised into different sittings. Some guests return each year. Then, for four days, we focus on tours and carols, which are a more relaxed format. We hope people will pause if the weather is not too inclement to sing together in the middle of the day. Otherwise, carol singers can be found cheerfully singing in different corners of the Castle.

Carols, in terms of religious songs celebrating particular events, have been around for centuries but really came into their modern, recognisable form during the nineteenth century when they began to be collected together and printed in books or pamphlets. It is thought that the concept of a Christmas carol service was invented in Truro, Cornwall, in 1880 by Edward White Benson, who later became Archbishop of Canterbury.

As a result, many of today's most popular carols are rather dignified nineteenth-century offerings with tuneful melodies, rich harmonies and Christmassy sounds abundant. Either way, they make wonderful singing for all age groups.

For the weekend, we turn to celebrating Christmas with Champagne, canapés and the local Military Wives Choir to help our carolling. Luis usually nearly runs out of Champagne and Sally sells an awful lot of small gifts from a table within the saloon.

As everyone leaves the floodlit Castle, the dark Christmas firs lining the drive make the lights pop even more and contrast with the sparkling decorations. These are the magical moments in life.

The first year we began this Highclere tradition, Sally was unprepared for her own success and for some reason many of the guests paid with cash. At the end of the evening, John asked her for the takings, in order to lock them away before banking them on the Monday. Sally handed over the stuffed cash tin from the table and then proceeded to pull out handfuls of banknotes from her brassiere. John did not know where to look and the rest of us collapsed in hysterics whilst Sally explained she had no pockets and it had seemed the safest place at the time. As she neared the end, John asked if she had a white rabbit and a pack of cards in there as well. Sally had done very well and definitely deserved more Champagne.

We also do talks about Christmas and afternoon tea with the Friends of Highclere before we set out the chairs and stage in the saloon for *A Christmas Carol.* By this point, Highclere's Christmas visitors have consumed 6,000 portions of fruit cake, the same number of mince pies and nearly 7,000 scones. One hundred and fifty bottles of Champagne are drunk in just two evenings, not to mention all the hot chocolates, coffees and teas. No wonder our fridges look rather empty.

If there was a *Downton* Christmas in July and then a whole series of Christmas events at the end of the year, there would still be one more type of Christmas to come and that is our own family Christmas. Usually, we alternate, celebrating Christmas or else New Year in the Castle, to help the staff, but once we had three Christmases in a year when manager John is not keen even on one.

These last few days leading up to the Winter Solstice are the shortest of the year and it gets dark before 4 p.m. Most noticeably, the chickens have almost entirely stopped laying eggs and their efforts do not begin again until well into the New Year.

The kitchen and banqueting team have some time off before Christmas and the office team begin to wind down and disappear to spend the holiday with their own families. By now it's all done – the decorating, the wrapping, the cooking, the carol concerts, nativity plays and pantomimes, the office parties and the shopping. We have all got to where we need to be geographically and the day itself is nearly upon us.

Christmas makes most of us turn to home. Home is about family and friends, some of whom may travel to stay with us, about beloved dogs and the nostalgic familiarity of re-enacting our parents' traditions.

I am always hoping for properly cold winter weather. Here, snow is less likely than frost even if every adult and child is offering special prayers. Nevertheless, frost transforms Highclere's world into something entirely magical. Even at this time of year, the outside world orders each day – there is the desire to be in the light, however brief the opportunity.

Early-morning tiny icicles edge each blade of grass and leaf, making them glitter, and the effect is especially striking where the land sweeps down the southern slopes away from the Castle. Hoar frost transmutes the gardens and parkland into a work of art. As frost rolls downhill, the coldest pockets at the foot of the wildflower meadow stay a deeper wintry white for the longest time, preserving the otherworldly beauty throughout the day.

The word 'hoar' comes from the Anglo-Saxon word '*hār*', meaning 'of great age, grey and white', which perfectly describes the trees and bushes that look like white hair with feathery patterns of frost painting each leaf and stem. It is nature's translucent artistry.

Frost frequently features in the stories and myths of fireside evenings on the short dark days of winter. Jack Frost is an elfish creature, both full of mischief and a hero. He seems to be responsible for the artistry of the whorls of frost occasionally visible on windowpanes – a well-remembered feature of my childhood – as he is often depicted with paintbrush in hand. In parts of the world where the different types of snow and frost have a greater significance than they do here, there are many different words to describe all the nuances of freezing weather whereas these are fading from the English language today.

Whenever the late-afternoon rain clears, the ragged pillows of December cloud take on hues of pink and blue. The air feels so fresh, all senses sharpened by December's bareness. Pockets of puddles are left in the golden pea gravel around the Castle. They are perfect for children to jump into and splash around or for the Labradors to lie down in. When stillness returns, you can see reflections of the Castle and sky in them. The depths are obscure and imaginary; the reflected world and sky tranquil and unbounded.

—

Whilst some families celebrate with feasting on Christmas Eve, Geordie and I follow our own tradition of welcoming Father Christmas and all his reindeer on 24 December and sitting down to a family lunch on Christmas Day. Christmas is a lovely story, both simple and complex. The heart of the festivity is to remember that its message should not apply just once a year and that giving is more important than receiving – 'For it is in giving that we receive.' Never easy for children to understand when Santa does not read the present list.

My nieces still believe or wish to believe that Father

Christmas will travel through the night delivering presents, pausing en route for light refreshments for both his reindeer and himself. In the Castle, Luis is adept at helping with all the preparations for Father Christmas's arrival, remembering the need for a little brandy and the fact that we must let the fire go out so it is not at all hot for his arrival down the chimney. Geordie reads out the poem ''Twas the Night Before Christmas', managing the interruptions before we check outside hoping for a good clear evening to allow Father Christmas (or Santa Claus) to steer his way deftly across the rooftops, calling his reindeer by name: 'Now, Dasher! Now, Dancer! Now, Prancer, and Vixen! On, Comet! On, Cupid! On, Donner and Blixen!' Without forgetting Rudolph, of course.

We slowly make our way upstairs as, one by one, all the bedroom lights go out. Just a few of the gallery lights remain, highlighting the doors Father Christmas needs to find, and soon everyone is fast asleep despite the anticipation.

Who does not love the excited sounds of children discovering stockings full of often rather hastily wrapped presents? Father Christmas is very busy after all so has to be forgiven if the wrapping is imperfect.

An aficionado of cold-water swimming, I begin Christmas Day with a cold swim, watched by the dogs who obviously think I am quite mad, before I (and perhaps they) deserve breakfast.

It is the one day of the year when everyone stops. Some may call it just a holiday, others acknowledge it as 'Christmas'. The word 'holiday', however, comes from the phrase 'holy day', so no one quite escapes the spiritual underpinnings of this time of year, which celebrate life and hope. We do all go to church for the 11 a.m. service: given that Christmas is about celebrating Christ's birth, attendance is something of a three-line whip here, before we return to the prospect of opening presents under the tree. We have turkey for Christmas lunch, which was what our parents used to offer, with chestnut stuffing, forcemeat stuffing, Brussels sprouts and all the trimmings, followed by Christmas pudding and brandy butter.

Food and memories are central to this time of year. My mother used to insist on Christmas crackers that contained whistles, each one supposedly being one of the eight notes of an octave. Theoretically, it was therefore possible to call out the numbers and conduct a carol or simple song. It is always a disaster and very untuneful but we always do it. After which the dogs really need a walk and we all do too.

In the past, wintertime was about feasting and music as people occupied the sixteen hours of darkness that make up a winter's day. Having feasted too well, some of us play the piano in the drawing room, but for the rest of us, thoughts turn to acting.

Whilst Gerald Dickens may have performed an outstanding play for our visitors before Christmas, it is now our turn (if I have a big enough cohort of sisters staying) to create a little video for the modern Castle on Instagram. As always, some of the party are very keen and others disappear, preferring the peace of doing a crossword puzzle. My mother used to write little plays for all my sisters and me to act out for friends, which were pretty dreadful – *Prinderella and the Cinse* being an example – thank goodness no record remains.

In the digital world, records do remain but we can luckily edit and agree the final version before we publish. One of my sisters, Georgie, is dance director; another, Penny, is music director; whilst others may be general director and producers.

Geordie takes the lead role and nieces and nephews aid and abet him, coming up with ideas and amendments. Everyone else is doubled over with laughter. With continual disagreements, the video is eventually put together and later editing may take a little time on my phone – I am the DOP (director of photography). There is much excitement the next day when we are ready to post.

Perhaps the most curious holiday experience occurred at 9 p.m. one Christmas Day. With much excitement and fanfare, ITV announced the *Downton Abbey* Christmas special which made it, in some ways, the fourth Christmas of the year. We all sat slumped in front of the television, as actors on-screen came in and out of doors in the room in which we were currently sitting and Lady Mary walked down the staircase that my nieces had just run up. It was all rather surreal.

For many reasons, there is only one television in the Castle, although there was nothing at all when Geordie and I took over, so this is a 100 per cent upgrade. Our first set did not work particularly well and my son Eddie got rather fed up about it. So, at the age of ten, he managed to ring up a TV aerial company and proudly announced to us that they had quoted £78 or something like that to fix the aerial and that this was the standard price with everything included. On the appointed day, at the appointed hour, the aerial man duly arrived and Eddie was thrilled. I remember the man standing in the corridor, suitably dressed to go on the roof, but explaining that in fact this would not be the standard-fee job as this was not a standard house and definitely not a standard roof, and that we would therefore definitely need a quote. Eddie was crestfallen but I just thought he had seen a problem and sought to solve it, which I was rather proud about.

The subject of the *Downton Abbey* Christmas special came

up on another evening. A successful business was celebrating at Highclere and had built a marquee on the south lawns to welcome 350 family and friends. They had left the opening reception within the Castle and were sitting down enjoying dinner, looking forward to the entertainment they had arranged. I had just arrived back from Harrogate where I had been asked to give a talk for the *Yorkshire Post*. Very appropriate, I thought, given *Downton Abbey* was supposedly set in Yorkshire. I had walked into the library to see if everyone was all right and found a very nice man waiting to go into the marquee to entertain everyone. I hoped he'd had something to eat and asked him his name. He explained he had just been in Yorkshire too. I asked him if he had ever been on TV? And he said he had. In turn, he asked me if I had watched *Downton Abbey* on ITV on Christmas Day? I confirmed, 'We all did.' He said he was on the BBC at the corresponding time and that his name was Michael McIntyre.

He then asked if we had a TV? I explained that we had one under a table concealed by a curtain. Laughing, he commented, 'Big Castle, small TV; small council house, big TV.' I felt rather embarrassed and said I hoped he might return if he had time, with his family. I later rang up my sister Lucy to ask if she had heard of someone called Michael McIntyre, and she squealed down the phone at me for my ignorance. I still feel guilty.

During Covid, my sister Lucy sent me a video Michael McIntyre had put together about going to see someone who read crystal balls. He played both parts and it was all about drinking wine at 10.30 a.m. on a Wednesday, finding our roots (no hairdressers) and becoming teachers – bad ones. It was and is hilarious and I always feel grateful for the laughter he engendered in such bleak times.

After all the build-up to Christmas, the day itself passes by extraordinarily quickly, which means it is another 364 days away once again. Each day after it is, thank goodness, a little lighter, and as a household we spend time going out for long walks with the dogs, who spend much of the journey looking for some mud in which to bathe en route.

Inevitably, we go to say hello to the Green Man, the legendary figure we had carved into a huge cedar trunk. He does seem quite jolly if also a little intimidating.

As we gaze up at his face, we remember that the Green Man symbolises rebirth and represents the cycle of new growth that occurs every spring. He reminds me every day of the connection clearly felt by our ancestors to woodland and the land generally.

Nature owes us nothing but we owe nature everything. To value December is to enjoy the frost and the cold, to appreciate the fleeting nature of each year and the beauty of the stark silhouettes of the trees. These peaceful days between Christmas and New Year are precious, without schedules and tasks, days in which to wander, plan and think. The shortest and most valuable commodity for most people these days seems to be time, and moments when the world just comes to a stop are rare. Christmas is a time of gifts but, ironically, the biggest gift it brings for many is this free time.

One of the most sheltered corners of the gardens here is where the land drops down, screened by a mixed evergreen hedge. A huge old dark-grey statue sits half-hidden under some tall yews between the arched walls of the Monks' Garden and a gate to the Secret Garden. Permanently in shade, the statue is often overlooked by visitors. Like many other families, mine included, Geordie's family claims kinship to this ancient king and here at Highclere this statue is a colossal reminder of him – Charles the Great, Carolus Magnus, otherwise known as Charlemagne, who was crowned Holy Roman Emperor in St Peter's Basilica on Christmas Day AD 800.

I often wonder if the face on the statue is in any way similar to that of the real man, but it would be pure serendipity were it so given the centuries that have passed. There are some similarities: a ninth-century contemporary records that he was 'heavily built, sturdy, and of considerable stature', with 'large and lively eyes, a slightly larger nose than usual, white but still attractive hair, a bright and cheerful expression, a short and fat neck'.

Part of Charlemagne's success was due to his skill as a warrior, but he combined this with those of an administrator and ruler, and he had a great admiration for learning and education. He enjoyed books and music although, apparently, he found it hard to sleep. He was a practical man and in some ways was ahead of his time. His religion taught him that life began in a garden, in Paradise, but he took it a stage further. In order to ensure every subject of his lived well, the Emperor promoted a list of ninety-four plants to be grown in every city – '*Capitulare de villis*':

> It is our wish that they shall have in their gardens all kinds of plants: lily, roses, fenugreek, costmary, sage, rue, southernwood, cucumbers, pumpkins, gourds, kidney-bean, cumin, rosemary, caraway, chick-pea, squill, gladiolus, tarragon, anise, colocynth, chicory, ammi, sesili, lettuces, spider's foot, rocket salad, garden cress, burdock, pennyroyal, hemlock, parsley, celery, lovage, juniper, dill, sweet fennel, endive, dittany, white mustard, summer savory, water mint, garden mint, wild mint, tansy, catnip, centaury, garden poppy, beets, hazelwort, marshmallows, mallows, carrots,

parsnip, orach, spinach, kohlrabi, cabbages, onions, chives, leeks, radishes, shallots, cibols, garlic, madder, teazles, broad beans, peas, coriander, chervil, capers, clary. And the gardener shall have house-leeks growing on his house. As for trees, it is our wish that they shall have various kinds of apple, pear, plum, sorb, medlar, chestnut and peach; quince, hazel, almond, mulberry, laurel, pine, fig, nut and cherry trees of various kinds. The names of apples are: gozmaringa, geroldinga, crevedella, spirauca; there are sweet ones, bitter ones, those that keep well, those that are to be eaten straightaway, and early ones. Of pears they are to have three or four kinds, those that keep well, sweet ones, cooking pears and the late-ripening ones.

I have included the whole of the list as I find it entirely fascinating: diverse, sensible, and offering the basis for a good life, both in terms of ensuring a ready supply of food but also in preventing urban areas from becoming too cut off from the countryside.

Highclere at Christmas seeks to bring together familiar traditions and to be welcoming to as many people as possible. We hope that here happiness and dreams can co-exist for a time with the mixture of reality and fiction that seems to characterise this place. It is also a time to say thank you and to hope that we are further along now than we were at the start of the year. None of us ever quite finds what we are looking for, and perhaps we are looking for the wrong thing in any case, or maybe Epiphany will bring a much-needed revelation. Up on the ancient Wayfarer's Walk above Highclere, many a weary traveller in times past probably wished for a guardian angel at this time of year. Both metaphorically and physically, some journeys and roads are safer than others: 'so an angel guardian is assigned to each man as long as he is a wayfarer'. What more could any traveller ask?

Downton Abbey has shone an extraordinary light on Highclere. Unlike this time of year, it was not wholly dark, but it did need a little illumination. In Hindu writings it is said, 'Lead me from the unreal to the real.' That advice seems peculiarly apt for life here at Highclere Castle.

Acknowledgements

As ever I owe a huge thank you to all the Highclere team.

I write each book around my other work here and it may well begin in the evening and continue long into the late hours. I am grateful to everyone for bearing with me during this time.

Thank you above all to Geordie, as everyday Highclere is a story of partnership and love. Thank you to all the team for their stories, time and editing led by Geordie, Sally Popplewell, John Gundill, Lucy Aitken, Simon Andrews, the two Hannahs and their dogs Cariad and Wilma, the kitchen team for offering food, Luis for offering bubbles, Laura, Jo and Caitlin for endless tea and cake; we are indeed a family and a community. There are many other members of Team Highclere, in offices, gardens, accounts, IT and farm – thank you all.

My son Edward remained calm, positive, helpful and encouraging, and my beloved Labradors kept me company when I was writing and stayed to protect me when we encountered the odd ghost.

Finally, a tremendous thank you to Jonathan Lloyd and Rachel Goldbatt at Curtis Brown, and Zennor Compton and her team at Penguin Random House for believing in the book and asking James Nightingale to aid with editing. Much appreciated.